THIS BREATHTAK

AROUND THE WORLD BY BICYCLE 1997-1999

21,688 MILES (34,701 KM)

TIM DOHERTY

Published by Lulu, Inc.
www.lulu.com

ISBN 978-1-4452-2150-2

Text copyright © 1997-1999 Tim Doherty

All rights reserved.

No part of this book may be reproduced or transmitted in any form or by any means, electronic or mechanical, including photocopying, recording, or by any information storage and retrieval system, without permission in writing from the copyright owner.

The right of Tim Doherty to be identified as the author of this work has been asserted by him in accordance with the Copyright, Designs and Patents Act, 1988.

All photographs copyright © 1997-1999 Tim Doherty

All map illustrations copyright © 1997-1999 Tim Doherty

All sketches copyright © 1997-1999 Tim Doherty

Layout and Graphic Design by Tim Doherty, 2009

Dedications, Ten years on...

This year I will turn 40, and it will be ten years since I finished cycling round the world. But life goes on with new and ever greater happenings. I moved to Austria, where I found a car design job and married Verena, in 2002. We now have two wonderful children; Tommy, aged four and a half years, and Hannah, aged 18 months. This book is dedicated to them all, my Austrian family.

But I also owe a big thank-you to my English family; my mum Berlie, my dad Gerry, my sisters Janna and Sally and their own partners and families. Without their encouragement I would never have finished the tour or the book.

Finally, this book is also in memory of my grandfather Walter Hollingsworth, who died in 1995, aged 93. He had many nicknames, like Grandpa Hoylake and Little Man, and he was with me in spirit on this trip, with his love of travelling, his passion for writing and his crazy sense of humour.

Graz, Austria, February 2009

CONTENTS

6   MAP OF ROUTE

7   PREFACE

10   ONE : ENGLAND TO ITALY
          JULY TO OCTOBER 1997

30   TWO : ITALY TO THE MIDDLE EAST
          APRIL TO JULY 1998

84   THREE : INDIA TO THAILAND
          SEPTEMBER 1998 TO JANUARY 1999

162   FOUR : THAILAND TO NEW ZEALAND
          FEBRUARY TO JUNE 1999

238   FIVE : CANADA, IRELAND, HOME
          JULY TO OCTOBER 1999

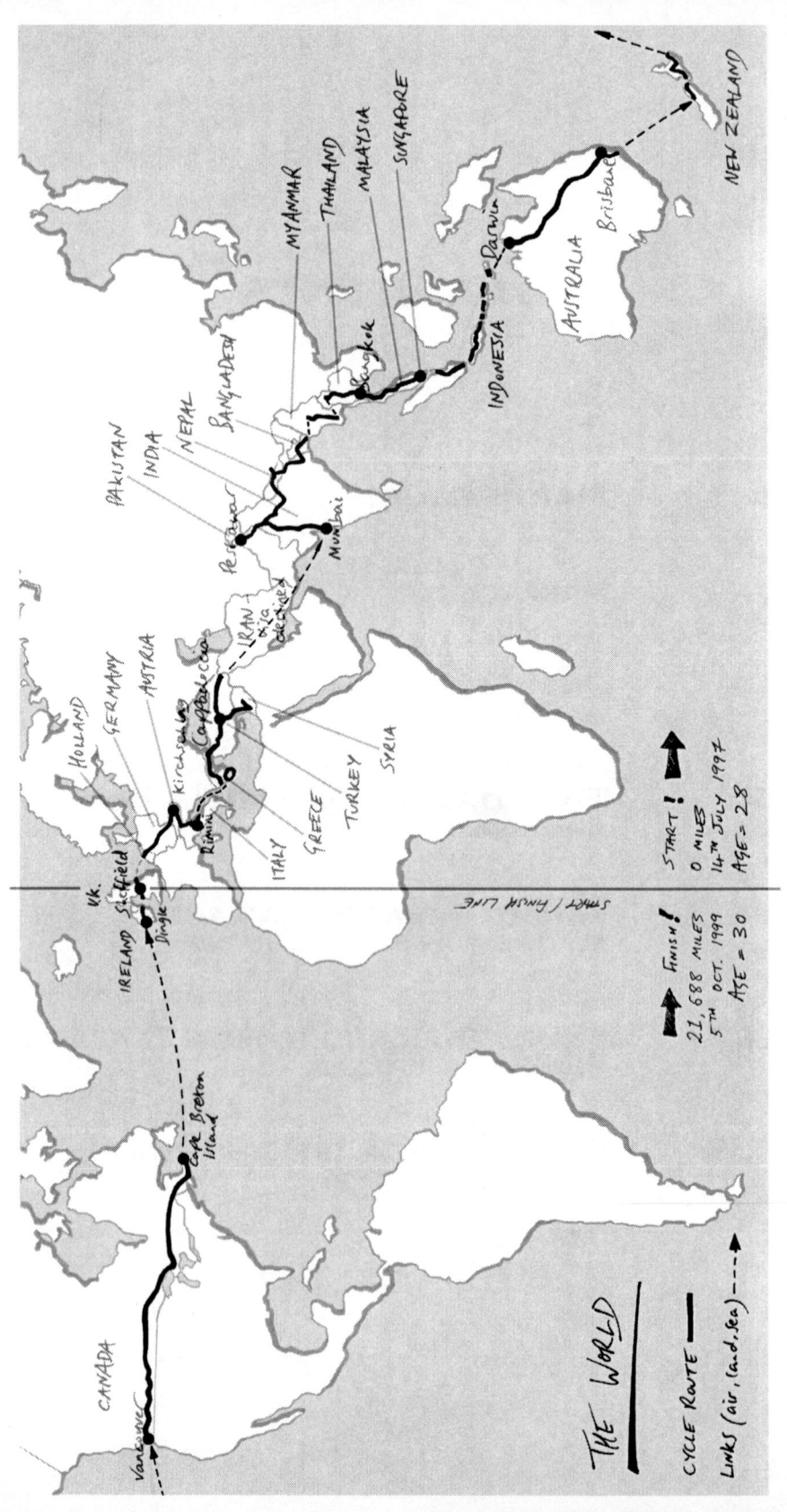

Preface

I'd dreamed of cycling round the world ever since my late teens. A tour of France with my school-friend Andrew Hindmoor set the scene, and almost every summer after that saw me touring in some part of Europe. Books by Dervla Murphy, Josie Dew and others helped to fuel my fascination, and anyone I met who had been to Australia or India became my hero.

The dream suddenly came into sharp focus in 1995 when I was flying home from Vienna with my friend Hugh Colquhoun, after we'd ridden there from home, via Prague. I just didn't want to go back to England; Italy was just down the road. Beyond Italy was the rest of the world! I decided on that flight that I was definitely going to do it.

I first met Verena the following July, in Leamington Spa, where I was starting my career as a car designer. She was intrigued by my round the world plan but didn't think I'd actually do it. She was working at a hotel in Leamington, and we had eight happy months together before she had to go home to Austria. Her contract had expired and she was needed back at her parents' hotel. We decided that my route would pass through Austria, and that her village, Kirchschlag, would be my first resting point.

"You'll have to stay with me for a few weeks or so!" she told me.
"Cool!" I said. "I'll get there before our first "anniversary"!"
"And stay until my birthday. I'll be twenty-four then!"
"I know. I hope you'll be able to get some days off."
"Well, you don't know what it's like at home! It's probably easier for you to work in the hotel, at least we'll see each other then!"
"I could fix things!"
"Yeah, like the broken chairs in the restaurant. And you could work behind the bar."
"No way! I'm not working behind the bar! I'd be the worst barman in the world! I don't even know the names of the drinks in English,

let alone German!"

"German wouldn't help you very much! You'd need to learn our dialect! It's called Kirchschlagerisch."

"Oh no," I groaned. "I'll be a disaster!"

With only a few months left until my departure, I began to prepare in more detail. I bought a bullet-proof Orbit Expedition bike (a tourer with mountain bike wheels) from the factory in my home town of Sheffield, and replaced my old cycling and camping gear. I stored all the old stuff at my dad's house, including my ageing Dawes Galaxy tourer, in case of loss or theft of the expensive new equipment.

I sat outside on the driveway with my sister's boyfriend Richard, while he showed me how to light my new petrol stove.

"What you do is this….." he said, pumping the handle on the side of the stove. "You've got to get it up to pressure, before letting a bit of the petrol through the pipe and onto the pre-heating dish."

He let some of the fuel out, then held a match to it. There was a loud "POP!" and a fireball nearly engulfed us.

"Wow!" I said, flinching. "D'ya have to do it like that every time?"

"You do, but you'll get used to it…. It'll heat the water in no time!"

"Yeah… it's a bit scary though… I'll wait till I'm really starving before I use it!"

With an idea of the countries I wanted to visit along the way, I found out about the visas I'd need and how to access or exchange my money. I visited the doctor and told him where I would be going, had all the necessary injections and bought enough malaria tablets to last me for a year.

I finally got round to handing in my notice at work. After four and a half years in the same design consultancy, in a converted Victorian school in Warwickshire, it felt like I was leaving my own family for good. I left a legacy behind, though; I sold my rusty old Datsun Sunny for £100 to my colleague, Dave.

In addition to the personal challenge of the trip, I wanted to do something constructive to benefit other people. I contacted a charity called Intermediate Technology (I.T.), and asked if there were any projects I could contribute towards, preferably to help asthma sufferers in Africa. My Tanzanian pen-friend John Laizer had told me about the terrible respiratory problems that people have in his country. I suffer from asthma myself, and I'd already raised about £450 for the National Asthma Campaign when I'd ridden to Prague.

The Appeals Officer for I.T., Sue Lodge, was excited by my planned trip, and told me that I could help them with getting funds for a project in Kenya. She said that I should think of a name for my fund-raising effort, so that they could make reference to it in their newsletters. The project name I thought up, "The Breathtaking World," seemed to be catchy and pertinent. I set out to raise and collect as much as I could before setting off, as Sue said they wouldn't be able to wait two or three years for the money! The idea behind the project was to help people to replace the traditional, smoky, wood-burning fires in their homes with more efficient clay-built stoves. Made from local materials, the new stoves had a flue to prevent the house from filling with smoke. I managed to collect and donate £1200 towards the project in just a few months, with a bit more trickling in later on.

I tried to find a travelling companion, as I didn't particularly want to go on my own. Five different people said they'd join me for various stages, but one-by-one they dropped out, having decided that the prospect of it wasn't as appealing as they'd first thought. Never mind, they all came to my leaving do, a cracking night out at the Lescar in Sheffield. After that, I was on my own...

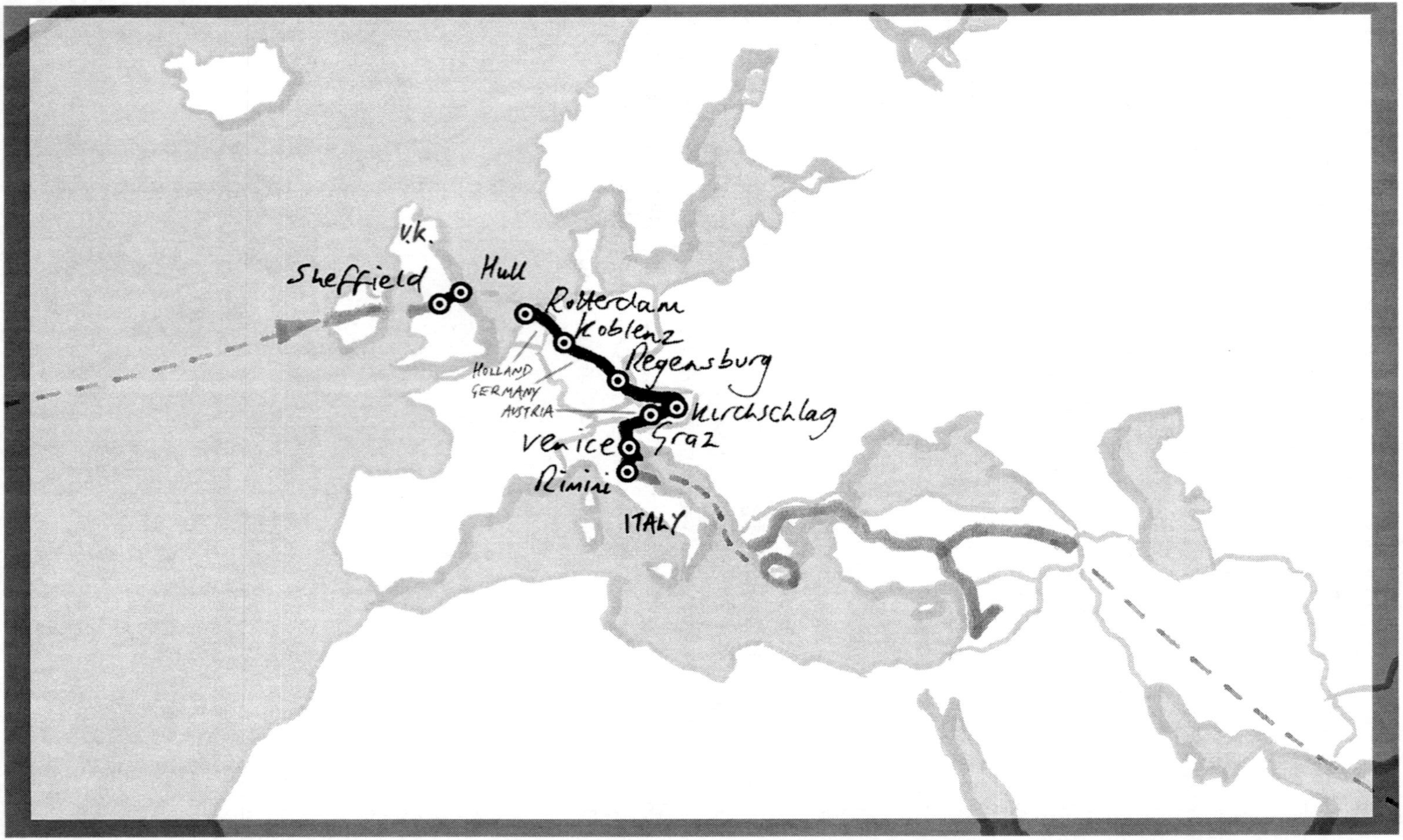
U.K.
Sheffield
Hull
Rotterdam
Koblenz
Regensburg
Kirchschlag
Graz
Venice
Rimini
HOLLAND
GERMANY
AUSTRIA
ITALY

ONE

ENGLAND TO ITALY
JULY TO OCTOBER 1997

The next two days were very cold, wet and lonely rides, taking me to Koblenz. Crawling out of the tent on the morning of the fifth day, I was tempted to give it up; in my haste to pedal ninety-four pounds of loaded bike to Austria, I'd practically destroyed my knees already...

Sheffield, England to Kirchschlag, Austria

Day one of cycling round the world was a difficult thing to get my head around. On the one hand, the thought of so much solitude and danger scared me to death, but I reckoned that I'd be okay once I got going. On the other hand, this was what I'd been waiting for, and I knew that I'd be having experiences and adventures far greater than anything that I'd yet come across. All that I could really think of, however, was the fact that I would be seeing Verena in a couple of weeks, then having a relaxing month or so with her. The rest of it was too distant to really matter yet.

I set off from home early on the morning of July 14th 1997, with good-byes and some little tears. I went down the road for a cool getaway, rather than riding up the road at a snail's pace. I later found out that my mum was convinced that she'd never see me again.

Dear Verena

Tim's just set off, and I could tell that he was really fired up. He'll be fine, Verena! He should be getting to you in about two weeks. You must be <u>so</u> excited! Please ask him to ring me when he arrives.

Love Berlie

With enough sandwiches to last me until next Easter, I raced through Sheffield, Doncaster and Scunthorpe, crossed the Humber Bridge, and got to Hull after five hours. That evening I boarded the overnight ferry to Rotterdam and slept on the floor in my new sleeping bag.

I had to ride 110 miles to Germany the next day, to avoid the need for Dutch currency (as yet there was no such thing as the Euro). What with the tendency for Dutch cycle lanes to meander all over the place, and most of the turnings not even being sign-posted, crossing Holland in a day was never going to be easy! The best bits were;

sitting on a bridge, stuffing my face and laughing out loud because everyone else was at work; and riding the last thirty miles because I knew the way already, having spent five months near Eindhoven as a design student. I reached Germany at ten p.m., just as night fell.

Two long days later I reached Koblenz. I'd ridden across Germany twice before, once en-route to Switzerland and once en-route to Prague and Vienna with Hugh. I'd come through Koblenz both times and now I wanted to see something new!

I kept the pace up, as much as my knees could take. Down the Rhine Valley to Mainz and across to Bavaria. I was taking the straightest route possible, be it main roads or hillside tracks. In the four months since Verena had moved back to Austria, we'd only seen each other for a few short days in May. She'd flown over mid-week, and I'd had to make a deal with my boss so I could take a couple of days off to be with her, then work all weekend to catch up!

Eight days after leaving Sheffield, I reached Regensburg on little winding back roads with birds of prey flying overhead. Regensburg was absolutely awesome. Near the river's edge is a medieval "Sauskuechen," a sausage kitchen. It's been there ever since 1612 or 1320, depending on whether you believe the book or the sign. Well, it was old anyway, and is still used for its original purpose. All the way up the walls the tidemarks told of past floodings. Another building had a huge fresco of David and Goliath. Breathing in the architecture and the colours of Regensburg Altstadt, I felt like I was finally getting somewhere. Being back in a town was a strange feeling after camping out in the Bavarian forests. I walked around a bookshop, grinning because of all the books and magazines around. I felt like a kid in a toyshop.

On a bridge I saw a raving mad canoeist, steadied by three of his mates, all wearing colourful buoyancy aids and wet suits. They counted to three and a gathering crowd watched as they launched him into thin air, plummeting into the fast moving Danube, thirty feet below! When he surfaced he was carried downstream at twenty miles per hour, and huge cries of glee came from all four multi-coloured lunatics.

The three still on the bridge then jumped as high as they could off the edge, one after another, emitting cries like "Hobblajobbla-ka-bobbla!", "Jinna-jolla-janga!" and "Ayeekazemabadoo!" On hitting the water, they too disappeared at immense speed. They all clambered out onto a quayside fifty metres downstream, then one of them got onto a bike and cycled away. A bungee rope attached to the bike was held at the other end by one of his mates. The cyclist turned around and pedalled as fast as he could till he reached the quayside. Crying "Chimma-lamma-hoola!" he flew off, complete with bike, into the Danube. MAD!

The ninth day was an epic 131 mile ride from Regensburg to Linz; an unforgettable day. The first fifty miles were a bit dull, but then my knees warmed up and the sun came out. The cycle path left the main road and snaked along right next to the Danube, and the valley closed in until it was a narrow steep gorge covered in tall conifers. I reached Passau, on the Austrian border, having just overdosed on Coca-Cola and Tortilla chips.

I looked round the town, which was even more amazing than Regensburg because of the narrow valley around it. Everything was stacked up, practically falling into the swollen river. To get down to the bridge I had to ride down a steep winding street, which went through a tunnel hewn from the rock, with houses tottering precariously on top. I thought "I'll just get to Austria before camping." I crossed the border at six o'clock and saw a sign saying "Linz 80 km." I'd told Verena I'd ring her from Linz. Those eighty kilometres were meant to be the next day's ride, along a beautiful stretch of the Danube. I thought, "Sod it, I'll do it now!"

A few more bananas, kartoffelsalat, sarnies and gulps of Coca-Cola and I headed off, reaching Linz as darkness fell. I found a phone-box and rang Verena for the first time since Sheffield. I told her I'd be with her in two days, and she said, "Can't you come tomorrow?"

Finding a campsite was less than fun. I got lost and found myself cycling around an area of huge industrial sites. Feeling tired and anxious, I managed to find the Danube cycle-path going towards Vienna. I followed it for half a mile in the dark, when I looked behind and saw a bike light. "Oh my life," I thought, "I'm gonna be murdered!" I was too worn out to race away, so I pulled over and slowed down. The cyclist rolled alongside and said something in German. Does this mean "Your money or your life?" I asked myself. Then I realised he'd asked, "Are you looking for the campsite?" I told him I was, although I didn't actually know that I was heading for one. He then showed me the way and didn't murder me, but gave me a hearty handshake, saying, "Gute Reise."

Day ten, from Linz to Kirchschlag was a 152 mile, twenty-hour killer. I lost weight on that day. The choice for the night was my tent or Verena's house. Hmmmm! Kirchschlag lies only 15 miles from the Austrian / Hungarian border, so I still had a <u>long</u> way to go.

I started pedalling before the crack of dawn, but came across a washed-away bridge, and when I took a forest track instead, it just turned into a muddy, nettle-lined quagmire. My bike was beginning live up to its name; "Expedition." I found the road again and stared over to the other side of the tributary and the remains of the bridge. Just a few slippery girders were left. It was still only six a.m. I went back to the previous village and a cyclist went past. I shouted, "Die Bruecke ist kaputt!" He eventually took me on an alternative route, once I'd convinced him that there was no bridge. He left me on the road for Vienna and told me, "This is your road. Many cars, not good for your nose." Then he shook my hand and patted me on the back. I could tell he thought I was crazy.

It was a hot, hilly and humid day and by two o'clock I'd practically given up, not even half way. I read a newspaper in Melk then thought, "There's no way I'm sleeping in a tent again tonight." Totally knackered from the last nine days, I broke my number one asthma management rule; I stoked myself up with Coca-Cola and junk food for the second day running. I justified it in all sorts of ways; I don't HAVE to get there today, but one day it might be a matter of life and death, e.g. getting bitten in the middle of nowhere by a rabid dog. Also, Sheffield to Kirchschlag in ten days sounded impressive, and it was good training. The only really important aspect of this first stage was to actually get to see Verena. The temptation to jump on a train was strong, but I wouldn't allow myself to "cheat," and I told myself that if I didn't keep on pedalling, I'd never get to see her again! I thought about the time we'd spent together in Leamington in May, walking along the Warwickshire canals and exploring Oxford. How distant that now seemed.

Though my knees ached if I stood up on the pedals, my legs felt like they would just keep going till I self-destructed. Having crossed the last mountain pass on the eastern end of the Alps, I reached the valley floor just as it was turning dark. A thunderstorm broke, so I sat in a bus shelter and ate loads of food. Ten miles away was Wiener Neustadt, which I reached thinking, "Verena said it's only twenty-five kilometres to Kirchschlag from here." I eventually found a sign saying "Kirchschlag 49 km." I cursed and plodded on in the rain, following the empty main road for over an hour, to a turn-off.

   I edged slowly skywards for what seemed like another hour, next to an invisible, whispering stream, with massive trees and hills silhouetted against the cold night sky. The climb finally levelled out then rolled away to an eerie ten-mile descent through silent, mysterious villages on a pitch black, deserted road. It was one of those magical moments, which made the whole day worthwhile.

   I dropped into Kirchschlag with the same nervous feeling of excitement and trepidation that I'd had on reaching the Czech border with Hugh in '95. Before I left home, Verena had sent me a house-key, a sketch map and some photos. I recognised the Hotel Post and the ruined castle, found her house and let myself in. I left the bike and crept upstairs, tripping over some shoes on the way. I found myself in a dark living room and saw some more stairs. I climbed upstairs and quietly opened each door in turn, my heart beating almost out of control. I checked all of the rooms, then turned the handle of the last door and crept inside. I could make out a mattress on the floor and the faint sound of sleep…

   Verena's parents soon found plenty of work for me to do in their hotel, in return for as much food as I could eat. As well as the summer festivals there was a wedding, where the bride, Verena's cousin, was "kidnapped" from the hotel. In line with the local custom, the groom then had to lead the wedding party from one Gasthof to the next, until she was found, and a drunken war of improvised singing ensued to win her back.

   The people in Kirchschlag treated me like a pop star, buying me beers or coming up to me in the village, saying, "Du bist der Englander!" They even put me in the regional newspaper, the Niederoesterreichische Nachrichten, with a story of my planned trip and a photo of Verena and I standing with the bike. The world-shattering headline translated as, "Twenty-eight year old Englishman in Kirchschlag."

Verena and I visited the Alps and Hungary, Vienna and Tuscany, but after six weeks I had to go. We planned to meet up in Sydney a year later. Meanwhile she and her friend Petra would be backpacking in South America and Australia. Our goodbyes were the most painful thing ever, and Verena had to wear dark glasses at work because she kept bursting into tears. Eventually I just had to get on with it. I loaded up the bike with all the gear and rode out of the village….

Kirchschlag, Austria to Venice, Italy

So, I'd done it; I'd finally broken away from Kirchschlag. Riding up the valley, I was thinking, "What am I doing? I could have gone to South America with Verena and had the most guaranteed gorgeous time ever!" And yet, here I was, riding to who-knew-where. I was navigating with a photocopied map of Austria, and rode down to Graz (my future home!) and on through the stunning county of Styria, with its orchards, vineyards and fields of pumpkins...

In southern Austria I passed the lakes and mountains of Carinthia. After a few days, I was nearing the Italian border. It was a hot day once the clouds had lifted, and I rode on through a stunning landscape. The craggy peaks of the Dolomites towered above, marking the borders of Austria, Slovenia and Italy. The road dived through tunnels and pine forests, and I stopped for photos of the landscape.

On the go
Tim Doherty set off in July on a round-the-world cycle. "The Breathtaking World" was inspired by the asthma sufferer's pen-pal who said that cooking at home in Kenya was a very smoky process. Tim has already raised over £1,200, helping Intermediate Technology study methods of smoke reduction.

There were a few other cyclists along the road and soon I was crossing into Italy. The border official couldn't believe that I'd cycled all the way from England. Next thing I was whizzing down the road with the river crashing on one side and the mountain-tops like fingers pointing into the sky on the other. I found a campsite and met a Belgian cyclist who looked like a Victorian Mr Strongman, and spoke with a comedy French accent.

The last day was long, hot and humid, with far too much traffic. A strong headwind slowed my progress, but I was motivated by thoughts of Venice and a rest. I explored some magnificent places, though, like Cordovado, a medieval brick-built town with historical

plays in progress. Rather than actually cycle into Venice through the mess of Mestre, I decided to camp at Lido di Jesolo and visit Venice on the ferry. I pitched the tent, went down the beach and laid eyes on the Mediterannean.

For the next two days, I travelled light, with just a camera and some Lire. Approaching Venice by ferry has to be the best way. There was something magical about the way it first appeared across the green waters of the Adriatic, muted in a cloud of mist. Gradually its features were revealed as we drew closer. The bell tower, the Ducal Palace and the Piazza San Marco stood proudly in front of the ferry as we docked.

As I walked round I was thinking, "Venice has just overtaken Prague as my favourite city ever!" There are so many tiny alleyways and canals, there's a different world around every corner. You stand and photograph a tiny bridge with its curved railings, the pale pinks of the plastered buildings, their green shutters and white lintels and sills, the pan tiles and the faint blue sky. An old lady appears on the bridge, walks a few steps and is gone. Then you can hear an accordion player, getting louder and louder, but there's no one there. You look round and, out of a side canal a gondola appears.... the front has disappeared before the back is in view. In the middle sits the accordion player, singing and playing to a young couple. Then, right next to you, two feet away is the head of an empty gondola. It streams silently past as the gondolier kicks off from the pole next to your feet and ducks as he disappears under the bridge.

Even the decrepit state of the buildings, crumbling into the canal, adds a pathos to the city's beauty; an ephemeral charm which will ultimately decay into the mild, green water.

It's all too easy to forget that people actually live here. Everyone seems to be a tourist, or somehow connected to tourism, but occasionally a little motorboat goes past with two little kids on board, chattering away excitedly, or a doorway opens and a Venetian steps onto the streets. Behind the iron-grilled windows, people file away noisily, turn their drills on or sit reading beneath angle-poise lamps. Just like anywhere else.

Venice to Rimini, Italy

I lay awake all night, strait-jacketed inside my sleeping bag, my dried-out skin on fire, till finally I was so exhausted I fell asleep. The sun drove me out of the tent, bleary-eyed and unwilling. The temperature was already rising as I loaded the bike in the empty meadow, shook off my weariness and set off up the hill. As soon as the first needles of sweat stabbed out, my skin felt as if it was covered in acid, burning pain flaring all the way up my arms and body…

I headed around Mestre for Chioggia. It was a stupidly hot day and all the excitement and magic of Venice was completely gone. I was on a road full of huge trucks with trailers cutting me up, and a long, boring stretch of it faced directly into the wind.

After the fun of Venice came the hard-hitting reality of what I was actually trying to do. I was facing two years of solo pedalling in the heat, in unfamiliar places, and it scared the life out of me.

My eczema, which had been getting steadily worse, absolutely flourished in this hot, dry, salty air. The campsite at Chioggia had "hot" showers, but they were not really hot at all and I had been stinging all over all day. I tried to chat to some people at the campsite, but nobody seemed interested, and the language barrier didn't help.

I went to bed and sweated. In the morning I got up and pedalled into the same wind, with the same heat and the same traffic. Thoughts of Turkey, India and Australia came up and seemed absolutely awful. How could I possibly expect my skin to survive those places? Riding through arid landscapes in a strong sun, with sand everywhere and no showers for weeks on end, is a terrible prospect for someone with eczema.

Not only was it spreading rapidly but the rash itself was worsening. It was ironic because my asthma had completely disappeared.

I'd been diagnosed as having eczema when I was six months old, when an abscess had appeared behind my ear on Christmas Eve, 1969. All through my early school years I'd suffered hideous wounds which I'd scratch and scratch until they ran with blood, my only thought being to soothe the pain. The joints were always the worst affected areas, as any flexing of hardened skin or build-up of sweat in the folds would set off another ferocious scratching session. Occasionally, I had to be carried around the Primary School by the teachers, the backs of my knees locked solid by a mess of congealed blood and scabs. By the time I went to college, however, it was more controlled. I had a nasty rash on my arms and neck through the winters, but nothing more, if I was careful.

As for the asthma, it had been there since I was six years old, but it came into its own after I'd finished college. The pressure of work and a busy social life led to a dependency on my inhaler. Too many late nights, too much time in smoky pubs or in the dusty workshop, too much hyperactive cycling and too much bad food. Never mind, the inhaler would always give me a kick and I could keep on partying, just like my mates. Then one day, and it really was that sudden, the inhaler stopped having any effect. I was referred to a specialist in acupuncture and reflexology, who concluded that my adrenal glands were worn out. For the next two years I struggled by without the inhaler, no mean feat as there were smokers at work and in my shared house; once or twice a month I'd have an attack which would last for days on end...

On a long, straight road in this Italian heat, my thoughts were turned to Verena. I could see myself four months down the road, just plodding along day after day, wishing the whole time that I was with her. Those two days were a taster of what the rest of the trip could be like.

This was me at the crossroads. One way lay danger and adventure, the other way was happiness with Verena. I'd always thought I would choose the first – after all I'd been planning this trip for years. But now that I was actually at the crossroads I knew that it was not what I wanted anymore. I couldn't be with her and follow my dream. My mind was in turmoil. The eczema had flared up with such ferocity because of the dilemma I was facing. At the time, though, I was convinced that the turmoil was a result of the eczema, not the other way round. Even so, I began to think about her more and more.

She grew up in the hotel in Kirchschlag, and as a young girl she'd sit quietly in the bar, listening to the regulars chewing the cud; politics, the war, the affairs of the village, and endless jokes. Her family has been running the Hotel Post for five generations, and photos on the wall show Russian tanks cruising down the street outside, and the petrol pumps that once stood there. Verena's grandmother used to wipe the pastry from her hands before pumping the petrol, then go straight back into the hotel kitchen!

Verena studied at Catering College in a town next to the Yugoslav border. Slovenia was fighting for Independence and she said that there were bullets coming across the border, hitting the Austrian houses. She first left home in 1992; intelligent and analytical, interested in everything from art and history to travel and languages. She went to Paris to spend six months as an au-pair, learning to speak fluent French. As for her English, she makes mistakes so rarely that, when she does, it sounds comical. Once she bought me some cuff-links, but told me that she'd got me some handcuffs!

She's warm-hearted and affectionate, an open and genuine person with what my mum says is "real quality." On the one hand she's a true lady, delicate and subtle, yet, on the other hand, an adventurer. She travelled once for two weeks by camel with the Bedouin in Egypt, sleeping under the stars with a lacework of ice forming on her sleeping bag....

So, just two days after leaving Venice, I completely changed my plans. I'd give up cycling round the world because there was no way I could do it with my skin in such a state. Two days is a long, long time when you're on your own.

I'd called Verena from Venice to tell her how wonderful and exciting it was, and now I rang her again to tell her I was giving up. I'd return to Austria and go backpacking with her instead. I could sense the deep relief in her voice when she said, "Oh Timmy! You've no idea how happy that makes me feel!"

I decided to try and reach Rome before throwing in the towel completely. I headed into Tuscany where the hills turned into mountains. It was cool and I was barely sweating, so my eczema felt okay. Over on a hilltop I could see the Republic of San Marino, raised above its surroundings as if on a pedestal. The campsite I was heading for was closed for the season, as was the next one. As much as I love free-camping, the fact that I couldn't have a shower that night was bad news for my skin.

The morning was crisp and clear, the dew sparkling in the September sun. Perfect cycling weather under normal circumstances, but the damage had already been done. There was a youth hostel in forty miles and then I'd be only two days from Rome, which seemed like as good a place as any to finish the trip. But forty miles the other way, back down on the coast, was Rimini, and it would be downhill nearly all the way. After half an hour sitting on a wall feeling totally defeated, not knowing what on earth to do, I couldn't face cycling up any hills to a hostel that might be full or closed.

So I freewheeled down to Rimini. This was a painful and demoralising thing to do. I was actually turning back now – the end of the line. That night I wrote in my diary:

My head is still spinning!
- It's dead hot – I definitely don't want to cycle round the world.
- I finished Ffyona Campbell's book – she made it (on foot!). I still want to go round the world!
- Finding the Rimini hostel was a pain and I have that problem every day – I don't want to........
    - I met two English blokes cycling home from Greece. Told me about their mates who had ridden
    round the world – I still want to.....
    -Maybe I could persuade someone to join me for all the horrid bits...
-I can't do it anyway, because of my eczema.

What a downer!!!

and round, and round...
I don't think this dream will go away very easily.....

Towards the end of our backpacking adventure, I formulated my plan of what to do after Australia. Somewhere on the Barkly Tableland, between Three Ways and Townsville, we parked our beaten-up Australian Ford and stared out over the vast expanse of the

Outback. For some reason, this place had a cathartic effect on me, something to do with the emptiness and the lack of distractions. Everything seemed to fall into place and become clear; I had set out to cycle round the world, and I'd given up because of my eczema. But that had long-since healed, and the worry that Verena and I might not survive the separation was now much less likely. The last few months of travelling in each other's pockets had set our relationship in stone.

The other factor was that I now felt much less daunted by the thought of going to the Middle East and Asia. The thought of it had scared the life out of me in Italy, because I'd never been out of Europe before. But I'd now been to Argentina, Chile, Bolivia, Peru, Brazil and Australia, so I felt that I'd done an apprenticeship in world travelling.

We'd done some amazing things, like hiking the length of the Inca trail, and climbing the odd volcano. On successfully climbing the 6075 metre (19,931 feet) high Chachani Volcano in Peru I'd discovered, by first-hand experience, something that would eventually get me through the next two years; whatever happens, keep going. It sounds simple enough, but if you really want to get there, you will.

"How about if I ride to Istanbul?" I asked as we stared out across the Outback.

"You can do what you like, Mr Doherty, as long as you're back in four months," Verena replied.

"Five. You could even meet me there!"

"Oh Timmy, I think I just want to get back to work now!"

"Okay... I'll go back to Italy, ride across Greece to Turkey then work out the rest from there! I might even be able to get to India. England to India doesn't sound too bad does it? I'd have done something that most people never do."

"Good. Now shut up and let me have a think!"

By the time we flew from Sydney back to Vienna, I was determined to do a few months' cycling, resurrecting my round the world route, but that I'd just see how it went. The idea of doing the whole thing still seemed too daunting to think about. I stayed for a week in Kirchschlag while I worked out a plan of action. I loaded up my expedition bike again, saving weight by leaving the front panniers and rack behind, along with all of the non-essential gear. I decided to take the train right back to where I'd left off seven months before; Rimini.

I boarded the train in Graz with the bike, with only a minute to spare. Two guards got on behind me and I couldn't get back to Verena to say goodbye. I went further along, until I could see her outside the window, looking anxious. I ran to the far end of the carriage and found an outside door. We had about half a minute together, with Verena crying her eyes out. The train started to pull away and she ran alongside. It was absolutely unbearable, like a poignant scene from a film. Gutted, I slumped down into a seat and stared blankly out of the window as Graz disappeared in a blur of colours…

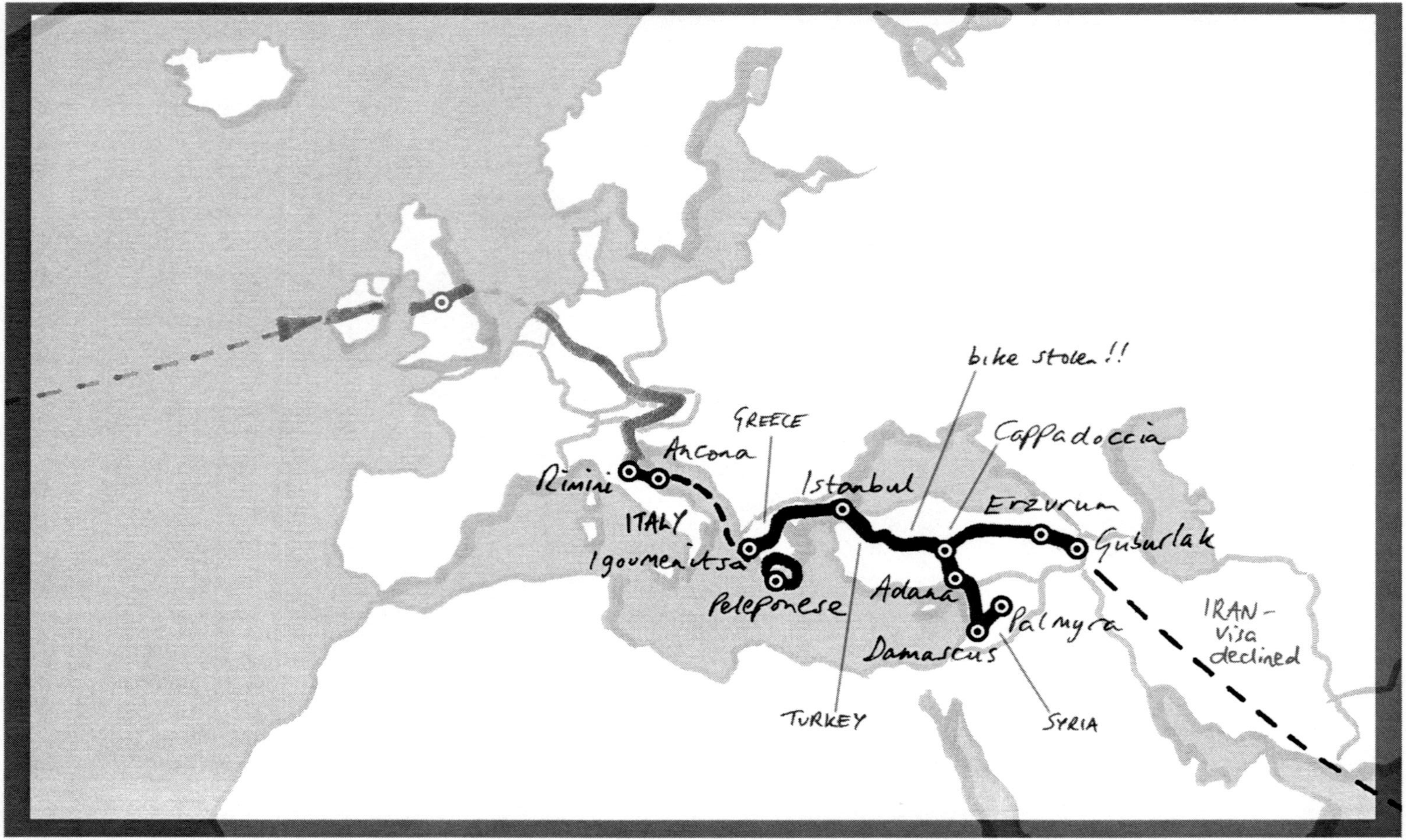

bike stolen!!
GREECE
Cappadoccia
Ancona
Rimini
Istanbul
Erzurum
ITALY
Igoumenitsa
Gusurlak
Adana
Peleponese
Palmyra
IRAN-
Visa
declined
Damascus
TURKEY
SYRIA

Two

Italy to the Middle East
April to July 1998

I was starving when I arrived in Rimini, on a Sunday afternoon. The only food I could find was McDonald's, which wasn't very appetising. I didn't really know what I was going to do with the next few months; my plans kept changing all the time…

Rimini, Italy to Peleponese, Greece

I did two short days of cycling, taking it easy, to build up the strength in my knees. Being back on the road felt lonely, but the spring weather was kind to my skin; no worries about eczema for the moment. Those two days took me to Ancona and the ferry for Greece, a good psychological boost as I'd put Italy behind me, and I'd never been to Greece before!

Hi Verena!
Tim just rang me from Italy! I've been investigating flights to Greece to meet up with him. The only place I can get to apart from Athens is Corfu, so I've booked a flight! When he phones you, tell him that we don't have to stay there; we could meet at the airport and go to the mainland.
Anyway, it's all very exciting!
Love to you both,
Berlie xxxx

The ferry went past Corfu, where I would be going in two weeks to meet my mum for a holiday. In the meantime, I thought it would be cool to ride around Peleponese, to get back into the rhythm.

It was worth going to Greece just for the first day! In Patra I bought a new bike tyre, bread, razor blades, and a map. The shopkeepers were welcoming, and most of them shook my hand, telling me how they used to work on the ships going to Cardiff, Liverpool or Newcastle. The guy in the bakery gave me an extra bread cake, saying, "From me!" After feeling like a nobody in Italy last year, I wondered how anyone could ever feel lonely in Greece.

I left Patra and headed into the mountains, overflowing with vibrant spring grass and dotted with tall poplars. I rode through simple villages of pretty whitewashed houses, where donkeys and goats shaded themselves under trees bursting with oranges. I saw a woman who must have been about two hundred years old, painting the kerb outside her house, even though she could hardly bend down. Everywhere I stopped, people came to talk to me and point me in the right direction. The road climbed steeply to skirt the isolated rocky ridges of Mt. Skollos before bombing down; twisting, turning and free of cars.

Getting used to the road-signs, written in Greek letters, was a bit tricky; trying to navigate on such little roads was no mean feat, but luckily my map had the names in both English and Greek. I came speeding down a hill and round a corner to find that the tarmac just disappeared. The road became a dirt track with another track crossing it, and no signs. I just stood there in middle, laughing. A farmer started shouting, "Olympia, Olympia!" whilst pointing to one of the tracks. I waved at him and carried on... luckily I wanted to go to Olympia!

I saw a cycle tourist standing in the middle of a junction. I went up and asked him where he was from. He said, "France." He was going in the opposite direction to me, having just come from Olympia. We had a chat for half an hour in what must have been the noisiest place of the day, with a digger truck farting around and a lad messing about in a BMW.

It turned out that this French guy, Paul, was on his own and was cycling round the world in stages. He's been at it for ten years, on and off. He keeps going back to France to get some work. He was heading back there now, this current stage having taken fourteen months so far. The place I most wanted to know about was Syria. He said it's his favourite country in the world;

"Ahh, Syria, I love Syria so much! You can never get very far - people always invite you into their homes!" he said, enthusiastically.

"That sounds great!"

"I think you will really like it there.... You must go. If you are going to Istanbul, you must continue to Damascus."

"People have already told me how brilliant it is!"

"Oui. And it's so cheap as well. The only thing I bought in Syria was a visa, and also a new wheel. I was there for four weeks and I only spent $50!"

"So you stayed overnight in people's houses as well?" I asked, intrigued.

"Of course! Sometimes for four or five days!"

He was a mad, straggly character and his mountain bike was a wreck... the bottom bracket was completely shot, so the pedals wobbled all over the place. His cranks were different lengths, and he had this nasty steel wheel from Syria. His trip sounded fantastic, but the downside was that his obsession has split him up from his wife and their five year-old daughter. He seemed to accept this as an inevitable consequence, but I was determined that the same thing wouldn't happen to Verena and me. Regular phone calls and faxes, once every five days, were the least I could do to keep her mind at rest.

   I left him to find a place to free-camp, while I carried on to Olympia, thinking about everything he'd said. He was definitely an inspiration, and to meet him only three days after resuming my uncertain tour was significant. I'd only met two others like him since I left Sheffield, nine months before. They were also French; the pair that were doing it on a tandem. They'd crossed the Salar de Uyuni salt lake in South America, and I'd met them on the flight to Australia. I remember thinking, "If they can do it, why couldn't I?"

   After camping in Olympia I found a mountain road to the south. I'd definitely brought the right bike for the job, as a lot of the roads were stony tracks. Outside the bars and cafes were groups of elderly men, but never any women. A skinny, toothless old man in a ragged jacket gave me some directions in a dark, smoke-filled cafe with creaky wooden chairs and tables. His hand described, in twists, turns and swooshes, the way the road to Tripiti would go. Then he and two of his croneys came outside to wave me off.

   Halfway there, I stopped for a rest and watched a guy playing with his goats in a steep field which disappeared into oblivion. He kept looking over and waving. He came out of the field, crossed the road and started talking to me. He had a big hairy boil on his face. The conversation went something like this…

   "Italia?" he asked.
   "No, England!"
   "American?"
   "No, England!" I repeated.
   "Anglia………(pedalling motion)…..Peleponese?"
   "Yes, I've cycled from England," I nodded.
   "Athina?" he smiled.
   "No, No Athens; Patras"
   "Patras?" he sounded confused.
   "Patra."

"Patra?" he shrugged.
"Patra, Patras," I tried.
"O, Patras!" his face lit up.
"Patras? Patra? Yes!" I was now as confused as he was!
"Olympia?"
"Yes, Olympia!"
"Mystra?" he pointed to the road ahead.
"Yes, Mystra, Nafplio..."

Suddenly, he excused himself, legged it over the road, slammed his gate shut and started yelling at the goats and throwing stones around like a madman! I thought, "Fair enough!" I cycled off and the man waved.

In the village of Andritsena at the top of the hill, the shopkeeper had to get her daughter to translate for me. After that, I decided it was time for me to learn some Greek. I wrote some key words on a piece of paper and put it in the map holder on my handle-bar bag, so I could learn whilst cycling along.

On those mountain roads I hardly saw any cars at all. The roads went via all of the villages on the mountain, even if one was at the top and the next one was at the bottom! Up and down I went, from near sea level to well over a thousand metres and back again.

I saw an old man sitting sideways on a donkey, his bum over one side and his feet over the other, gently swinging his heels against the donkey's belly. He held the rope in his hand and nonchalantly waggled it around, encouraging the donkey to keep up his steady trot. All the time, he was talking to himself or the donkey, and he waved as I passed him on my way to Megalopoli.

I free-camped in an olive grove over-looking a steep valley, with flowers all around, the smell of mint in the air and a high cliff rising up behind me. All this scenery, the lack of traffic and tourists, the laid-back way of life and the friendly people made my ten-day circuit of Peleponese the perfect way of getting back into it, after what had happened in Italy the previous year. When the April sun came out it was beautiful, but even the plentiful rain didn't put me off. I would simply laze about in the tent and read, or find some shelter, get my petrol stove out and cook up some pasta. I was perfectly happy, and my confidence was growing by the day.

I reached the eastern coast and visited the old Venetian city of Nafplio, before heading cross-country, back up towards Patra. One afternoon I dropped down a tarmac road, round the hairpin bends and into a deep valley with nothing but olive groves and a tiny village called Amphithea. There the tarmac ended and I stopped to have a look at the village, just a handful of humble cottages.

Two men wandered over to talk to me, undeterred by the language barrier. One of them invited me into his house for some food, which I gratefully accepted, once I'd worked out what he meant.

His living room was modest, with a black and white television and an old telephone. He motioned for me to sit down on a spindly chair on the concrete floor, next to a couple of beds. A tea towel, laid out on the threadbare couch, was covered with fresh fruit. On the table were a newspaper, a pack of playing cards and a few religious trinkets. A dusty mirror was nailed to the wall, next to a fading photo of a woman, and the ancient curtains were practically falling off their rails.

The man was the perfect host, extremely generous considering what little he had. Using the basic Greek I'd learnt, I told him I was twenty-eight. He told me he was eighty, but he looked about a hundred years old, really gaunt and small. We managed to have a few laughs, despite the language problems, and he wrote his name in my phrase book, with a slow, unsteady hand; Pano, Filipaki.

He gave me a bowl of salty cabbage soup with beans in, and had some himself. We cut some hunks of bread, and some strong-tasting cheese, which looked like translucent edam. While I was eating, he disappeared out of the house for a minute, coming back with a handful of olives. When I could eat no more, he poured me a glass of potent local wine, to wash the whole lot down.

I thanked him for his generosity and offered to give him some of the food I'd bought earlier on, but he wouldn't take anything. As I was leaving, he gave me the rest of the bread, two cakes and a bag full of olives. Then, patting me on the back, he led me out into the sun and pointed out my way to Patra; a steep tractor track winding its way up through the olive groves.

Igoumenitsa, Greece, to Istanbul, Turkey

Terrified, I escaped up a side-road, away from the relentless river of mud and the malicious trucks. Thunder broke, the rain lashed down even harder and lightning cracked above the wires. I came to a standstill in the middle of the road, frozen to the spot. The next bolt of lightning was directly over my head, and I decided that I just had to keep moving. I found an abandoned house and hid there to regain my composure.

I continued on my way. I'd finally reached Istanbul but getting to the centre was proving impossible; this peninsular-bound city of ten million people sprawls out for miles. I reached the coastal road and followed it for an eternity. The drivers were impetuous but I was too cold, wet and tired to fight for space…

Once I reached Patra I took the ferry back up to Corfu to meet my mum, Berlie, for a week's holiday. It was the first time we'd seen each other since I left Sheffield. We had a mad time, blowing out the touristy bits and hiring a car on the mainland to explore the mountains in the north. At the end of the week we dropped off the car, picked my bike up and walked over to the ferry. We were in Igoumenitsa, on the western coast. My mum got the ferry back to Corfu for her plane home, while I turned around, ready now to tackle the route to the East.

Dear Gerry

I was delighted to receive your recent letter enclosing cheques amounting to £117. This brings Tim's total to a magnificent £1,357.00 to date.

I am so glad to hear that Tim's eczema has improved. It must have been disappointing to have to abandon his ride in Italy because of this. I hope things go well for Tim's ride to Greece, and that the Spring temperature is a little more conducive to cycling activities.

Please pass on our good wishes to Tim when you next speak to him.

I MISSED THE FERRY! GREECE '98.

ME IN GREECE '98

Yours sincerely

Sue Lodge
Appeals Officer
Intermediate Technology Development Group

After a very hilly ride I got to Ioannina and found a campsite, where I made friends with a girl from New Zealand. She'd been travelling on her own for over a year and she was raving about Istanbul.
"It's such a fantastic place," she said, "really *ixcellent*!"
"Well, that'll spur me on then!"
"Don't cyclist's raise money for charity, to give them the incentive to carry on?"
"Yeah, I was doing that before. I raised quite a bit, but I've done that now. I asked everyone I could for donations, so I'm happy that I did my bit."
"Well done."
"Yeah, thanks! Anyway, I've not really got a proper plan now. I'm just going to get as far as I can, before I go back to my girlfriend."
"Next stop Istanbul!"
"That's right. Next stop Istanbul!"
The following day's ride was even hillier than the last. I did nothing but pedal all day over one big mountain, down again and up over the Katara Pass. Even after that, when I turned onto a smaller road, it still went up. But the view behind, of snow-covered mountains and lush green meadows full of flowers, was inspiring. The road was lined with snow poles and I passed a ski slope. At last I started to descend into a cool pine forest on a dirt track, losing altitude rapidly. I pitched the tent by a spring and cooked some spaghetti, followed by a "choc-n-orange" hot drink that my mum had given me.

Once I left the mountains, the landscape became much more arid, with nothing but wheat-fields and poppies. Another series of mountains and another plain led me all the way to the sea and a hostel in the City of Thessaloniki, whose name means "Victory in Thessali". Historically, it was an important city on the trading route to the Balkans. It also happens to be on the Ignatia, an ancient Roman road connecting Rome with Constantinople (Istanbul).

Near Lake Volvi, I stopped in a village square and sat down to write my diary. After a while I looked up and saw three giggling girls, about ten years old, sitting a few yards away. The oldest one came over to me and gave me a hand-full of pistachios. I gave her some biscuits in return and she went back to her friends.

I went over with my diary and pen to ask them their names, as one by one their friends joined us. Antiopi was eleven years old and could speak some English. She sent her sister Natassa home to bring her English textbooks. Angela, their younger sister, was the loudest one. She thought I was a bit dumb because, no matter what she shouted out, I couldn't understand. Her way of asking me, "How long has it taken you to cycle from England to here?" was to shout at the top of her voice in English, "HOW MANY… MOTORBIKE?" When one of the lads made out that she was in love with him, she went to great pains to explain the word "Tsemmata," as in, "It's a lie." She even found it in my phrase book and wrote it down, pointing emphatically at it whenever anything else untrue was said.

Kris said he was fifteen years old, but I didn't believe it for a minute. He liked making rude insinuations and strangling his mates. Then there were Tollis and Polina, two kids called George and two called Danny. This went on for about an hour. I was surrounded by hyperactive, laughing kids, half of whom were trying to murder each other. It was cool! I asked them if I could take their photo and all but Kris and Polina lined up. Natassa took a picture of me with the others, and I gave my chocolate biscuits to Antiopi to share out. I cycled off as they waved and shouted, "Thank you! Thank you!"

The next day I saw another cycle tourist coming towards me, and he pulled over and stopped.

"Hi, how are you!" I asked

"I'm fine! Where are you from? I am from Iran!" he smiled.

I can't remember his name but he was a crazy bloke, thirty years old, with a scraggy beard, and his mountain bike loaded up in a complicated way. He was a good laugh and we shared his coke and my biscuits while we chatted for an hour.

"Where are you going?" I asked, munching a digestive.

"I am going to Germany. I left home one month ago, and I have two months left."

"Why do you have to go back? Is it because of your girlfriend?"

"No, I don't have a girlfriend. If I did, I wouldn't be able to do this!"

"My girlfriend didn't stop me!" I said, feeling very lucky.

"Well, she is unusual! If I can't go away with the bicycle I become upset. Whenever I travel, it is always by bicycle!"

"But two months is a long time to reach Germany."

"Ahh, I will also visit Austria and Switzerland, maybe France as well. But I always travel slowly, slowly. There is no hurry!"

"Did you meet the French cyclist, Paul? He's been through Iran and Turkey."

"No, but I did meet an Italian man in Turkey. He was walking to Israel! He was pushing his wardrobe along in a wheelbarrow!" He cracked up, tears of laughter rolling down his cheeks.

He told me that travelling in Turkey was easy for him, saying that he's a Muslim and that his mother tongue is Turkish. He told me that the Turks come from a part of the world that is now Iran, Azerbaijan and Uzbekistan. In the end it was too cold to stand around any longer. He grinned and shook my hand and off we went; me towards his homeland, and he towards mine.

In the picturesque port of Kavala I saw the first sign for Istanbul; "Konstantinoupolis 460 km," and a week after leaving my mum on the western coast of Greece, I reached Alexandroupolis, near the Turkish border.

Getting out of Greece and into No Man's Land was easy. Crossing the river Evros, the actual border, on a steel girder bridge in the sunshine with armed guards at either end, was an indescribable feeling: "THIS IS IT!"

The Turkish customs was all chaos, confusion, stale cigarette air and run down concrete huts. I changed forty Dollars for ten million Turkish Lira, my three-month visa was made and I was allowed to go.

I cycled out, past the last row of guards and a little way down the road before exploding in a "YEE-HA!!!"

The sun was out and everyone beeped or waved. Trucks filled the road and I was being extremely cautious because I'd heard lots of horror stories about Turkish roads. I was wearing my cycle helmet and looking over my shoulder every few seconds. The Iranian I'd met the other day had bought a rear view mirror for his bike. I decided I'd need to get one in Istanbul.

Something very scary happened after I'd been in Turkey for about an hour. I was already feeling nervous because of the traffic, when I came to the top of a small hill to find three evil dogs coming at me, out of a lonely cottage. They caught me up with frightening speed. One was tearing along, snapping at my ankle. Another was just behind, level with the pannier bags. The third was right by my front wheel, just as I started to accelerate down the other side. I could see his vicious teeth and I tried a new trick, which worked first time. At the top of my voice, my eyes coming out on stalks, I shouted, "GET LOST, DOG!" All three of them suddenly legged it over to the other side of the road.

A bus came zooming up towards them and the driver blared his horn at them but made no attempt to slow down, and I could see that one of them wasn't going to make it. I heard a thud and watched over my shoulder as the back wheels went over the dog, kicking it into the air. It landed on the road and its mates gathered around it. I was going downhill fast, half retching, and I wasn't going back. I kept telling myself that it's not just Turkey; I've seen dogs getting run over before.

It was a sobering sight, and as the darkness closed in I was stuck with nowhere to camp, just open fields everywhere. The next morning I woke up in my jammy free-camping spot in the pouring rain, after not much sleep and lots of worry. I'd found it after ten minutes of total darkness, right by the road but set down off a little track, completely screened by a line of trees.

It was not a nice morning's ride. Strong headwinds, rain and trucks hampered my progress, but I passed a very significant sign; "Istanbul 160 km." Other road signs were not so encouraging, telling drivers not to smash into each other; this is obviously not considered to be common sense in Turkey.

The next day I rode the last seventy miles to Istanbul. This was the most uppy-downy, roller-coaster of a day I've ever had to endure, and I didn't even get to see any of the sights. I left the rip-off, muddy campsite early to get going. I ate only junk food because I didn't have time to cook and eat properly. It was simply a case of "Whatever happens, I'm getting to Istanbul today!" And stuff did happen – plenty of it…

The rain and wind were intermittent at first and the traffic of lethal trucks and buses built up gradually. A motorway had been built but none of them use it, probably to avoid paying a toll. The only way I could cycle without endangering my life was to use the hard shoulder or the occasional small road running alongside, but riding on these was painfully slow; all mud, puddles and potholes.

One of the things I'd been anxious about was the back tyre; it had brought me all the way from Sheffield and was beginning to fray on the side. I went over a speed-hump on a side-road, and the tyre exploded. The inner tube had poked out of a small hole in the tyre wall, become compressed and blown.

Within seconds, people and kids surrounded me in the pouring rain. The two men who offered to help me were like chalk and cheese. One was a friendly local, who acted as the translator, from Turkish into German. The other was actually a native of Bulgaria. He was incredibly arrogant, taking over and refusing to listen to me. Bashing the wheel around, he insisted that he had to go to his house to get another tyre, but I HAD to put my spare tube in first, just so that I could wheel the loaded bike along. This he just couldn't understand!

We ended up with bits and pieces all over the pavement and he cycled off in a foul mood on his old bike, to fetch the tyre from his house. As soon as he came back around the corner I could see that he'd brought a twenty-seven inch tyre, which was too big. I told the German speaker, "Dieser Reifen ist zu gross!" The Bulgarian pedalled up, all cheesy grin, showing off the tyre. He offered it up to my wheel, which passed clean through it!

After I lost a tug-of-war, he took off with my wheel to a bike shop. The German speaker and I had to follow by car, having dumped my bike in his house. Neither of them believed me when I said the new tyre might be too WIDE! The bike shop turned out to be a wooden shack in the middle of some muddy waste-ground, with old frames and tyres on the roof.

The Bulgarian guy fitted a knobbly twenty-six inch tyre onto my wheel, and when we went back to the house we found that it only just had enough clearance in the bike frame. If he'd only let me do it myself, or at least listen to me, the whole affair would have been very simple. What he left out, despite all my protests, was the tyre liner which I always use. This magic stuff was the only reason I'd got this far from Sheffield with no punctures. Sure enough, only an hour after this fiasco, on a horrible wet main road, the new tyre let a nail through and went flat!

I found a garage and asked to use their facilities, but they fixed the puncture for me, "as a present." They too couldn't see the point of the tyre liner, and they certainly wouldn't let me fit it myself, but I insisted, as nicely as possible, and it was re-installed.

The rain kept coming down in buckets, and the riding was slow because of the new knobbly tyre. The road gradually became a fast-flowing muddy river, and it was impossible to see the many potholes lurking underwater. My brakes were having no effect and I was being splashed and honked by all the cars and trucks. The thunder and lightning only added to my fear and misery. In a word, it was awful.

I asked someone how far it was to Sultan Ahmet, where the hostels are. He said, "Four kilometres." I thought, "I've made it!" I pedalled on for another hour, fell off my bike, carried on and then asked another guy. He said, "Twenty kilometres." Disillusioned, I joined a main road and it started pissing it down again. The road once again became a river and I hatefully watched the lunatic drivers as I stood under a tree, bitterly cold and with no idea how far I had to go. Suddenly, I completely lost my nerve and screamed, "All I want to do is get to the Hostel!"

A moped went past and the rider lost it in a drowned-out pothole. He stood there and eventually got the engine started again. I watched him ride off, then set off along the pavement, but merely crossing the junctions proved almost impossible.

I noticed a sign ahead and did a double-take; "CAMPING." I couldn't believe it! I went into the office and the guy sat me down and gave me a little green fruit called "Eric." A Dutch lady came in, and while I sat there shivering uncontrollably, she told me all about her three-month motor-home trip with her husband.

I pitched my tent in the rain, then sat inside, still shivering, with no food to eat. I said to myself, "I wish one of these nice couples would invite me into their motor-home for a meal and a chat." Just then, I heard a woman's voice saying, "I was just looking for you!" It was the Dutch lady, coming to invite me into their motor-home for a meal and a chat. And some beer! It sounds silly, but I almost burst into tears.

After a boiling hot shower I joined Mr and Mrs Dutch-people and had a wonderful evening. The next day they left a note outside my tent saying, "Have a nice journey, Jeanne and Jan, Holland." I rode the last three or four miles to Sultan Ahmet in the rain. My rear cantilever brakes failed terminally on the way but I didn't care; I could see the Blue Mosque!

"Hallo!"
"Hallo! Ist Verena hier bitte?"
"Ja Hallo Timmy… Moment bitte…. Verena… Der Tim!"

Blue Mosque, Istanbul, Turkey '98

"Timmy! How are you!"

"Oh, I'm cool, Lady! I just had to try seventeen phones till this stupid card worked!"

"Are you in Istanbul yet?"

"Yeah, I got to the old bit yesterday. The ride was an absolute nightmare, all those trucks trying to run me off the road, and it was chucking it down!"

"Oh, honey, don't worry, you can have a rest now!"

"I know. I've found this really cool hostel. I'm in a dorm with a load of travellers. I reckon I'll stay for another week. I've got to get the visa for Syria sorted, anyway!"

"Have you seen any of the sights yet?"

"Oh, you can't miss them! I went into the Blue Mosque this morning… it's absolutely huge, and really beautiful. I went in the Aya Sofia afterwards, and that's even more amazing…"

"Why?"

"Well, it's stupidly old, fifteen hundred years or something! Everything is absolutely massive, and it was converted from a cathedral or whatever, into a mosque! The minarets were added later!"

"It sounds really interesting, Timmy!"

"Anyway, right, and next off I'm going for a kebab, even though I only had one an hour ago.."

"Timmy…!"

"Yeah, and I've got to buy some new brakes for the bike, see the Palace and the bazaar, slack about in the hostel…"

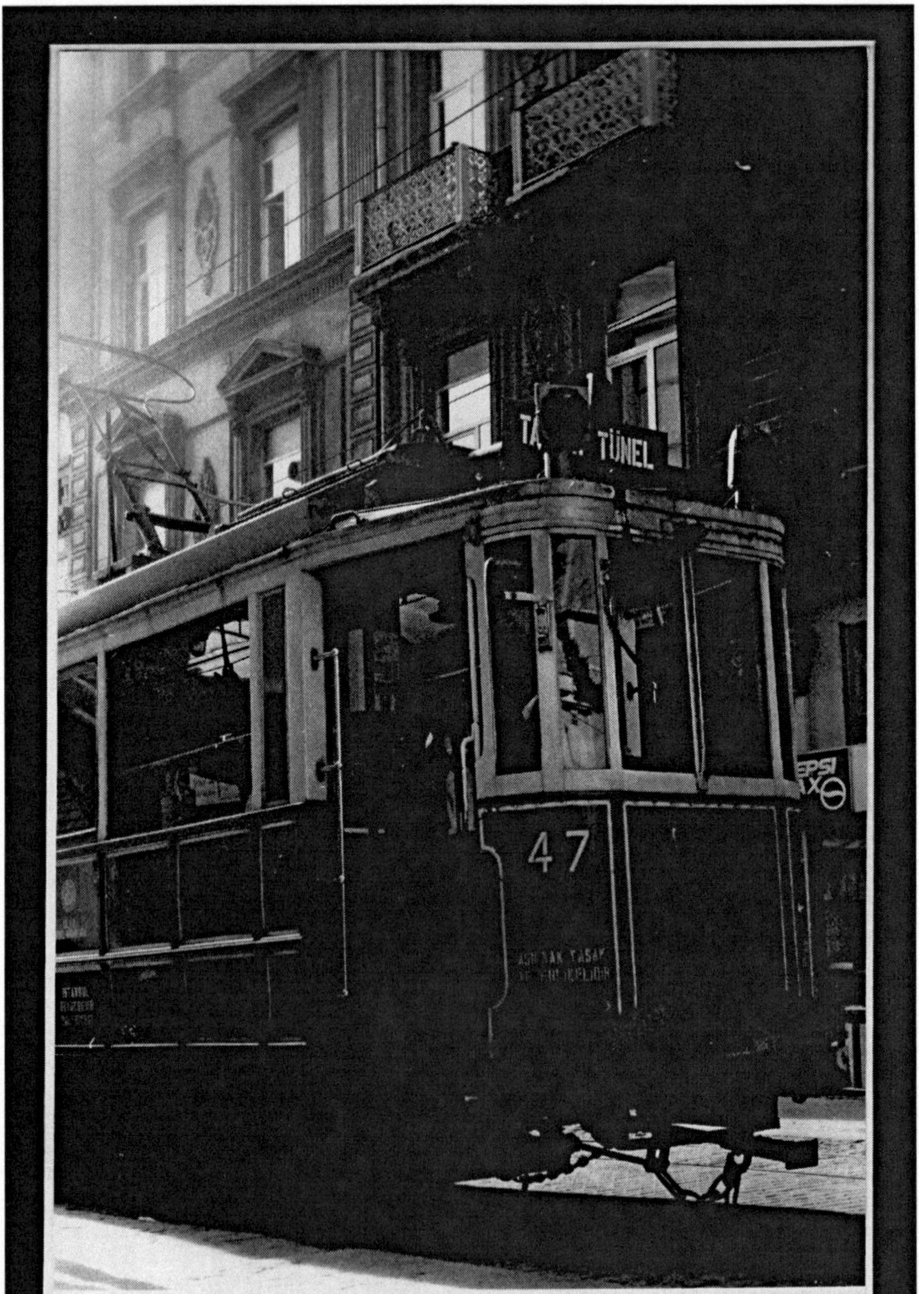
TÜNEL
47
ISTANBUL, TURKEY, '98.

Central Anatolia, Turkey

...I was bundled into a transit van with five armed jendarmes, and we blasted down to Cimsit and the scene of the crime. One of them kept cocking his pistol and pointing it at his head, pretending to blow his brains out. They were all hyped up at the prospect of going on a raid to help an English cyclist, and Urcun was doing his level best as translator. Joking about what they were going to do to Mr. Bilgin, they mimed his execution. Urcun told me, "We will string him up!"...

The very same day that I left Istanbul, I met a Belgian cyclist with his panniers full of the fruit he'd scrumped. He said he'd like to go with me to Syria, but knew he wouldn't be allowed in as he had a stamp from Israel in his passport.

So it was that I continued alone again, which was fine at first because the mountains around the Marmara Sea were beautiful in the May sun. But then the boredom set in again as the weather deteriorated and I headed across the endless plateau for Capadoccia. My skin started to go again as I had to do a week's free-camping with no showers. I was having a bad day of knee problems when I stopped in the middle of nowhere for a rest.

As I was sitting, cooking my tea, late in the afternoon, a minibus pulled up because it had a puncture. The passengers got out while the driver changed the wheel, and a man with two donkeys came over from one of the fields to see what was going on. He came over to me, his donkeys surrounded by orbiting flies. He then went off, sitting right on the back of one donkey, chasing the other one whilst making "Eeyore" noises and waving his arms around. When the minibus had gone, he came back and tried to talk to me in Turkish, asking if I had any cigarettes.

He asked if he could have a go on the bike. I let him ride it down the road and back, whilst I was eating. He pointed the other way, up the road, and I told him he could go that way for a bit. Meandering off up the road, he showed off to his mates in the field. He got further and further away and I packed up my stove and sat waiting.

When it was became obvious that he wasn't actually going to come back at all, as I thought might be the case, I stood up and had a look around. There were no houses in sight, and nothing at all on the drab horizon. I stood there with my handlebar bag in one hand, and a pannier bag in the other. It seemed that my bike had gone, and I wasn't really bothered, as I'd been having such a bad day of knees and eczema. If I had no bike anymore, then it would be the end of my journey, which seemed just fine. He also had the other the pannier bag containing the tent, my sleeping bag and some odds and sods.

One of the other shepherds came over, a stubbled man with dark skin and kind brown eyes. I took out my dictionary and pointed to the word "name." He pointed to the next word down, which was "naïve" and then pointed at me! He wrote down his own name, Fikret Kobkovo, and his phone number. He also gave me the thief's address and I took his photo, just in case. The other shepherds came over and told me the thief's name – Mr. Bilgin.

We tried to flag down a few cars, but with no luck, until a taxi came along. He drove like a madman to a Jendarmerie twenty miles up the road, and wouldn't accept any money. I tried to explain to the soldier at the gate and he blew his whistle to summon an English speaker. A lad called Urcun came to hear my story. I was allowed in, and once they'd sat me down inside the building, Urcun explained to his seniors what had happened. One of the men, a doctor, asked me to clarify the story by writing it down. I wrote:

"My bicycle has been stolen. It was taken by a shepherd..."

I burst out laughing when I saw what I'd written; it looked so ridiculous. It was decided that I should return to the scene by transit van, accompanied by Urcun and four others. Fikret had moved on with his sheep in the meantime, but we soon found him and we shook hands, then he talked to the driver and went back to his flock. We drove to a tiny village and I thought, "How do we know that this is it?"

The fact that my bike was in the shed right in front of me was a dead give-away! This was obviously Mr Bilgin's house. I inspected the bike, then brought it out and laid it on the grass. Bilgin had obviously managed to crash it. The handlebars were bent, the brake levers were damaged, and the third water-bottle cage was twisted.

Urcun said, "Be grateful to God that you have it back. Don't examine." He had a point. The thief wasn't around, so we couldn't go into his house to retrieve my other belongings. The entire village gathered around us, and there was a hysterical woman who must have been Bilgin's mother. For two hours we awaited his return, until well after dark.

A beaten-up Renault 12 turned up with five more jendarme crammed inside. Urcun's colleague made the silly mistake of telling the villagers how much the bike was worth, and two of them started fighting. The situation rapidly developed into one of edginess and anger, as one of the fighters pointed at me, shouting venomously, and the armed soldiers tried to break up the fight. I was made to sit in the van for my own safety, and I watched with Urcun through the dusty window. The scene looked just like one of those harrowing items on the news; the village with its simple adobe houses, barred windows and muddy streets, the peasants arguing amongst themselves and the soldiers trying to break it all up. I could just imagine one of them taking his pistol and shooting a peasant in the head, to shut everyone up.

Thankfully, that didn't happen, but I sat there feeling guilty for having brought this upon them. One of the men in the fight, it turned out, was Mr. Bilgin's uncle and he was on my side. He said he was sorry for what his nephew had done, and he even brought Urcun and me some tea, bread and a plate of macaroni!

I'd only just started tucking in, when the jendarmes jumped back into the van. It was obviously kicking off time. We drove to another Jendarmerie where I was entertained and asked about Manchester United, whilst they plied me with tea, along with chicken and vegetables. But I was still worried about the rest of my stuff.

At ten p.m. we got into the van again, drove for a while and stopped in the middle of nowhere. I had to get out and wondered what was going on. I realised that we were back outside Mr. Bilgin's house, and there on the grass was all my stuff. Actually my trousers weren't there, Bilgin was still at large and was probably wearing them, along with my garish swimming trunks, but I didn't care. I just wanted to get out of there.

I told them everything was there, shaking hands with the uncle and the mother to show my gratitude. I sat in the van and she came over, looking timid, her brow furrowed with worry. She wiped her hands as if to say, "Is that all over and done with, then?" I did the same to say, "Yes". Six hours after the theft we drove off, as the whole village waved goodbye.

The two vehicles raced each other along an old narrow road. As we followed only inches behind the Renault, it struck me that Turkish drivers say, "Turkish drivers are dangerous," without realising that they are talking about themselves.

We got back to the first Jendarmerie, alive, and spent the next two hours making reports on old klanky typewriters. One of the men, an incredibly tall and lanky soldier, asked me to write a letter to their Headquarters in Ankara, saying how grateful I was, so that his boss would get a pat on the back. His energetic miming and fast Turkish talking were hilarious, while he tried to explain what he wanted me to write.

At nearly one o'clock in the morning, Urcun showed me a selection of photos of himself trying to look beautiful, posing by blossoming trees. The idea was that I should take one of the pictures back to England to help him find an English girlfriend. This happened every few days; Turkish men wanting either an English girlfriend or a visa.

    I finally got to sleep in the soldiers' dormitory, without having had a desperately needed shower, because Urcun forgot to ask his boss, but you can't have everything! The beds in the dorm were far from clean, but everything was folded up and positioned exactly. Urcun woke me up at half past seven from a very deep sleep to ask if I wanted some breakfast. I ate in his office and he said he'd been up working until three in the morning.
    He told me that he couldn't wait until he's finished his National Service. He worked in a hotel before, and after he's finished he'll work in a Camel cigarette factory. Another lad said he was working as a DJ on a Turkish rock radio station in Istanbul, and he'll go back there afterwards.
    Urcun had to put on his smart clothes and shiny shoes to nervously take me to the big boss man to finish the diplomatic stuff. The big boss man was all smiles and handshakes. I thanked him and Urcun profusely, and soon I was back on the open road. I had to ride the first twenty miles just to get back to where the bike had been stolen. A rainstorm stopped me for an hour, just two miles beyond that place. I sheltered at a petrol station and glued my eyes to the bike.

Cappadocia, Turkey to Aleppo, Syria

A couple of days after the bike robbery I finally managed to get a shower, by staying in the basic "Otel Banana" in Kirsehir. From there it was an easy day's ride to a place of magical beauty, where people live in houses hewn from the very hills; Goreme in Cappadocia. The valley came into view, and countless rock pinnacles covered the land, stretching beyond the horizon. As I gathered speed down the twisting road, I could make out the doors and windows carved into these peculiar towers. I cut through the hot air, driving off the aches and pains of the last week on the cold plateau, enthusiastically leaning the bike into the fast curves…

CAPPADOCIA, TURKEY '98.

I found a campsite in the middle of the village, and the man brought me a table and chair, a blanket and a glass of apple tea. When I went for a wander and saw the houses up close, I couldn't stop laughing. It was such an extraordinary place, and many of the strange, conical rock pillars are still lived in after almost two thousand years.

Over the hill from Goreme is a valley of unbelievable, timeless beauty. There were more houses carved into the rock pillars, with farmers walking along the meandering pathways to their fields. Green and in full blossom, the valley could have been a wonderland from a fairytale. Birdsong and the humming of bees filled the milk-warm air, and young children played between colossal rock toadstools.

I went over to a horse to take a photograph. An amiable farmer appeared with his wife, their baby and their eight-year old son. They welcomed me to their home, and the son stayed to watch me take some pictures of the horse, Sahil. I went back the same afternoon, bearing gifts of bread, honey, pencils and so on, but I couldn't find them anywhere.

Back on the campsite, I was joined by a couple of other cyclists, on their way to New Zealand. Martino was an Italian and his wife, Evelyn, was Swiss. We cooked up a big meal together and sat around, eating and talking. They told me that they weren't cycling all the way as sometimes they preferred to chuck everything on a bus. Their next country would be Iran, which had them both worried. They had hoped that their visas wouldn't be granted, but they were, so they had to go.

The next day we went for a walk together and found an intriguing Byzantine church, carved inside the rock, complete with integral pillars, alcoves, pews and a second room beneath. Ancient frescoes adorned the walls, pillars and ceilings, the faces of the figures having been erased by the Muslims, centuries ago.

We found a secret valley, which I explored that evening. I followed the small sandy gorge, only just wide enough to walk up, with rock pillars towering up on both sides and the windows of ancient dwellings visible high above. I had to climb a ten-foot high, trickling waterfall chute, then the riverbed squeezed its way through a series of long tunnels. These were natural but had been widened, perhaps hundreds of years ago, to make it possible to walk up. The tunnels were intimidating, devoid of any light. I had no torch and had to feel my way around the corners till I could see the light, my sandals slipping into the wet hollows in the riverbed. Eventually I surfaced, miles from Goreme.

I spent the evening with Martino and Evelyn, plus some other Swiss campers who invited us for a barbecue. Before diving into our tents, I told Martino and Evelyn that they were lucky to be able to travel together.

"You've really got it sussed!"

"I know!" said Martino.

"You can do this, and still be with your wife!"

"Well," laughed Evelyn, "it doesn't always work that easily… sometimes he'd rather cycle, when I want to take the bus!"

"Yeah but you seem to sort it out okay. And you've got everything with you… even a kitchen sink!"

"A foldaway plastic bowl, you mean. We've got too much really. Martino even has a spare pairs of shoes!"

"Well, that's the thing; I wouldn't want to be dragging all that stuff around. The little trailer looks cool, but it must be dangerous when a truck suddenly blasts you off the road!"

"Oh, it's not so bad! Anyway, we must get some sleep. If we don't see you in the morning, have a nice time in Syria!"

"Yeah, thanks! And send me a postcard from Iran… maybe I'll bump into you again…"

Months later, when I rang home one time, my dad Gerry told me that there was a postcard for me from two people called Martino and Evelyn, saying how much they'd enjoyed Iran.

As I rode south from Goreme, towards a range of alpine mountains, I had the same dilemma going on inside me that troubled me almost every day. I really felt that I was now capable of cycling around the world, and that I wouldn't be able to settle down unless I'd done it. I'd be riding along thinking, "Yes, I'm going to do it!" Then, half an hour later, I'd be sitting by the edge of the road, crying my eyes out because I couldn't stand being away from Verena.

She'd given me leave to go off for a few months, to see how far I could get. I hadn't known what I would do, but I was starting to get more of a long-term plan together. I was now heading for Syria, and would return to Cappadocia before riding to the Turkish / Iranian border. I would then travel by bus all the way back Austria to spend a few weeks with Verena, and somehow tell her that I wasn't yet done;

I wanted to get a visa for Iran and carry on. This would be an incredibly hard thing to tell her, as she was expecting me to take her back to England that October. The decision to let me go on would rest with her, because if it meant losing her, it wouldn't be worth it.

My gorgeous alpine road took me through simple hamlets, where the only thing belonging to the twentieth century was the occasional tractor. As in Greece, the cafes are patronised by the men only, who take their time over glass after glass of chai, and games of cards, dominoes or backgammon. I would join them with my basic Turkish, my phrase book and lots of miming. This was the perfect way to escape the sun and the road, and it took my mind off other things.

I was free-camping for most of the nights, and walking about in the grass in my sandals was a bit risky. The Youth Hostel man in Istanbul had told me that he used to be a shepherd and was always afraid of the snakes; "I'm walking…….with my sheep….and maybe I see…quickly…..it's him snake! And I go "Wahhh!"……and maybe, me brother, he got…rifle, and if him quick…he "PAM!"…shoot him snake......I don't like snake....And then, we bury dead snake outside house...Sometimes, in the night, him fox come, dig up dead snake, eat 'im all up...in morning – no more snake! Also, sometimes, we hear wolf or we see....him wolf...I scared of wolf! When I walking in grass with my sheep... I always looking....him snake...him fox......him wolf...When you camping in the night....you be careful....him snake bery bad!"

The tranquility of the road was suddenly lost when it joined a main road at the confluence of another valley. It was back to trucks, fumes and grime, all the way to Adana on the south coast. I dropped down to sea-level from seventeen hundred metres and the temperature soared as I descended. In the space of an hour, I went from lush green vegetation with trees and flowers everywhere, to semi-arid coastland. I couldn't see the sea for the haze, but I knew it was there.

East of Adana I saw some fascinating vignettes of Turkish life. Gypsy camps with plastic sheeting for walls, covered in layers of thick grass. An old woman kneading dough, sitting on a carpet of straw, the ruined façade of some forgotten Roman or Greek building behind her. Old Renaults with twelve passengers overtaking donkeys loaded high with straw. Rivers crowded with boys, playing in the water under a scorching sun.

I made it to Iskenderun one night, now very close to the Syrian border. In a Lokanta (a basic restaurant) I had a plateful of rice with bean and pork stew, plus a plate of boiled chicken with potatoes and vegetables, all for less than £1. In the morning I got some money from a cash machine, but as the banks were closed I couldn't change it for Syrian currency. I had to set off anyway, on a hill-climb from sea level to almost eight hundred metres in the searing heat. I dropped down on the other side, into a totally arid and swelteringly hot valley. I had a strong tailwind and for a while I was doing motorbike speeds, until it became a side-wind, sapping all of my strength.

Everything was burning and I was drinking constantly. Some people were working in the fields, but most were just lazing around under the trees by the road. At five o'clock I reached the Turkish side of the border. A guy filled in a form for me and then demanded baksheesh, but I told him to get lost! I sat in a café and had my last Turkish toasts and tea for a few weeks, washed down with several litres of cold water.

The formalities of leaving Turkey took seconds, and then I was in no man's land. A tight valley wound around for a couple of kilometres, full of wrecked cars and old tyres.

Then I reached Syria! Approaching the gate, I saw three men sitting around a bed in the shade. On the bed was a border guard, fast asleep. A very amicable guard checked me in before sending me to Passport Control. There I had to fill in my visitor's card, but the guy stamped it before I'd even finished, saying I could go! All of the signs in English were extremely polite.

Next, I cycled up to the second gate beyond which lay Syria proper. There was a big fat man wearing an immaculate white outfit, and behind him was his Mercedes. He reeked of money but displayed only courtesy, a genuine interest in my trip and an eagerness for me to enjoy myself in Syria. The border guards were in no hurry, as there was no other traffic. Eventually, one of them eased himself out of his chair to walk with me to the gate. He undid the padlock and pushed the gate open, its hinges creaking loudly as if to say, "Nobody has been across this border for years."

Further on was yet another gate, and these guards were also slumped in their chairs. They let me go after a few sociable questions, and I had two hours of daylight left to cover nearly thirty miles to Aleppo.

Luckily I had a tailwind again. The heat had dropped and the sun was behind me, adorning the flat-roofed stone houses with a fantastic golden light. Everything zoomed by at an astounding speed and as I flew through the villages, people tried to wave me into their houses.

There was hardly any traffic, and most of the time I was given plenty of space by passing mini-buses. People seem to drive just as fast as in Turkey, but they don't try to run you off the road. Bystanders would stare at me until I acknowledged them, then they'd start cheering, waving and clapping as I rode by.

I passed many dark and dingy auto repair shops, most of which had ten-year old boys working there, covered in grease and dirt. As darkness fell I reached the outskirts of Aleppo, a city of three million people.

I met a local guy on a racing bike and he said he'd lead me to the centre so I could find a hotel. Going through the night traffic was scary and I had to trust that he knew what he was doing. Despite the crazy route, he was keen to have a conversation on the move. It turned out that he'd taken part in the "Tour of the Czech Republic" bike race, so he must be fit as a fiddle.

He left me outside a hotel, where enthusiastic people surrounded me. Before I even made it into the hotel I was whisked into a tyre shop to meet everybody. Brothers, uncles, fathers, some dressed in grey Kaftans and others in jeans or boiler-suits. I was delighted but more than a little overwhelmed. In Syria, it seemed, hospitality and greetings come before the things you need; phone-calls, showers and sleep are put on the back burner! Eventually I got into my hotel room, had a shower to cool the sunburn off and slept like a lamb under the spinning fan.

Aleppo to Palmyra, Syria

It turned out that I had a serious money problem in Syria. My Visa card was useless and my Turkish Lira was only worth half of its actual value here. I'd been planning to stay for four weeks but actually I only had £20's worth of Syrian Currency. My only option was to spend some of this money to send a fax to Verena and see if she could send me some Dollars....

I met a shifty character who said he could help me to send the fax. I arranged to meet him at four o'clock outside the mosque. In the meantime I explored one of the ancient Souqs, similar to the Grand Bazaar in Istanbul. This particular one was the textile Souq, spinning with the commotion of a thousand colourful market-stalls in a seven hundred-year old labyrinthine building. Bicycles, horses and small vans squeezed their way through the crowds. The air hung thick, layered with dust, exhaust from the two-stroke engines, and the constant sounds of bartering.

The people I met were either genuinely friendly or they would suddenly spring a sales pitch on you, halfway through a conversation. Miraculously I came out of the Souq at the same place I'd gone in, weaving my way amongst the tea-sellers in their fantastic costumes, people carrying huge bundles on their heads, men in Kaftans and veiled women, covered in black from head to toe.

I entered the Mosque, where a man beckoned me over to a cloakroom to put on a long garment and remove my shoes. The tiled floor, under the blazing sun, was too hot to walk on. Time slowed down as I sat in the shade, marvelling at the majestic courtyard and its fountains. The vast space around me was framed by walls of ochre-coloured marble, with a pure blue sky and sharp contrasts between light and dark. Dwarfed black figures drifted in the brilliant light; praying, carrying out their ablutions or relaxing in this oasis of tranquility.

The dodgy guy with the fax machine appeared on time, but after he'd taken me round the houses to his office, it turned out to have broken two days before. I then found one at a hotel but the minimum charge was £6.50, so I went to the Post Office, where at last I was lucky.

Verena
Got No Money.
Fax charged per minute, so keep it short.
Please send me $150 to the Post Restante in Damascus, A.S.A.P.
Pay you back later!
Love, Timmy xxxx

The fax didn't get through but the lady re-sent it and only charged me once, having read my desperate message! The reply came after five minutes:

Timmy
No problem, I'll do it straight away. Do you want cash or travellers cheques?
Verena

Arrgh! A question! I had to pay for another fax!

Lady,
Cash.
You're a star!
T. xxxx

I set off in the midday sun on the road to Damascus, two hundred miles to the south. I took four days over it, as it was cheaper to live on the road than in the city. After thirty miles I found a petrol station and asked for a shop, but was immediately invited in for chai.

While I drank this, I was introduced to everyone, and one of the men invited me to his house for some food. I followed him on his ancient motorbike along the dusty street. We passed a shop on the way but I never had the chance or the need to use it. The man was the petrol pump attendant, but he was running out of petrol! We parked up in his little garage and opened the door to the courtyard. An elderly man in a Kaftan and headscarf was sitting in the shade and I was introduced to him.

I was shown into a room with straw mats on the concrete floor and cushions round the edges. My friend introduced me to his three young children and his brothers. His wife came in briefly but she was busy in the kitchen preparing the food. I thanked her by saying "Shukran" when she brought the tray in, but she didn't respond. I think I was expected to show my gratitude to her husband, because he was the host.

Three of us took part in the eating, while the others sat around talking, and I was encouraged to finish almost everything off. We had a pile of thin round chapati, from which you tear a piece to pick up the scrambled egg. There were two bowls of onion, tomato and cucumber salad, and I made a note of as many Arabic words as I could.

I showed them the Christmas photo of my family, explaining about the winter clothes they wore. The old man was fascinated by the gloves, hats, scarves and jackets. Chai was served as we all sat around cross-legged. Then I thanked them profusely and set off down the road. I couldn't believe it! The temperature had already dropped, and I cycled on into the night, which was gorgeous. The air was silky and cool, and the road was much safer than any main road in Turkey or England. Even so, crazy things were going on; it's perfectly acceptable for cars to drive up the wrong side of a dual carriageway with no lights on!

I camped on the edge of a field and woke up at six o'clock. The sun was up and the air was fresh. Everything was golden, with a slight haze of dust around. I saw some strange adobe storage houses, like five-metre high beehives. A group of women were loading a cart with big pans full of grain, tipping them in and going back for more. A girl kept yelling at me, "Give me your camera, give me your watch, give me your bicycle," while the others fell about laughing. One of the girls stole my cap and I never got it back, which was a problem as the midday temperature hit forty-two degrees.

Elaborate trucks passed me as I cycled down the road. They had loud tune-playing horns and the buses had their radiator grills open wide to let the air in, and more colours, lights and stickers than I thought possible.

Again I went off into a village and again I never made it to the shop. A group of men sitting in the shade called me over, and I was there for over three hours. Coffee was served in tiny cups and one of the men invited me for food. Ten minutes later a huge silver tray was brought by his wife, who again I barely met, with bread, scrambled eggs, goats cheese, tomatoes, hot milk and tea. He turned out to be pretty good at making himself understood with his limited English, which he'd only studied for four years at school in the early 1970s.

His name was Ahmed, and he was open-minded about the problems of the world. He was deeply upset when he told me about how many children were killed by the Allied air-raids on Iraq.

I was invited to stay for five days if I wanted, to learn Arabic and help him with his English. This was a kind offer, but I thought that his wife probably had enough people to cook for already, what with six kids and Ahmed himself. We sat in a bare concrete room in his house, and he wanted to let me watch his television. I felt like I was in a different world as he got a screwdriver to fix the aerial box, whilst constantly throwing his head back to keep his long Arab's headscarf out of the way.

Later on, I met some men in a park and they told me a little about

Syrian society. Two of these men were actually heavy drinkers, but they all firmly believed that no way can a woman touch a drop. Also, men have to remain covered from just above their belly button to just below their knees, but the women can only show their faces and hands, and some have to cover everything. They all agreed that this is how it is, because Allah said so.

They wanted to know if women and men are allowed to take a shower together in England. I said yes, which they found fantastic. Ten yards away a couple of Christian girls were sitting and the men asked, "Why don't you go and chat them up?" I told them about Verena, and that I wasn't interested. They took this to mean that I was under Verena's thumb. They couldn't believe that I, a liberalised Westerner, didn't want to try my luck with these two women. I explained, "Because Verena is my girlfriend and I don't want anyone else." They said, "So it's Love!" They all thought this was great, and gave me five!

Further down the road, I cycled into a village and this time I actually made it into a shop and bought a few things. I didn't get any further though! The men sitting in the porch invited me to join them, then one of them said that I could stay the night. As we sat around drinking chai and eating ice cream we were joined by the local kids.

One of the men asked his wife to bring some food, which she did, but of course she didn't join us to eat. The Arab way of eating is very relaxed; no knives or forks, no tables or chairs. Everybody picks from the same plates with their fingers; chips, fried aubergines, and tomatoes, are loaded onto torn-off pieces of bread and dipped into the yoghurt. Burping, dripping the yoghurt and talking with your mouth full are all part of it.

When I told them about my experiences with dogs on the road, my host showed me a wound from a dog bite. He said he shot the dog with his Kalashnikov rifle. It turned out that he was a policeman. He was fifty-four but hardly had any teeth left. Only the kids in the village had white teeth, and even the eighteen-year olds' teeth were stained from smoking.

Back at the policeman's house I was able to have a shower. After more chattering we drank tea again before the children had to go. Suddenly the life disappeared from the conversation, and one by one everybody went home. I had to sleep on a mattress next to the big fat policeman, on the roof of the house under a mosquito net! I don't know where his wife slept.

I'd only cycled about twenty miles the next day before I was invited for more chai. I'd already turned down loads of other offers, and I started to wonder if I'd ever get to Damascus! Paul, The French cyclist I'd met in Greece, was right about Syria!

In this particular village, everyone belonged to the same extended family, with the children having an idyllic upbringing. Families will help each other out in times of need, and the elderly are looked after, usually in the home of the oldest son.

Some families are huge, with eight, ten or even fifteen kids. A Syrian man will build the house for his family, firstly as a bungalow with a flat roof and the steel rods poking out of the top of the concrete. At any time in the future, one or two more floors can be added for the children to live when they get married. I was told that unemployment is unheard of and AIDs is practically non-existent, as

69

both extra-marital sex and drug abuse carry big penalties.

    The day I reached Damascus was definitely a desert day. It was a hot, dry landscape with hardly any vegetation, just stones everywhere and some mountains bordering Lebanon to the west. I saw some road signs to Beirut and to Baghdad, not so far away. By two o'clock the heat and the wind had almost killed me. The villages were now much fewer but I found one and pulled off the road.
    The very first people I saw were three teenage lads sitting in the shade. They sat me down on the dusty earth and we spent a couple of hours nattering, which was great. It just so happened that in their bags they had a jug of chai and their lunch of bread, hard-boiled eggs, goat's cheese, tomatoes and cucumbers. They insisted on giving me everything, and what I said I couldn't manage, they gave me for the journey, and they wouldn't take anything in return. Four hours after leaving them, just as the sun dipped behind the mountains, I photographed myself by the sign I'd been waiting so long to see, "WELCOME TO DAMASCUS."
    The following morning I woke up in my hotel room with the fan still spinning. It was in an old Damascene house, all stained glass and marble with a central courtyard and a little marble fishpond on a plinth.
    There was a fax and a phone so I was able to contact Verena. There was cable TV and a dozen other travellers, and I was told that I wouldn't have to pay till I left. All of this cost just £2.50 per night! I spent my twenty-ninth birthday there, and received more phone calls and faxes from Verena. I went to the post office and her money had arrived. She'd sent it by express delivery in two separate envelopes ($75 in each) with the money wrapped in writing paper, and it had only taken three days.

    Hi Timmy!
    Here's the money you wanted. It's Sunday evening and I closed the restaurant at 22:00. Today was really stressy. Dad was feeling ill for a couple of days – he's simply working far too much. Christoph is lying in the hammock – I guess he'll sleep out there tonight – it's lovely and warm at night.

Oh honey, I just know one thing: our relationship is the most important thing to me in my life – I wouldn't know what to do if you weren't there anymore. Promise me to look after yourself. I want you back in one piece – so don't nearly kill yourself twice a day. I love you LOADS and I miss you.
See you soon –
Verena

I had to change some of the money on the black-market and the man invited me up into his shop for chai. He showed me some beautiful silk-woven tablecloths, some depicting designs in the ceiling of the Azan Palace in Damascus.

I went to the Omayyad Mosque, said to be one of the most beautiful treasures of the Islamic world. I had to don a long black skirt to cover my legs up, and as soon as I walked through the gate I thought, "I could spend all day here!" The Omayyad Dynasty was apparently the first great Muslim Dynasty, which moved the capital of the Islamic world from Medina to Damascus. The city exists because of the Gaouta Oasis, otherwise it's all desert. This, so I was told, is the oldest inhabited city in the world. Persians, Greeks, Romans and Muslims have all ruled during its seven thousand-year history.

Before even looking around the Mosque I hooked up with two of the other travellers from my hotel, James from Australia and Cormack from Ireland. They were good company, and we looked through the Souqs together while munching corn on the cob. We looked for the strangely named "Street called Straight" to find a bar, then drank a couple of very strong beers.

To celebrate my birthday, we went to a cheap restaurant with two others from the hotel. One was a German cyclist and the other was the man that everyone referred to as "the Guru." He, Martin, has been to almost every country in the world over the last thirty years; cycling, motor-biking and backpacking. Everyone was taking the mickey out of me because Verena kept ringing up the hotel, even at three in the morning. Luckily the receptionist didn't mind waking me up!

"Well, we should give you the birthday bumps!" announced Cormack.

"How many is it, anyway?" asked Martin.

"Twenty-nine!"

"Twenty-nine bumps then!"

"Err, I don't think so!" I argued. "I'll throw up after all that food!"

"Don't worry about that; your girlfriend will ring up to make sure you're alright!"

"Yes, James, very well put!" said Cormack. "If I want to talk to my girlfriend, I have to ring every week at a pre-arranged time, to a phone-box in Cork!"

"No way! Verena wouldn't put up with that. Anyway, when you're on a bike you might not even be anywhere near a phone-box!"

"You're completely tapped, mate," said James, "riding round on a bike in this heat…"

After a few days in Damascus, I set off across a hundred and fifty miles of desert to Palmyra, an ancient oasis city built by the Greeks. I started at five p.m. and covered the first fifty miles. The last two hours was in the dark, which was sublime because I was in the desert, but a few scary things happened. I couldn't see anything, and at one

DAMASCUS, SYRIA '98.

point I ended up on the gravel, on the wrong side of the road. I stopped, shone the light at my sandals and saw a scorpion!

Later on, a couple of vicious dogs started chasing after me. This is much worse in the dark than in the daytime. I realised that it must have been my flashing back light that was driving them mad. The other frightening thing was that a truck went past with another one directly behind, completely invisible as it had no lights.

Even in the middle of the pitch-black desert there were people around on the roadside, standing by broken-down trucks, but talking to them wasn't scary. But when I reached a roadhouse and was warned about the "many beasts... mastiff" on the way to Palmyra, I accepted the offer of a bed for the night.

First I ate an enormous meal whilst watching England defeat Romania 2:1 in the World Cup. Twenty-five people were trying to talk to me at once, and at midnight the barman showed me to my room, a brick outhouse with half a dozen truck drivers crashed out on the floor. He pulled out a thin mattress and stole a blanket from a snoring man, saying, "There you go!" I asked him to wake me at five a.m., but the roadhouse's diesel generator kept me awake anyway.

I left at half-past five for the last hundred miles to Palmyra, just before the sun rose. Soft morning light bathed the Mosque next to the roadhouse. The nomads and their camels were asleep on the dusty desert floor, and the drivers snored beneath their trucks.

As the sun climbed into the empty blue heavens, fantastic colours brought the stony desert to life. Subtle shades of pink, green, blue and red floated from the mountain range on one side to the endless plain on the other. The smooth black tarmac was a tightrope to the horizon, often without a curve in sight. Early on I found a petrol station, where I was invited for a welcoming breakfast of olives, bread, tomatoes and cucumber, followed by yoghurt and cherries and washed down with glasses of chai.

The temperature rose relentlessly during the day but a strong tailwind aided my progress. It was just as well, as an eight-strong pack of wild dogs appeared from nowhere and tore after me, going for my blood. They came for me when I was riding up a hill, and I had to pedal for my life to escape their dreadful jaws.

They're used by the Bedouin to tend the sheep and protect them at any cost. From then on, every time I saw a group of tents or a flock of sheep in the distance, I approached with terror and with legs ready for a furious sprint. Whenever I had a headwind I felt even more vulnerable, with no chance of escape. What with that, the night-time traffic and the scorpions, I decided that the desert is not a place to be messed with. There's more to it than making sure you've got enough water.

In the blistering midday heat, I came across a sign saying "Palmyre 30 km." I could make out the oasis, a tantalising vision in the distance, just a smudge of green palm trees and the faint outline of ancient Greek ruins…

Cappadocia, Turkey to the Iranian Border

A colossal crash shattered the silence. Dust filled the air. Confusion. Waves in the ground beneath my feet. A loud juddering sound. People running, petrified, silent. Escape the buildings. RUN! Bus station wall cracked. Scattered dust, rubble, glass.

I was on my way from Palmyra back to Cappadocia by bus and train. On June the twenty-seventh I was waiting for the bus from Adana to Goreme, when the earthquake struck.

The bus arrived an hour later. A fifteen-year old girl and her mother sat in front of me, and the girl said that she'd been trapped in her bedroom by the earthquake; her wardrobe had fallen over and blocked the door. The news came on the radio and she translated it for me. The earthquake measured 6.5 on the Richter scale. Six hundred people were injured, fifty were killed. The next morning I woke up on my campsite, back in Goreme, where I'd been three weeks before. I sorted out the bike, ready for the seven hundred and fifty-mile ride to the Iranian border...

Depending on how much I enjoyed the next ten days, I'd be returning to Austria with the intention of telling Verena that I wanted to continue all the way to India. After an idyllic ride past the houses in the rocks, I sailed through some small villages towards a snow-capped mountain. The weather was perfect after the unbearable heat of Syria, feeling more like an English summer.

Over a breakfast of fried eggs, bread, cheese, and honeycomb the next day, a man told me about the PKK terrorists. He said that on my way to the Iranian border I would be going through three areas where the terrorists were prevalent. These areas are patrolled from eight a.m. to five p.m. by armed soldiers.

He said that these Kurdish separatists are pretty much under control now. In 1984 they started to become a big problem, with 1990 to 1994 being the worst time. He said that he used to be a soldier himself, and has seen the PKK shooting babies and children in the head. He himself was shot in the hip and spent fifteen days in hospital. I didn't know if everything he told me was true, but I had to err on the side of caution.

I rang Verena and she said that the Adana earthquake was on the international news; one hundred and twelve people had been confirmed dead so far. The worst hit area was in the slums on the outskirts of the city, where over-population and poorly built housing blocks were a time-bomb.

I continued on my way, but before dark I became worried about the PKK. I stopped at a petrol station to ask if I could camp there. They said it would be okay, but they weren't exactly over-friendly. In the tent I could hear the locals, gathering for a look at the strange plastic house in their midst. A shepherd went past, singing beautiful songs. He was drowned-out by the Muezzin at the Mosque, who couldn't sing to save his life. I woke up freezing cold in the night. I went out to relieve myself and stood under a black sky with a million bright stars.

Eastern Turkey is so much different to the west that it's like being in a different country. The road was almost empty, but whenever the trucks appeared on a stony section, flinging dust and stones in my face, the pleasure of being there would be quickly eroded.

For a number of days I rode across the high plateau of vast grasslands and arid hills. I got to Kangal, just before the first PKK danger zone. Over a meal in a lokanta asked the proprietor about the terrorists. He didn't seem worried, but when I stopped at a police station for a second opinion, they advised me to take the long way round. They said that the PKK don't go for tourists, but that any terrorist is a potential threat.

I still had several hundred miles to go before the Iranian border. I planned to do this by using main roads only, staying in town hotels for about £1 a night, only cycling during daylight hours and contacting the police every day to check the situation out.

I had a hilarious evening, writing a letter in English on behalf of a twenty six-year old lokanta owner, in return for a free meal. There was such a language problem that it took a couple of hours to get the story. The letter was intended for his forty nine-year old Welsh wife, to ask her why she won't help him to come to Britain. Apparently she doesn't love him anymore, although he was giggling so much when he told me this, that he didn't seem to be too bothered about her either! They met in Bodrum, when she was on holiday, and decided to get married when she next visited him. It was obvious to me that all he cared about was getting a British visa. She was obviously aware of this, as she'd informed the British Embassy in Istanbul that their marriage is null and void, thereby cancelling his visa application. She'd then written him a letter, saying simply, "It's over," and promptly changed her phone number.

On a mountain pass, halfway between Cappadocia and the border, I saw a tank at the top and a couple of men running around. My first thoughts were that this must be the PKK, before realising that they must be the military. In the next valley I was passed by three truckloads of soldiers. I stopped for a pee, but never did it because I spotted gunmen in the cliffs, frighteningly near to me. At the next town I went straight to the police but I was told that all I'd seen were more soldiers.

The next mountain pass, almost two thousand two hundred metres above sea-level, was safe between eight a.m. and five p.m., when the soldiers were on patrol. Another pass followed, at about the same altitude. Here the scenery changed dramatically from pretty alpine views with flowers and grass, lakes and snow-capped mountains, to a spectacular vista of dry, sun-baked valleys in all shades of bronze and copper. Ancient lorries crawled up the steep gradient against a backdrop of earth and rocks. This made me think of what I might see, if I were to carry on to Iran and Pakistan. The heat was phenomenal; I could feel my face burning. It was a race to get to Erzincan before the five o'clock PKK curfew time.

After a good night's sleep, I only covered twenty-two miles as the puncture I'd repaired in Istanbul began to leak. I was in the middle of nowhere when the tyre went flat. I had no spare tube, as I'd become complacent, sub-consciously thinking I'd never get any more punctures!

I thought I'd pretend that this was a real emergency. I stuffed the dead tyre with my spare clothes and put it back on the wheel, just to see what would happen. I rode a couple of miles but it was unbearably lumpy! As the next major town was a hundred miles away, I had to go all the way back to Erzincan. I stayed overnight again, then managed to get some new inner tubes. I decided to leave

EASTERN TURKEY '98.

my baggage in the hotel, as I'd be passing through again, on my way back from the border. I then raced all day, a fantastic hundred and twenty mile ride with a tailwind. At a petrol station, somebody told me that the death toll for the Adana earthquake had now reached a hundred and forty-three. He said that earthquakes are common up here as well. In 1992 about four hundred people died here, and fifty years ago there was an enormous earthquake, killing forty thousand people.

I stayed the night in Erzurum before covering another 130 miles. I reached a place that I'd been warned about, one of the strongholds of the PKK. The local police reckoned that I'd have no problems though, as the area had now been cleared of terrorists. It turned out to be one of the most memorable rides of the whole trip! From the town at the end of the valley, the road climbed to 2360 metres above sea-level. Half-way up the climb I saw a Land Rover with English registration plates. There were two lads trying to tie their gear to the roof-rack.

"You're English, aren't you!" I shouted, stopping near the car.

"You're very English!" they joked, climbing down off the roof.

"Well, it's true!"

They came up and shook hands, smiling in disbelief.

"Where's your food?" asked one of them, looking at my un-laden bike.

"In the next restaurant!" I replied, telling the truth.

They told me they'd been sponsored for their trip, everything "from the Land Rover to the hair gel." They were attempting to climb the highest mountain in every country in Europe, including the ex-Soviet Balkan states. They were here to climb Mt. Ararat, Turkey's highest mountain at over five thousand metres.

"No mountaineers have been able to climb Ararat since '86!"

"Why's that? Is it cos of the PKK?" I offered.

"Yep, that's it! We've visited the mountain and we're now going to Ankara, to try and get permits and organise a guide."

"But what about the terrorists?"

"Dunno!" They looked at each other and shrugged. "We were playing backgammon with these blokes last night, then we found out they were Kurdish rebels!"

"Blimey!"

"They were very friendly though!"

"I'm sure they were," I laughed. "I'm a bit worried about them though, but it might just be the police being extra cautious."

"Probably. Anyway, before you go, let us get a photo of you!"

"How do you want me... like this?" I said, posing.

"That'll do!" they said, clicking their cameras. "You meet the weirdest people in the weirdest places!"

"Thanks very much!"

They gave me a T-shirt because it was getting cold and wet. I said goodbye to them and carried on climbing. The rain didn't last long and the evening was beautifully warm. I passed a village of stone houses with flat roofs covered in living grass, and more adobe "beehive" stores like I'd seen in Syria. Skinhead boys chased after me, shouting at me to give them my money. Martin, the "guru" I'd met in Damascus, said that he'd cycled to Nepal in 1972 on a midwife's bike. The kids in Eastern Turkey had thrown stones at him and tried to put sticks through his spokes, and the lorries were constantly running him off the road.

There was one last ride to do before I reached the Iranian border. As I pedalled, I was already gelling the plan that would keep me busy for the next few months. Once I'd visited the border, I would have to put the trip on hold and travel back all the way to Austria by bus. I'd stay for a few weeks and gently break it to Verena that I'd be going off again. In Vienna I'd try to organise visas for Iran, Pakistan, India and Nepal. The raw excitement and wilderness of the last ten days had finally got me hooked. I knew that the Iranian visa might never be granted, because I'm British, but there was no way I could go back to England without at least visiting India!

I rode into a strong headwind for ninety miles on this, the last day. The scenery was spectacular, and as I climbed the last mountain pass, the ever-welcoming Turkish soldiers waved enthusiastically.

On reaching Dogubayazit, at the foot of Mt Ararat, I had an enormous meal before setting off for the last twenty miles to the border. I had to hide for a while under a bridge when a hailstorm hit; a black sky above and the mountains soaked in a misty golden light. Iranian trucks and buses drove by, along with the occasional tank. In the distance I could see Guburlak, the border town, and beyond it lay the mountains of Iran!

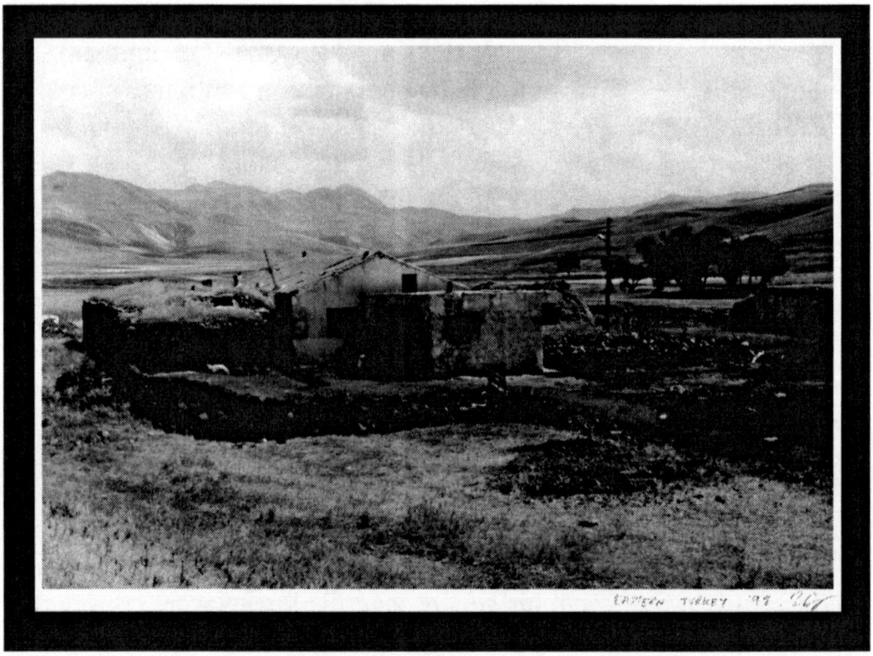
EASTERN TURKEY '98

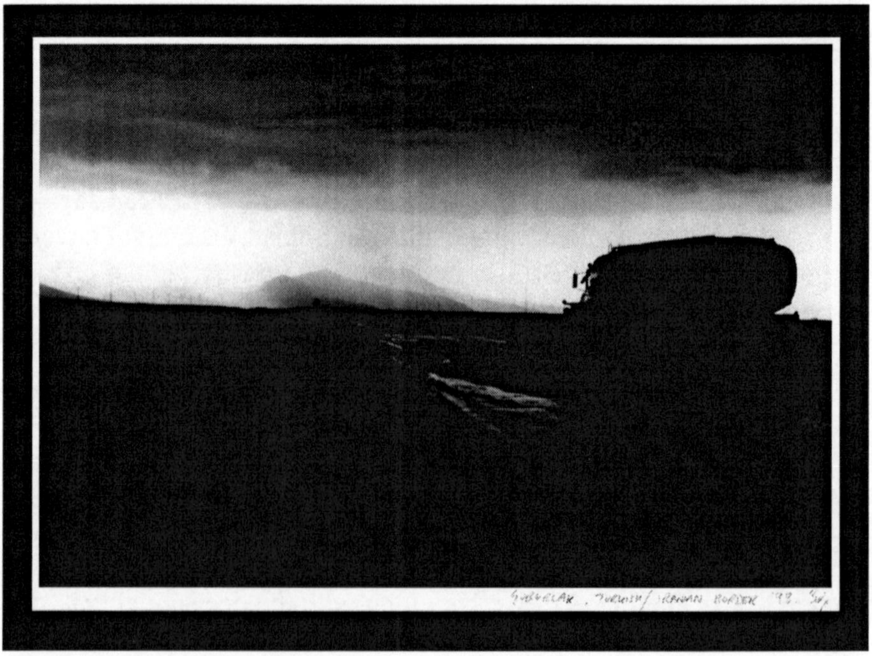
TURKISH/IRANIAN BORDER '98

Luckily, the first border guard I met spoke English. He was perfectly okay about the fact that I'd come for a nose around. I told him I was planning on coming back in a few weeks to cross over. I'd heard so much about Iran; a beautiful country with incredibly hospitable people. There it was, all I needed was a visa!

He told me about a meteor crater, just back from the border zone. I went piling off down a dirt track, past a tank and a Jendarmerie, and there was the crater. It was a massive hole in the ground, what else, with a sign in Turkish and very bad English, dubiously claiming that this is the World's second biggest crater hole, after one in Alaska.

Whilst I was there, a group of jendarmes turned up, laughing and joking, and I had to be in their photographs. All around us were lookout towers and army camps. We stood around for a while, talking and larking about, before the jendarmes patted me on the back and drove off.

I'd spent the last three months heading east, and now I turned around to face the west again, anxious to get back to Verena as quickly as possible. It would take four days and nights, on a number of different buses; through Erzincan to pick up my panniers, Istanbul, Bulgaria and Yugoslavia. It was now a year since I'd left Sheffield and, little did I know it, I had another fifteen months before I'd see my home again.

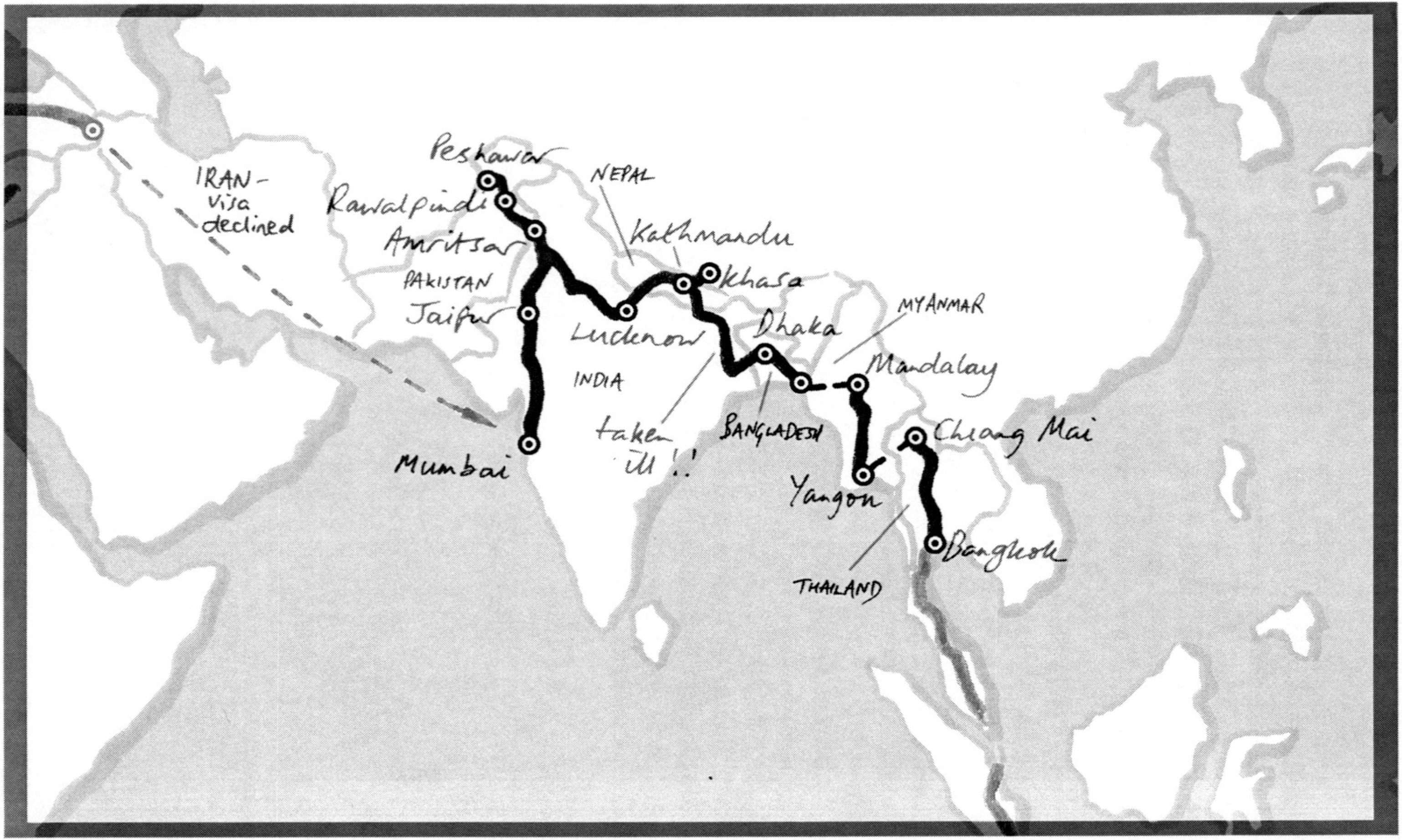
Peshawar
IRAN-
visa
declined
Rawalpindi
Amritsar
PAKISTAN
Jaipur
NEPAL
Kathmandu
Lhasa
Lucknow
INDIA
Dhaka
MYANMAR
Mandalay
taken
ill!!
BANGLADESH
Mumbai
Chiang Mai
Yangon
Bangkok
THAILAND

Three

India to Thailand
September 1998 to January 1999

Black machine-gun clouds sprayed the earth with bullets of rain. Dancing droplets leapt from the flooded ground, braving the onslaught from above.

As peace was restored, I stepped nervously into the retreating monsoon. I looked down at my sandals as they made the first tentative pedal strokes, slowly leaving the airport terminal behind. The tyres cut through the water, sending tiny ripples across the tarmac, unnoticed by anyone but me. In my mind, a quiet voice was telling me that I'd just started cycling across India.

Mumbai (Bombay), India

"I can't believe it!" I shouted, slamming the door.
"What's up?" asked Verena.
"The Iranian Embassy."
"Oh no!"
"Yeah, that's right. No visa."
"Why won't they give you one?"
"Well, I asked him what was the reason given. He said "No reason." That's what it actually said on his computer screen. "No reason." It makes me laugh!"
"Oh Timmy. That's awful." She came up and gave me a hug.
"All that precious time I've wasted. Six weeks and two applications!" I could have cried.
"And all that money as well."
"I know! How many times have I had to go to Vienna? Not to mention flying to London just to get that visa for Pakistan! The Iranian Embassy said I had to have the Pakistan visa first, so they knew I'd leave the country!"
"I know Timmy. But it wasn't the Pakistan Embassy that sent you back to London. It was the British one in Vienna!" she reminded me. "They refused to give their consent."
"Yeah, waste of space, they are! What are they good for if they can't even help me get a visa!" I was fuming. "Anyway, I can't even go to Pakistan at the moment. It's too dangerous. The US Embassy was bombed!"
"Well, you'll have to go to India then!"
"No, I can't go straight to India. I might as well blow the whole thing out."
"Look, Timmy; you've really hurt me by telling me we're not going back to England yet. I've got to stay here for another year because you want to carry on cycling round the world. So you'd better go and do it. Go to India, then go to Pakistan when it's safer, in a few weeks or so."
"I know. If I don't do it I'll only regret it and then I'll end up doing it anyway!"
"Exactly!" She pointed at me accusingly, with a cheeky look in her eye. "You've got to do it now. I'm not gonna go through all this

again. Go away for another four months, then come back for a month… that's the deal!"

"Well if I do it like that, in stages, at least it's broken down into easier chunks. But it's still dead scary… it does my head in!"

"And you do my head in, Timmy. Go off to India and come back at Christmas. You're gonna cycle till your bum falls off!"

So it was that Verena packed me off to Vienna for a flight to Mumbai via Paris, Rome and Delhi. I was convinced that some of my stuff would go astray. Sure enough, one of the pannier bags didn't turn up, and the bike never appeared. Three other travellers had the same problem; a Greek girl and a Spanish couple. We were told that we'd have to find a hotel and wait around for a couple of days.

We were exhausted from the flight, and as soon as we walked out of the building, the humidity hit us like a baseball bat. A line of ancient taxis stood beneath a thick grey sky and the taxi drivers lounged around under the palm trees. The last taxi alone had good tyres so we hired it for the drive into the city. Several times we came within an inch or two of a pedestrian or another vehicle, but nobody ever seemed alarmed about it, except us.

A couple of holy cows were dotted about along the way, but most of it was too overwhelming to take in, in my state of exhaustion. Because of a lack of available rooms, I ended up having to share a twin room with the Greek girl, and she turned out to be the roommate from hell. Whenever I saw her she would say, "I wan' my bag." Then she'd light up another cigarette and sit staring out of the window.

The view was a grey sea and sky, with an aircraft carrier in the bay and countless crows swooping around, occasionally landing on the open window. We went for a walk in the nearby streets and everything seemed strangely familiar, yet at the same time new and different. It felt as if we were walking through a film set for an inner city drama; over-the-top colour and vibrancy against a backdrop of exaggerated poverty and pathos. There was an almost surreal difference between the mood of the people and the conditions they were living in. The children were running round, laughing and coming up to shake our hands. Behind them their houses seemed to be on the brink of collapse.

The next morning my room-mate from hell told me a few more hundred times that she wanted to get her lost rucksack back. She gave up her one-day old no-smoking rule and bought an assortment of cigarettes and drugs to smoke. She promised not to smoke in the room, but that rule didn't last either. I went for a walk along the seafront to the "Gateway to India," a pretentious arch built to mark the occasion of a British Royal visit. It seemed completely out of place, surrounded by beggars, and a man with no limbs sitting in the rain with nothing on but a pair of shorts.

I walked into the city and watched the wacky rickshaws and angular red buses driving around. There was a cricket match and also a football match going on in the muddy park, then I found a series of market stalls. The heavy sky and the black smoke from the roadside fires made everything appear dark and broody. I was becoming anxious about my lost bike, so I phoned the airport and asked them to ring the hotel when they knew where it was.

I woke up with a start at three o'clock in the morning. Somebody was banging on the door, shouting, "Mr. Tim, telephone for you!" The news was good; I could collect the bike and the missing pannier bag in the morning! There was no news for the room-mate from hell, so she sat up all night on her bed, chain-smoking. I saw the Spanish couple when I got up. They told me that their bags had also come, so the three of us took a taxi to the airport.

The road was absolute chaos again, and the thought of cycling on it was far from appealing. Each pre-historic truck and rickshaw was hidden in its own cloud of exhaust fumes. The worst thing was that the kids ran out barefoot across the jam-packed road, hanging onto the taxi's doors and windows as we stop-started and weaved around. I felt sure that one of them would get killed, and the taxi driver kept closing in on the car alongside to force the kids to let go.

We turned into the airport and had an argument with the taxi driver. His metre showed nineteen rupees, yet he pulled out a chart to show that this really meant two hundred and twenty rupees. Needless to say, we lost!

When I got my stuff back I had to kill two hours, slowly setting the bike up, because of the torrential monsoon rain outside. A crowd of inquisitive people gathered around as I put the pedals back on and checked the bike over. Luckily they became bored after an hour, and

RAJASTHAN, INDIA '98

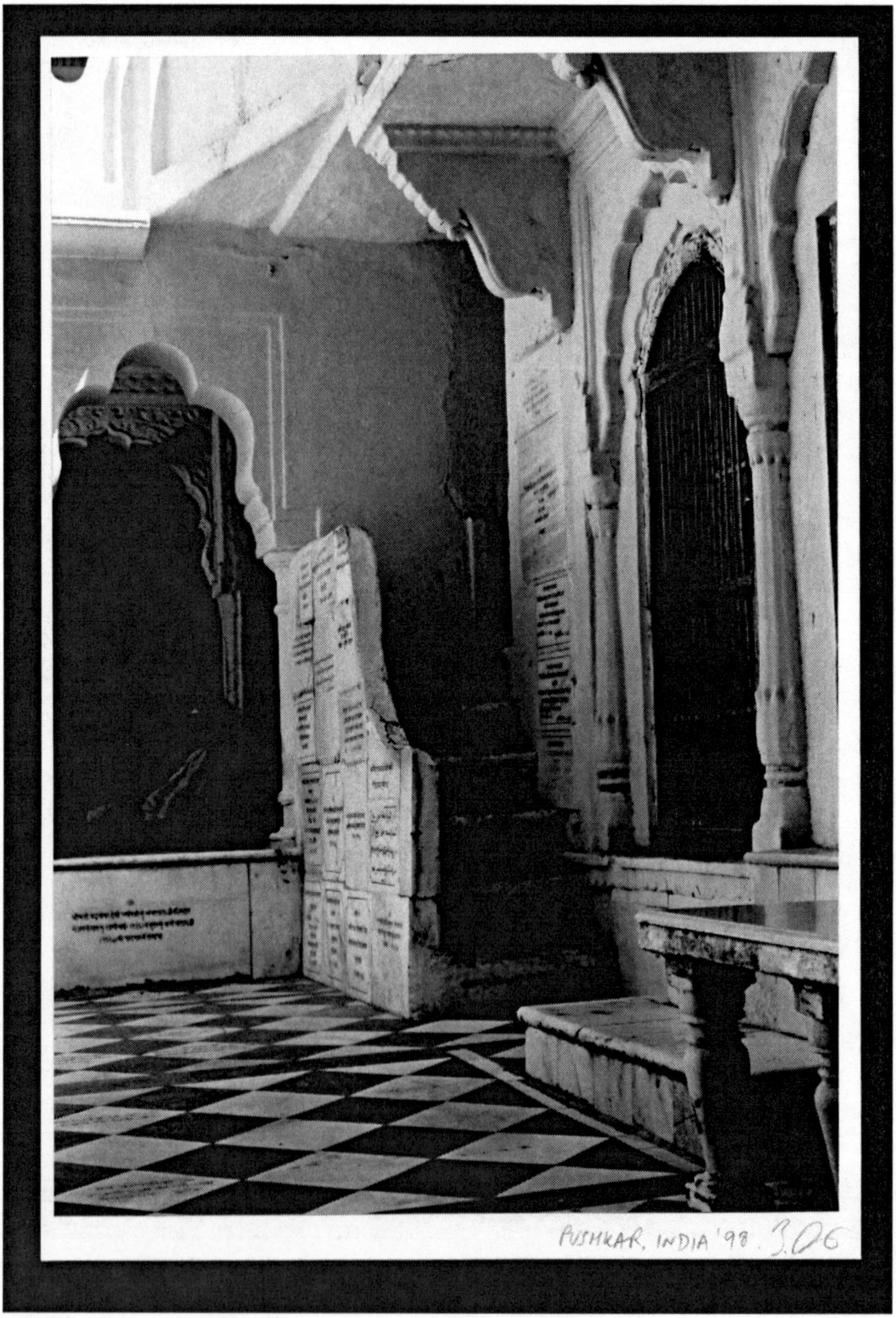
PUSHKAR, INDIA '98 3.06

that was my chance to retrieve my money. Officially it's illegal to bring Indian rupees into the country but, like everyone else, I'd done just that. To be on the safe side I'd smuggled most of the money in with the bike; four thousand rupees in the saddle stem, and a further one thousand rupees inside the front tyre!

The rain died down and I cycled away from the airport and along to the main road with a feeling of trepidation. The first ten minutes were serene, and when I waved at the rickshaw drivers, they waved back enthusiastically. But then the traffic became much thicker and I approached an impossible junction; I'd reached the highway. I had to get to the other side so I muscled through, with countless farting rickshaws and grinding trucks, over a road made almost entirely of gravel and potholes. It was an obstacle course of people, bikes, cows, dogs, tractors, cars and buses. Nobody could go in a straight line because of all the holes.

Makeshift dwellings lined the way, with half-naked children running around and playing in the puddles. The road itself was almost too much, and I spent most of the time riding through the mud at the side. But after twenty miles I was finally clear of Mumbai, heading north through tropical Maharashtra.

Dear Verena –
The first two days I was in India, I was too scared to eat anything but biscuits. Then I had stomach ache after a lentil curry, but after two hours of farting I was OK! The first proper meal I had was absolutely gorgeous. I could have been in an Indian restaurant in Birmingham – everything was exactly the same!

The people are really friendly and most speak English, so no problems there. At the moment I'm just doing about fifty miles a day. It's an extremely relaxed pace for me, but I reckon if I avoid getting over-tired then I'll avoid all sorts of other problems. I'll just keep plodding up north bit by bit.

I've just got to Jaipur, which is meant to be a gorgeous city so I'm going to look around. I've arranged to meet someone. He's a Sikh called Jeetpal. I first met him a couple of days ago in Ajmer and he showed me round all of the amazing temples; he knows everything

JAIPUR, INDIA '98

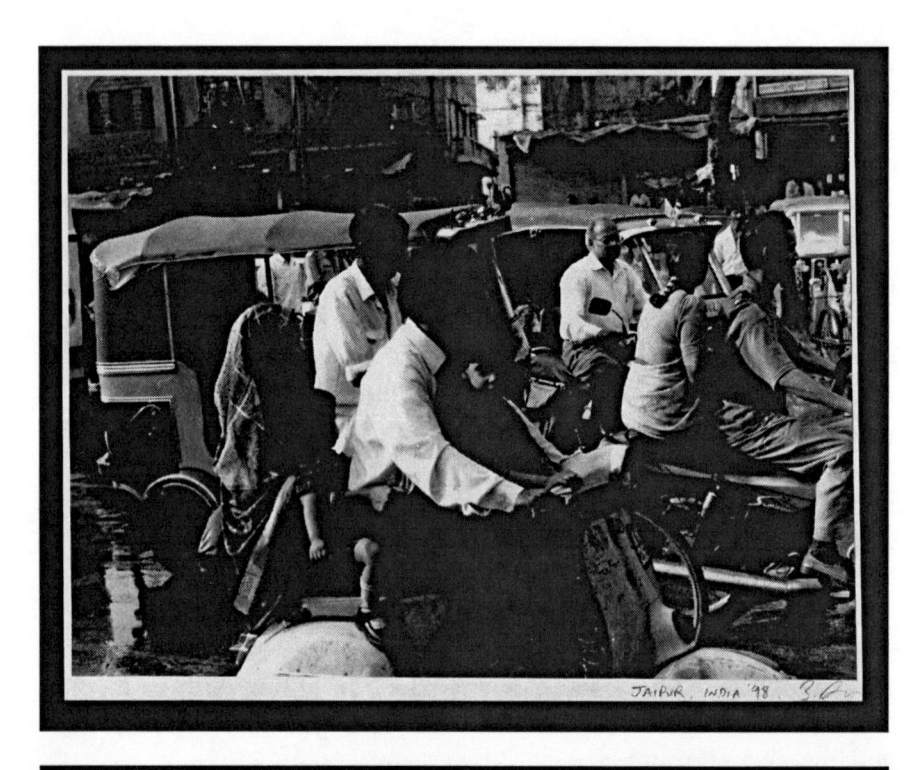

JAIPUR, INDIA '98

about them. Then he took me on a scooter to Pushkar, which is absolutely stunning. There's a lake with ghats leading down to the water, surrounded by light blue temples and houses, with the mountains of the desert behind.

Even so, I much prefer the sleepy little chai houses by the roadside, where I can sit with the old blokes and chat with the kids, and there are no tourists or touts around; it's a much more laid-back experience.

I'm really missing you but at least I'm getting on with the job of cycling across India – it's just a matter of time before I get back. You said you wanted to make some cups for our future house. That sounds like a cool idea, and it might take your mind off things. Anyway, what if we invite our friends round and we say, "Sorry, you can't have a cup of tea because Verena never made any cups!"
Only kidding!
I'll fax you again as soon as I can!
Love from Timmy xxxx

Punjab, India

Three weeks and a thousand miles of pedalling north of Mumbai, a Sikh on a moped pulled up alongside me. He was an English teacher in his early thirties, called Surjeet Singh. I was invited for lunch in his concrete house in Sardulgarh, and there I met his wife Amarjeet, a trainee teacher, and their tear-away son Kumwarpal. I ended up staying for four days and was invited to the wedding of Mr. Beldev Singh's daughter at the house next door, two days hence. In the meantime they decided to send me to stay overnight at Jagmalwali, a nearby Sikh mission...

Eight of us were crammed into an ancient looking Mahindra jeep and Mr. Beldev Singh instructed the driver to go slowly. It was a no-knee-room job, as I was in the middle at the front, jammed up against a metal box containing a knackered stereo. Punjabi songs blared out through tinny speakers, as we crashed along the bumpy road, and the driver kept forcing my knees to one side to change the cassettes.

Most people, including the three women of Mr Beldev Singh's house, were going for the day. Only the lad Vicky and I were going to stay over. Vicky's job was to look after me but he was so shy that it looked like I'd be looking after him. I was still wondering what on earth I'd be doing there, but this was India; just go with the flow.

As we approached the mission it struck me immediately as an unusual place. A wall about a kilometre long formed the facade, painted in bright colours, with that modern Indian architectural appearance of not quite hanging together, but very cheerful and informal at the same time. Halfway along the façade was a gateway set into a huge arch, on top of which were two bright yellow lion statues, rather crudely formed, more like badly proportioned cartoon characters than the serious lions which usually adorn such buildings. The strangest thing of all was between them; a model of a big silver aeroplane! Apparently this was the last guru's whimsical symbol for the vehicle that will take everyone on their final journey.

Once inside the gate, we were greeted with the words, "Dhan Dhan Satguru, Tera Hi Asra." Vicky told me that this translates roughly as "God be with you," and that I should repeat it to everybody I meet in the temple. We crossed an extensive courtyard in the burning sun, and entered a shelter where people were sitting on mats. Two elderly men were serving the sitters with lassi, dhalfry and chapatis. This was the traditional Sikh free-for-all canteen, and the accommodation was also free. Anyone from any caste, religion or nation is welcomed.

Dear Verena –
Hello, hope you're well! I just thought I'd write and thank you for forwarding Tim's fax from Jaipur the other day. I've no idea whether he got my reply because it went through our machine, but then it told us that there was an error. So next time he rings you, tell him I did reply! It's Sally's birthday in a couple of days so maybe he'll try and ring her. I hope his funny tummy is better.
Keep well and happy and get working on those cups!
Love, Berlie.

I was introduced to Praveen, a man in his late twenties who spoke perfect English. He wore the traditional Punjabi suit of Kemise and Pajamas, and he never really told me what his role was, but he seemed to be the Public Relations man. He lived in England until recently but had to return because his mother was sick. His British visa then expired so his English fiancée broke off the engagement. He said that he'd had a "BMW....Ferrari," but when questioned he said, "Actually the Ferrari was my cousin's." He told me about when he used to go clubbing in London, but now he says he's happy here, living with the Saddhus.

He was a nice guy and all, and he kept Vicky and me entertained for a couple of days, but really he was a salesman. Full of his own importance, he started to walk off, waving his hand in a beckoning way and saying, "Come," as if he was an important businessman showing me round a hi-tech factory.

A couple of old Saddhus came into the room where Praveen, Vicky and I were talking. They told me that they devote their entire waking hours to God, and that, as such, sleeping is a waste of time. Some of them, therefore, never sleep.

One of the old Saddhus was a wonderful character. He looked like an Ewok from "Star Wars," except that he was six foot two inches tall. His wrinkled face was dark brown, as were his warm eyes, and

THAR DESERT, INDIA 98.

his beard was bushy and greying. He couldn't stop giggling when I demonstrated my "I'm looking for a hotel" mime; putting my hands together and laying my cheek on them to pretend to go to sleep. He thought it was amazing that I could travel through so many countries and get by in India with little or no knowledge of the country's many languages. He didn't speak any English either, yet we had a laugh every time we saw each other. Whenever we met, he wouldn't bother with the formal religious greeting; he'd just lie down on the ground and pretend to go to sleep!

My next favourite character was the head cook. He looked just like Woody Allen and never stopped smiling. Then there was his underling; a small, energetic man with no beard or turban. He hung around with us all the time, and he thought I was a saint because I travel alone and do everything for myself, even washing my own clothes. He thought that my water filter and Swiss Army knife were the bee's knees.

We attended a meeting with a guru, where not much happened, other than everybody gazing at him admiringly. One man said that the guru looks like a man but has actually come from God and has incredible power. The intense emotions were clearly visible on the people's faces as they came in to see him.

After dark we were taken outside to see another guru. He was actually the leader of this place, and he sat meditating on a raised platform under a fan and a light, while the devotees sat around watching him. Beside him were an accordionist, a singer, a pianist and a tabla player.

Every now and then he'd clear his throat and the band would stop, then he'd mumble something into the microphone, and the band would carry on. This guru, I'd been told, must have come from God because he packed in his Law career to come here and work in the gardens, growing vegetables in the hot sun.

After about three hours, he got up and pointed at Praveen and I, summoning us into his personal quarters. We sat cross-legged on the floor in front of him, as he thoughtfully stroked his long white beard. Every two or three minutes he would ask me a simple question about myself, translated by Praveen. After a while he decided that I was okay. He'd been wrongly told that I was a vegetarian and that I didn't drink alcohol, and I let him go on thinking that, rather than confuse the issue. He therefore had only one sticking point; I should stop eating eggs. Otherwise, he said, I could become a Sikh. I didn't know how to tell him, without sounding offensive, that I didn't want to become a Sikh, and that I hadn't come here for that reason. So I just defended my will to carry on eating eggs, and presently he wished me a good evening and we left his room.

Later on I was talking to Praveen, and he kept telling me that I haven't got the self-control to give up eggs, and that I'm not yet ready to be initiated. I told him several times that, in fact, I don't want to give up eggs and I don't want to be initiated. I was less diplomatic with him than I had been with the guru. I told him that I don't believe in God, but he never quite got it. He suggested that Verena and I could come back and we might be ready to be initiated then, in two or three years' time. I told him I reckoned I was doing okay in my life and I didn't need anyone to guide me.

During the night I didn't sleep at all, for the first time in India. Praveen said I could sleep until three a.m., but I was on a blanket on a concrete floor with the light on. A noisy fan kept me awake, and Praveen was sitting right next to me, talking loudly with his mates. One of the Saddhus who never sleeps was going around all the rooms in the temple. He banged on the doors with his staff to wake everyone up so we could walk around the grounds with the guru, as they do every night. As we left the room, Praveen boasted about the fact he hadn't slept. I told him I hadn't slept either.

We had another hour of failing to sleep, again with Praveen and his friends talking away. One thing he kept saying was that I'd told him to "come to my country so we can spread the word." I'd never even said this, but he told them he'd definitely take me up on this offer. At nearly five a.m. we had to get up again. I told Praveen that I can't sleep in a room full of people talking. He allowed me two hours' sleep on my own, but my head was spinning. The thing that most troubled me was that the guru had said it was fine for me to marry Verena and have children, but I wouldn't be allowed to get emotionally attached to them, as this would take my mind away from God.

When eight o'clock rolled up there was a pleasant surprise; a party of people turned up at my door. It was the family of Mr. Beldev Singh, come to take me away...but no! They were picking Vicky up to go to a prayer meeting, and would collect me at four p.m. Until then, I was to stay with Praveen. I started counting the hours...

Dear Berlie!
Thanks for your fax – it's always nice to find good messages in the morning. Tim rang me yesterday – he's at a Sikh wedding and he just came out to give me a ring, because he had so much to eat; he needed some exercise, probably to get some space for more Punjabi food!

He sounded ever so excited; there were some brilliant dancers in saris, and the couple, Jaspreet and Sandeep, are really sweet. He said that, after the ceremony, those two had to walk around Jaspreet's father's house four times. Then they sat under a makeshift temple with a copy of the Adi Granth, the Sikh holy book. Two

Granthis read the book as the wedding guests came up to give money.

  Before the wedding, he spent two days in a Sikh Temple, which was an interesting experience. I've got a feeling he's planning to cycle to Pakistan after all. He said he'll send a fax to the British Embassy and let them know his route. And he'll contact me every day he's there.
  Anyway, only three months till he comes back!
  I'll keep you informed
  Big hug, Verena

NORTH-WEST FRONTIER PROVINCE, PAKISTAN

"Exercise extreme caution." This was the immediate reply to the fax I sent from Amritsar, India, to the British High Commission in Islamabad, Pakistan. "Always dress modestly (no short trousers) and if you see any sizeable crowds gathering anywhere, turn back. Don't travel at night, and you should register with the local police when travelling / staying in a rural area." They said that, had I written to them just two weeks earlier, I'd have been advised not to go, in light of the U.S. air-strike on Kabul and the subsequent bombing of the U.S. Embassy in Islamabad. This was why I'd initially flown out to India and not Pakistan. It seemed that the Anti-American hysteria was now starting to die down, so I rode across the border to Lahore. Three days' hard cycling later, I was within a hundred miles of Peshawar...

Lady –
Fax me back if you can! I'm in Rawalpindi and I've rung the High Commission again. I've spoken to some policemen as well, and they say that the road to Peshawar is safe; it's only the bit after that's dodgy. That's the way to the Khyber Pass and Afghanistan, but I'm not going there anyway!

Had a couple of problems this morning – it's been hilly all day (mostly up!) and after I took my malaria tablets I threw up, all over the handlebars. I was OK after that but then I noticed that the back tyre (the expensive one from Kirchschlag) was tearing in five places! I found a bike shop in a tiny town, full of old and new tyres all the wrong size! The lad pedalled off and came back with a brand new big chunky mountain bike tyre, made in Pakistan and a bargain at two hundred rupees! I had to adjust everything to make it fit, even swapping it with the front one cos there's more clearance there. Then we had to cut off some of the knobbles - only then would the wheel go round!

Sam, an English Pakistani visiting from Bradford, treated me to a big bottle of Pepsi, a tea and a bag of cakes, cos his Urdu isn't very good and he enjoyed our chat in English!

xxxx

p.s. Please forward to my mum again

I had an enormous breakfast, then set off from Rawalpindi, over the last of the hills before the Indus. I got carried away at having down-hills to play with, after a month's flat riding in India. I started overtaking all the trucks, but then remembered that I was supposed to be sensible on this trip!

My chest was back to normal after yet another asthma attack on the subcontinent. I'd be okay on the open road, but vulnerable in the evenings, trapped in a town or village where the air is choked with two-stroke exhaust fumes and dust kicked up by the horses and rickshaws. My lungs would close up, as if my rib cage were tightening, crushing the air inside. Every desperate struggle for breath would burn like a suffocating fire, leaving me cursing this breathtaking world.

At least I could see the funny side of it, remembering the first time I had an attack in Verena's presence. Lying awake till four o'clock in the morning, fighting to breathe and making strained wheezing noises, I was startled when Verena burst out laughing.

"Ha Ha Ha! I'm sorry, Timmy!"
"What's so funny?" I croaked.
"You sound like a doodle-sack!"
"What the hell is a doodle-sack?"
"You know, that thing that those Scottish men play!"
"What are you on about?" I could hardly get the words out.
"Those thingy Scottish men, you know, they wear those skirts!"
"A bag-pipe! You think I sound like a bag-pipe!"
"I'm sorry! I shouldn't laugh…"

I crossed the Indus, and was struck by its incredible blue colour and the thought of its journey, running for hundreds of miles from its source near China, past the site of the ancient Moenjodaro civilisation and into the Arabian Sea. It gives its name to India, yet it's now part of a different country.

Hello Verena!
I hope you're O.K.

I loved the fax from Rawalpindi – telling the tale about the bike wheel; amazing story! Thanks for sending it on to me! Anyway this is to say great to hear from you – it's lovely to keep in touch.

End of fax – When you next hear from Tim, tell him to put his malaria tablet inside a bit of dry bread or a banana if he thinks he might throw up again.
Love, Berlie xx

Twenty-five miles short of Peshawar, I got stuck in the town of Nowshera. It was four p.m. and there wasn't enough daylight left to do the final stretch. I wanted to spend the night there and continue the next day; riding at night was something I was not prepared to do in these parts. It turned out that both the hotels in town were full, and there was nothing I could do but chuck the bike on the roof of an ancient bus and climb aboard, bound for Peshawar. This was a big disappointment, since I'd cycled fifteen hundred miles from Mumbai to get here; I had to take another bus back to Nowshera the next morning to ride those last twenty-five miles in the safety of the daylight.

The bus ride was fun, just like Turkish and Syrian buses, with energetic Islamic music playing, flowers and decorations all over the dashboard and windscreen, and a driver who used only two things- the accelerator and the horn. At one point, we were held up by a horse-and-cart, overtaking another horse-and-cart on the dual carriageway; we went past on the gravel! Right next to the bus stand in Peshawar was a hotel with a smart twin room for a hundred and fifty rupees. After a rest, I went out to find a fax machine so that I could contact Verena.

Along the roadside of this frontier town, people were sleeping under any shelter they could find. A terrifying storm had blown up from nowhere. Dust was whipped up from the streets and thrown around in a blinding swirl. A heavy black sky shut out the daylight. Trees distorted in the wind and a cold rain came lashing down. In the distance, in a haze of red, stood the mountains and the mighty Khyber Pass, the border of Afghanistan.

Back in my hotel, the inevitable power cut had just happened. I was served with a mixed vegetable dish of potatoes, sweet-corn, spinach and other ingredients I could taste but couldn't see. The man at my table told me that it's an Afghan dish, and that he himself came from Afghanistan, as did most of the other people in the room. He'd come over from his home in Kabul twenty years ago, at the age of five; a refugee from the war. His father and older brother had returned to fight.

When the power came back on, I noticed a group of men squatting on mats on a raised platform, their backs to the windows. They had incredibly fierce-looking faces, and although they were slouching around, they looked like real fighters. When they'd finished eating they turned their attention to the television, which was showing

Indian women dancing in their saris. None of the men said anything to each other, but just sat there with furrowed brows. All had thick beards, and their faces looked windswept from centuries of mountain dwelling, very different from the soft features of the Sikhs in the Punjab.

I was served with a weak, green Afghan tea. My friend told me about the Korakoram Highway, saying it takes three or four days by bus to reach the first Chinese town, but the journey is absolutely stunning. He wanted me to help him with his English, so we spent a couple of hours going through his exercise books. The Afghan Civil War was obviously a major part of his life; his English text book asked him to fill in the blanks in the sentence "There has been some .... in ...." His two chosen words were "fighting" and "Kabul."

The book was very strangely worded in places, and often it was incorrect. My friend was confused at times, and the Afghan stubbornness came out; he insisted that the book was right and I was wrong! He said that the refugees have a hard time finding work in Pakistan. Sitting opposite us was an older man who was a science and maths teacher in Kabul, yet here the only work he could get was growing vegetables.

We were interrupted when the hotel staff came over to our table and started drawing some curtains around us. We were politely asked to move, as some women were coming to eat. The women had everything but their eyes covered, and as they sat eating in purdah at the little curtained-off table, the men continued to stare at the television screen showing Indian women dancing; all bare arms, shoulders and waist.

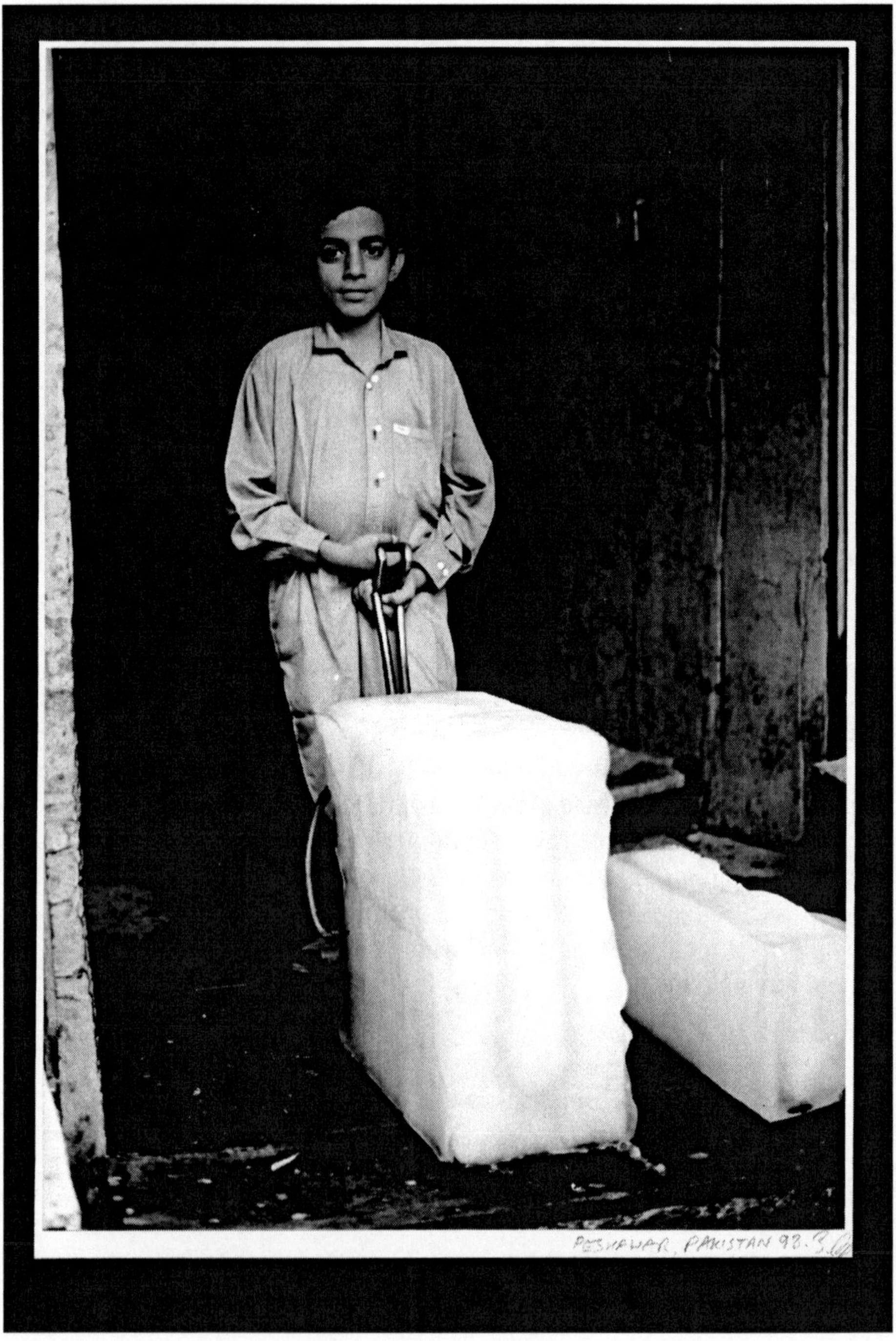
PESHAWAR, PAKISTAN 98.

Uttar Pradesh, India

Bound for Nepal from Pakistan, I was trying to ride across northern India as quickly as possible. It wasn't easy though; three days of rain had flooded all the towns on the way, and often I was riding through more than a foot of water. The things in my panniers were getting completely soaked, and I couldn't see the potholes and rubbish lurking in the water.

The route-finding was difficult too; I was cutting a huge corner off the Grand Trunk road to avoid Delhi, but this meant following little roads which didn't do what my map said. The road signs were in Hindi and nobody spoke any English! So it was that I rejoined the GT road and opted for an easy day, in the hope that I could have a restful evening...

After fifty miles I found a rest-house for eighty rupees. I washed my clothes using the Austrian Rei-in-der-Tube stuff, which lasts forever, then went to the crossroads where there was a market. I bought four hard-boiled eggs, then went to a dhaba for two chais, two roti and a plate of dhalfry, all for fourteen rupees.

Somewhere in the marketplace I lost my room key, amongst the mud, banana skins and plastic bags at the side of the road. I searched around until darkness fell, then went back to the rest-house to tell the owner. There was a lot of miming to do before he finally understood that I'd lost the key. He said I'd have to smash the padlock and give him two hundred rupees for a new one.

I returned to the market in the pitch dark. I'd seen a bike repair shop opposite the dhaba. It was just a ramshackle wooden hut with a few candles inside, but they had a hammer and a small crowbar. One of the lads agreed to go to the guesthouse with me, along with a banana seller who left his banana cart behind to come along for the hell of it.

By this time, the guesthouse was in darkness because of a power cut. The man was wandering around with a torch, muttering to himself. He approached my two companions and they exchanged a few words in Hindi. For some inexplicable reason, they disappeared for a few minutes while I sat in the dark thinking, "Why on earth hasn't he got a spare key?"

The banana man and the hotel man re-appeared, and the latter insisted on having his two hundred rupees in advance. I gave him the money and the two of them disappeared again, eventually coming back drunk as lords, stinking of whisky!

We went to the door of my room and they began hammering and bashing away at the padlock in the dark, like a couple of drunken clowns, swaying about and hiccupping! They explained to me in a drunken slur that they were finding it difficult to hit the target. I suggested that it might be easier if they turned the torch on and actually shone it on the padlock, to help them see. The hotel man saluted me, almost falling over in the process, then did what I said.

Then he opened the next room, saying that I could stay in there for another two hundred rupees, but I refused, and stood by my locked bedroom door to see what he would do next. Finally, they did what I'd suggested half an hour before; they brought a sober man with a screwdriver to take the padlock bracket off the door. Within five minutes I was back in my room.

From the window I could see the candle lights, not just there for the power cut but also because of Diwali; a peaceful Hindu festival of light, until the noisy fireworks started!

I left at six o'clock in the morning, saying goodbye to the hotel man. He was a lot friendlier than before, and a lot more sober. I'd slept quite well, luckily, as I wanted to cover the remaining one hundred and ten miles to Lucknow in a day. By ten a.m. I'd done the first fifty miles, and the whole day was plain sailing and dazzling tropical weather.

Monkeys ran across my path and jumped effortlessly between the palm trees. Pretty villages of thatched mud huts lined the road, and life went on outside in the sun and shade. Water was collected from the wells and the firewood was gathered from the forests. The boys stretched their fishing nets across the streams, while the women squatted on the banks, washing clothes. Men paused from their work in the wheat-fields to wave at the English cyclist going past.

I had a fantastic lunch with yet another variation of dhalfry, sitting at a dhaba while the truck-drivers kipped on the charpois in the shade

UTTAR PRADESH, INDIA '98.

of a huge banyan tree. I was joined for a section of the cycling by a group of six skinny men, all clattering and chattering along. Each had two milk churns strapped to his bike, as they were on their way to fetch the milk, a twenty-mile round trip.

I worked my way through a two-mile tailback caused by a truck crash. Elsewhere, other crashed trucks were having their re-useable bits unscrewed on the spot, for re-sale at one of the many roadside huts which display their finds, hanging up like strange mechanical sculptures.

Broken down buses were repaired by the roadside with two or three men crouched underneath, next to piles of cogs dripping in oil. Meanwhile, the bus passengers sat around in contented family groups, eating their picnics in the shade.

I reached Lucknow in the fading light, having covered six hundred miles since leaving Pakistan, eight days before. The old part of this former Moghul capital looked like a classic image of India; the sun setting behind the crumbling remains of an ancient empire, while down below, everyday life buzzed along with all its colours and chaos.

The Terai, Nepal

We passed into the gorge with a cold headwind coming down from the mountains. The road was steep and rough, a snaking river running far below. Ridaya had decided to come with me for the first few miles, just up the hill to a Hindu temple. Perched above a steep flight of steps, the temple overlooked the gateway to the Himalayas. Taking our sandals off, we climbed the steps, our bare feet feeling the cold of the stones. We found the Brahmin sitting before the shrines, and he dabbed my forehead with the customary red tikka mark.

Back at the road, I took a photo of my smiling Nepalese friend, then he free-wheeled back down the hill while I went the other way into the heights. The gradient soon got to me as I'd been riding on the flat for so long. I sat at a dhaba for some chai...

I'd crossed into Nepal the previous day, reaching the town of Butwal, where the Indian Plain butts into the wall of the Himalayan foothills. I'd been troubled for the last three days, since phoning Verena from Lucknow. She was obviously not happy, and later on she told me that she'd been tempted to say, "It's either me or that stupid bike!" I'd reached Nepal, but this worry had taken the pleasure away. I rang Verena from the border, but at £2.50 per minute, I only had enough money for a three-minute call.

"Verena, It's me!"

"Oh hi, Timmy!"

"How are you. Are you okay?" I tried to keep my voice and my emotions down, as I was in a telephone bureau, full of eavesdroppers.

"Oh, I'm really busy in the hotel... I'm working till midnight every night."

"Well, at least it takes your mind off other things."

"I know, I was so upset the other day," her voice quivered. "I just want you to come home!"

"Well, why don't you come and meet me in Kathmandu," I suggested. "I'll be there in a few days."

"Timmy, I'm much too busy... I can't just fly to Nepal like that!"

"Well I'll come and see you then!"

"No, you've got to save your money... You've got to get on with it!"

"I know," I said. "It's just a matter of time. I'm just cycling everyday and, before you know it, I'll be back with you. It's only two months till Christmas, so we're halfway through this stage already..."

Reassured that she was feeling happier, I headed off to Butwal. I stayed overnight on a chicken farm with its young manager, Ridaya, but curiously no chickens. The next morning was when I hit the mountains.

As I drank my chai, I saw something which I couldn't at first believe. A cycle tourist came round the corner and zoomed up the hill towards me! He was the first one I'd seen since Turkey. He was Japanese and as I waved at him, he waved back but kept on going, round the next corner and out of sight.

Half an hour later I was climbing a steep section. Tropical sun drenched the palm trees, the pink flowers and the monkeys. The walls of the thatched cottages were painted with an attractive terracotta colour, and the children came running out, shouting "Bye Bye, Bye Bye!" Excited, they followed me as I sweated my way up the hill. One by one they dropped behind, and I came across the Japanese cyclist again, sitting down eating biscuits.

"Hello!" I smiled, approaching him and laying the bike down.

"Hello. I am Mikur." We shook hands.

"I'm Tim, from England. Where've you been cycling?"

"In the Indian mountains. Cycling and trekking."

"So that explains why you've got so much gear!"

"Yes!" he grinned. "Very cold in Kashmir!"

"You've been there! What was it like?"

"Very beautiful," he said, offering me his biscuits, "but many soldiers everywhere."

"But you must have known that it was like that?" I said, taking a couple.

"Yes. My trekking had to be done with a guide, too dangerous to do it alone."

"Did you meet any other cyclists there?"

"Two Australians."

"What were they doing there?"

"They wanted to load their bikes onto a yak and trek to China. It's illegal, of course!"

"Sounds cool, though! I like the idea of that!"

We rode on until we found a dhaba which sold Sprite. We ended up being pretty well matched for fitness, though Mikur was slowed down because of his trekking gear. His mountain bike had a new steel wheel, four pannier bags, a hefty sleeping bag with the handlebar bag riding above it, plus a full backpack slung across the back. He'd climbed a five thousand-metre mountain pass on this bike and said he was getting ready to ditch some weight. He was a calm and thoughtful person though, a Buddhist. I offered to pay for the drinks but he wouldn't have it. We paid for our own and the deal was done; without either of us mentioning anything about it, we'd decided that we'd spend the next three days riding to Pokhara together.

Mikur didn't quite share my enthusiasm for waving at all of the children or replying to every single "Bye Bye." For me, though, that was one of the best things about the place, on top of the awesome scenery, the picturesque villages and the perfect weather. Another thing was that the women seemed to be much more open than in India, where I'd felt like I was in an all male world, with only the men coming over for a chat. The dhabas in Nepal aren't run by men for men, but are run by whole families; the front part of the house is opened up to allow for the wooden tables and benches. If they're not using a kerosene stove then it's a mud-built wood-burning stove, usually with enough room for three or four pots.

Mikur was very keen on a dish called momo, basically Tibetan ravioli. Instant noodles are easy to get, as are eggs. Otherwise, we were stuck with dhal bhat; a dull dish consisting of rice and noodles with some hideous extra bits, eaten very messily with the fingers.

The hill-climbs tired us out, but darkness fell at half-past five, so we found a lay-by and put our tents up for an early night. Mikur's tent was the kind of thing I'd been after. A narrow, free-standing dome tent weighing next to nothing, it didn't need any pegs and could therefore be pitched anywhere. He was telling me about Japan, and how expensive it is. He said that many people have no pride in being Japanese, as everything is ultra-modern and traditional culture is dying out fast.

I woke up at five-thirty in the morning, just as it was getting light. I got out of the tent to see that the land was drowned in a cold mist. I packed my gear away and sat waiting for Mikur. All that extra equipment of his took a long time to pack. It made me realise how efficient it is to travel alone; every single decision you make is entirely your own, and over days or weeks it can save a lot of time. Nevertheless, it was great to have some company for a change; it's best to be able to survive either way.

The views as we rode along were mind-blowing. Deep valleys scored the landscape. Terraced with countless paddy fields, the mountainsides were broken up into fantastic contour maps. Waterfalls blasted down to meet ice-cold rivers, and the road soared its way over the mountains and into the gullies. The descents were fast, twisty and hair-raising, on a pockmarked road peppered with stones, patches of sand and rivers, which cut across on the most dangerous bends.

Yet this was the Sidartha (Buddha) Highway, one of the few "main" roads in Nepal. There was hardly any traffic. The odd Indian truck or Chinese jeep would go past. Mostly it was buses with people crammed inside and on the roof, calling out to us, "Namaste," which sounds a bit like "Have a nice day." The sun burned away the last of the mist and it became very sweaty. The hill-climbs were never-ending, but there was so much to see that it didn't matter. We caught our first brief glimpse of the faint white peaks of the Annapurna Himal, way, way in the distance. That alone was enough to keep us going.

Mikur ate like a horse whenever we stopped; two bowls of Chow Mein, one buff momo, three cups of chai. I just couldn't fit so much in! In fact, I'd lost a stone and a half in the last two months.

We got to within fifteen miles of Pokhara and found a perfect spot for camping, with a breathtaking view of a wide valley, the sun about to dip below the mountains. Though only two thousand five hundred metres high, these "foothills" looked enormous. It became quite chilly so we put our tops on and munched on dry instant noodles. A group of village lads turned up to drink whisky and get on our nerves, but they went after half an hour because we pretended to be tired.

"I am glad they have gone," said Mikur, shaking himself awake again.

"Well, maybe they come up here every night to watch the sunset," I suggested.

"Oh, I don't know. The same thing kept on happening to me in India. Sometimes I just couldn't escape people. If they knew where I was camping, I would feel vulnerable."

"I hardly did any camping there," I laughed. "India was brilliant but it did my head in! If it wasn't for those cheap hotels, I'd have gone mad!"

"Yes, you have to have some space for yourself each day!"

"Especially when you've got a view like this!"

We woke up to another cold, misty morning, with another enormous breakfast at the first village to get us going. The sun lit up the mist on the steep mountainsides, gradually burning it away. Cattle stood around under huge straw parasols in the fields. Groups of women walked along the road, carrying tiny scythes for cutting the rice in the paddy fields. They wore baskets on their backs for transporting the rice, carried with a single strap around the forehead. Children ran past them, carrying their schoolbags in the same way.

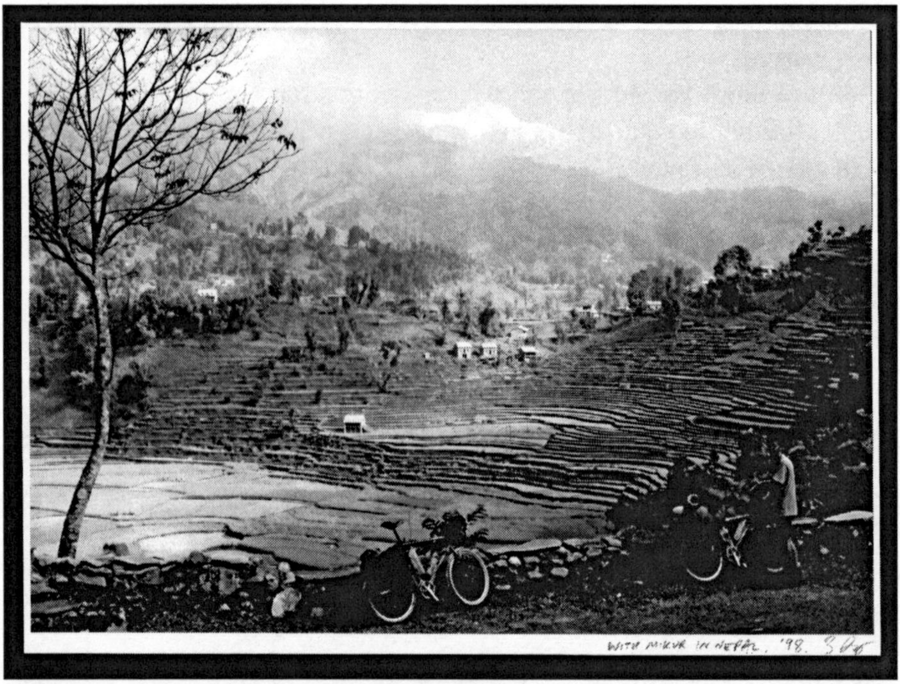
WITH MIKUR IN NEPAL, '98.

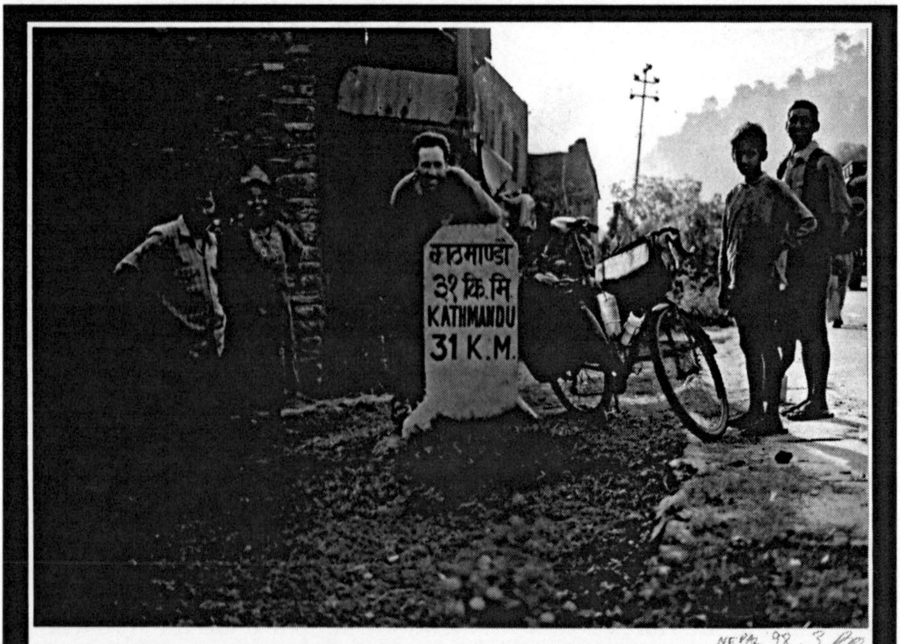
काठमाण्डौ
३१ कि. मि.
KATHMANDU
31 K.M.
NEPAL 98.

There was no such thing as a wheelbarrow in the places we passed through, and bikes were rarely used because of the hills. Most of the houses had no electricity, and water was usually collected from a fountain with a tap, in the middle of the village. The people washed themselves at the fountains or in the streams, the men taking off their topies (patterned tea cosies for hats) and stripping down to their undies.

We reached the top of a mountain pass and there, with Annapurna in the background, was Pokhara, far below in the valley. The ride down was a classic Alpine hair-pin descent, a welcome reward for all that hard work. In Pokhara we stopped at the lake for another reward; garlic steak and chips, with a glass of fresh pineapple juice. We followed it up with a couple of beers, to toast our safe arrival.

Mikur found a Japanese guesthouse, saying that he was going to spend the next few days relaxing with a Japanese book, before doing a two-week trek around the Annapurna range. I was keen to crack the remaining three days' ride to Kathmandu, so we shook hands and wished each other well.

Luckily for me, the road carried on going down for the whole of the afternoon, following the river. It felt strange being on my own again, and it took a while to get used to it. But then I caught sight of the Himalayas again, this time lit pink by the evening sun, whilst everything else in the foreground was a cool green. Suddenly, I went mad with excitement, shouting at the top of my voice, "HI-MA-LAY-AS!!!" and making noises like an idiot!

To Khasa, Tibet

The view disappeared into dense fog as I reached the mountain pass and a gateway saying, "Welcome to Kathmandu Valley." The city was a further eight miles, and at first it seemed to be a hot, dusty and confusing place. I found Thamel, the main backpacker's district, and a few people gave me approving glances as I cycled past; I was so dirty and scraggy that I'd obviously come a very long way...

After a night in the "Pheasant Lodge" Guesthouse, I woke up feeling like a skeleton, the last two months having finally caught up with me. A day later, I gathered together enough energy to look around, and made my way down to Durbar Square for the first time.

Colourful and theatrical, the square had a surreal quality. Surrounded by magnificent, ancient temples with triple-tiered roofs and elaborate carvings, I wandered around in a daydream. Smoke filtered out from the burning of incense, and petals lay scattered on the stone floor. Red sandalwood dust covered countless shrines. Saddhus in bright orange robes, devotees with tikka-marked foreheads, market-goers and awe-struck travellers melted past.

Standing at Indra Chowk, where for centuries blankets and bedspreads have been sold, I noticed a passageway. I walked through to a small square, almost filled by a central temple, with dozens of shrines around the edge, and people and pigeons buzzing around. Old ladies sat next to their piles of rice or vegetables. Children ran around, chasing each other between the shrines, and dogs lazed in quiet corners. The square was everything; a place of worship, a market, a meeting place, a home for the many people who sat peering out from the windows and tiny doorways.

Two days' riding beyond Kathmandu was the village of Tatopani, near the Tibetan border. I'd come here as a detour before heading back to India. One of the few roads to choose from in the entire country, the last twenty miles was a dirt track cutting deep into the Himalayas. Once in Tatopani, I thought I might be able to blag my way past the Chinese border guards for a quick look around, as I'd read about other people doing the same.

I found a guesthouse, where a crazy woman was trying to get her goat to go up the track instead of running into the building. I was put into a simple wooden room for a dollar, and was reminded of Dylan Thomas' boathouse. The name Tatopani translated as "Hot water," and at the top of the village, below a busy shrine, was a communal shower from the hot springs. This was a hive of activity, out in the fresh air, with a wall separating the women's showers from the men's. I went in, wearing my cycling shorts, and the water was wonderful, blasting out of a row of pipes just above head-height. People chattered away whilst covering themselves in lather, and it struck me that my shorts looked just like the mens' undies! I walked back down the road and people were asking me, "What 'appen? Where are your trousers?"

In the guesthouse I got chatting to a Tibetan teacher who lives in Kathmandu. He'd come here for a break, to let the springs ease his back. He told me that he works at a Buddhist monastery, teaching the Tibetan language.

MONKEY TEMPLE, KATHMANDU, NEPAL '98

"Before the Chinese wipe it out," he said. "I think they would like to do that!"

"So, why did you leave Tibet? Was it because of them?" I asked.

"Yes, my parents brought me here to Nepal, when the Chinese marched in and took over our country."

Two Chinese engineers came in. They were building a new hydro-electric plant just down the road. The teacher said, "They're crazy!" and that they don't have anything to do with the locals. They just came in, arrogantly ordered some drinks, didn't talk to anyone else, then paid and left.

"So, do you ever go back?" I ventured. "It's only five miles up the road."

"No, never!" he said, but he didn't dwell on the subject. "Now I'm on holiday. I am going to drink some more Raksi!"

"Let's order an omelette as well!" I suggested.

"Good idea. My wife, she teaches Kung-Fu!" He was drunk already, and got up to demonstrate. "She goes like this – Woo! Ha!"

"So she can protect you if you are attacked!"

"Yes! She is a red-belt teacher! Hoo! Ha!" He swung his arms around for a few minutes, practically falling over.

"Hey, here comes our omelette already," I laughed. "You'd better sit down!"

"Look at this! So much onion in one omelette! Small hotel, big onion!"

"I know!" I was in stitches.

"Tell me," he asked the proprietor, "Where did you get this from? Small hotel, big onion!"

The next morning I had chips for breakfast, followed by pancakes with marmalade. The lady really knew how to look after the English. I left my pannier bag at the guesthouse, having already left the other one in Kathmandu, and set off up the steep dirt track to the border. There were virtually no cars or trucks on the road, only children and goats running about, and women sitting out in the sun preening each other's hair. The boys chased me up the road, laughing as they held onto my bike.

The higher I climbed, the more basic the houses became, until they were just a row of wooden shacks by the roadside. This was now

Kudari, the border town. I'd just past some majestic waterfalls, and the river flowing in the gorge below looked wild and cold. I had a drink, then continued to the Nepalese immigrations. I asked the guy if I could go as far as the border-line painted across the middle of the bridge. He said I could go that far, but no further. I told him I'd read about people crossing this border with no visa, and cycling five miles up the hill to Khasa. He told me that it's impossible.

He kept my passport and I cycled up to the line on Friendship Bridge. Nobody seemed to mind when I set the camera up and took a self-timer picture of me and the bike; one foot and one wheel in Nepal and the other foot and wheel in Tibet! I thought I'd go and say hello to the Chinese guard at the other end of the bridge. I told him my passport was with the Nepalese immigration, and that this was as far as I could go.

To my astonishment, he waved me through! I pedalled into Tibet, wondering if my Japanese friend Mikur would have been able to do the same. His bike carried a huge "Free Tibet" sticker.

Suddenly, Chinese people surrounded me, curiously looking at my map. This part was a market, selling clothes and electronic goods. One girl walked past, kicking both wheels of my bike, which I found a bit curious. I told those people around me that I was going to cycle up to Xangmu, the Chinese name for Khasa. Nobody seemed to mind, so I went for it! It was a steep climb up a track of stones and dust, and it became noticeably colder as I climbed; the hot valley air was replaced by cold air coming down from the Tibetan plateau.

Though the condition of the houses was the same as those just down the road in Nepal, somehow everything seemed dirtier; everyone looked very scruffy, their clothes covered in dust or muck. There was none of the pride of Nepal, where people in the most basic houses still manage to look after themselves and their appearance. Somehow this place seemed a lot rougher and uglier. People were dressed in old Western clothes, and all of the beauty of Nepal had been left behind on Friendship Bridge.

I reached Khasa, where a crowd of Indian Tata trucks and Chinese DongPeng trucks crammed next to the customs point. After five miles in this autonomous region of China, this was as far as I could go. Crowds of workers hung around smoking, presumably waiting for something to carry. I squeezed past the belching trucks and went

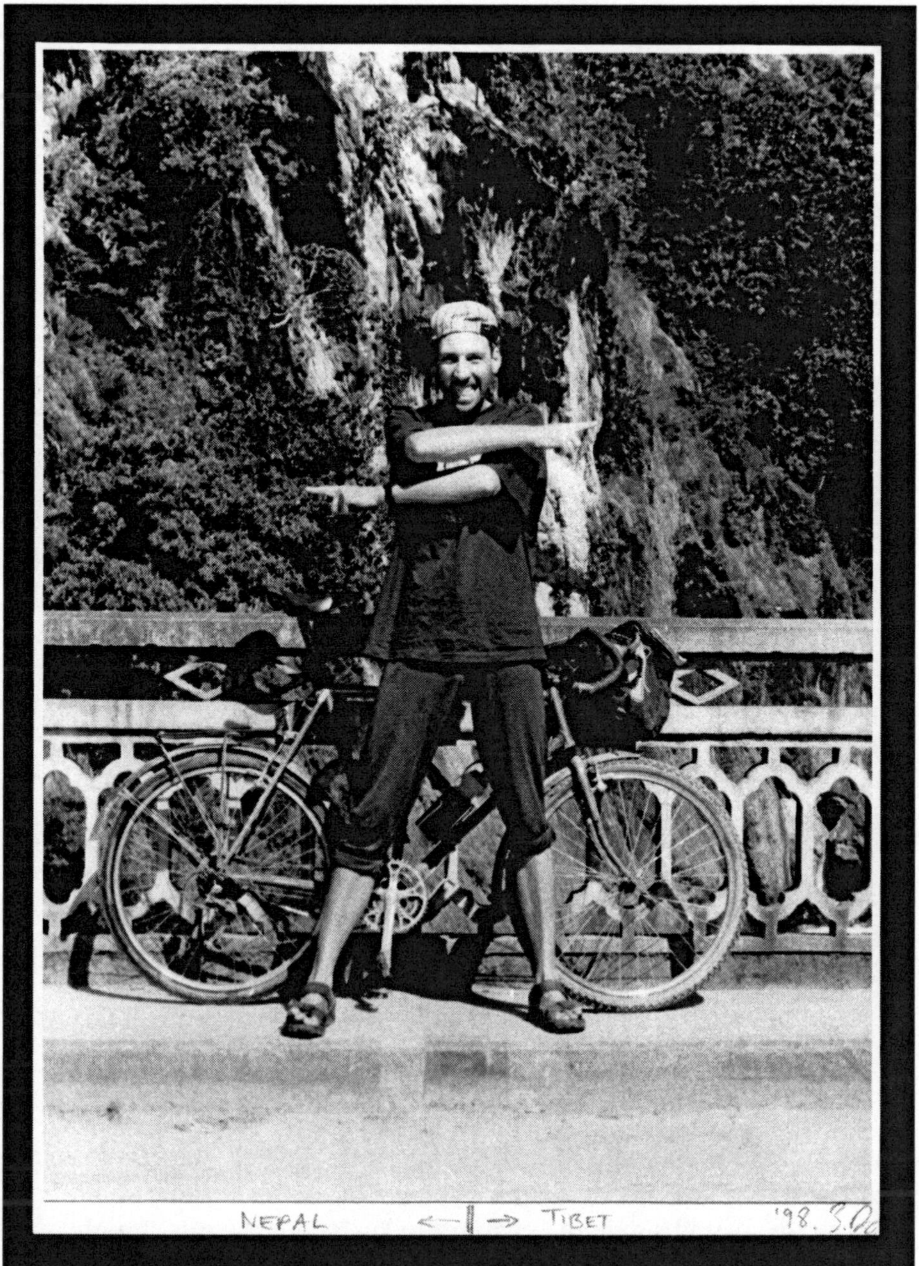
NEPAL ←|→ TIBET
'98.

up to the customs window. I explained the situation to the woman, just to confuse her and see what would happen, and she went outside to talk to one of her colleagues. I walked over to them, just for the hell of it because it meant crossing the yellow customs line.

In the end, four people came over and none of them seemed to know what to do with me, as my passport was still in Nepal, and I had no Chinese visa.

Eventually, one of them told me that as I'd been standing the wrong side of the customs line for several minutes, I should have a

stamp in my passport. I told him that was impossible because my passport was in Nepal! I told him I'd go back down to the bridge, and he knew very well that I wouldn't come all the way back up again just so they could stamp my passport to keep their records straight!

On the way back down, I photographed a group of Chinese workers carrying heavy loads on their backs. One wanted me to take a photo of himself alone, which I did. Then he started demanding money, and I told him that my money was in Nepal, which was a lie.

Three of them grabbed hold of my bike to stop me getting away, and even as I started down the road, the guy was running alongside, holding onto my handlebars. For a couple of minutes it looked as though things might have turned out nasty.

Finally, I escaped and bumped my way down to Friendship Bridge and the safety of Nepal, with the temperature way up again and Khasa just an ugly collection of concrete blocks on the hill above...

DARJEELING, INDIA

Starlight on steel. Too faint to see. Too cold to react. Tyre slides on railway line. Heavy bike loses grip, balance. Falling. Elbow strikes the tarmac...

After riding through Eastern Nepal and re-entering India, I came to the town of Siliguri, where the strike of the last three days had caused chaos and ended in a number of deaths through mob violence. I needed to change some money before heading south, but only just up the road was Darjeeling, not on my route but worth a visit.

I changed some cash at the bank, but I couldn't change any travellers' cheques because they needed to have proof of purchase, which no-one has ever needed before. There was an American who'd been here during the strike over the up-coming elections. He was sitting there, asking the guard if it was open yet upstairs, as there was nowhere to sit down in the hallway.

"Is it OPEN? Is it OPEN?" he strained.

"Sir, I don't know!" shrugged the guard.

"THREE DAYS, NO FOOD," he complained. "I do NOT want to go up there and have to come back down again."

"I am sorry sir, I do not know!"

"THREE DAYS, NO FOOD. For crying out loud! Is it OPEN?"

I couldn't help smirking, very secretly, and thinking, "What a donkey!" I'd just come back into India with only dollars, which nobody would take, but the hotel man said I could put my meal on the slate. How did this American guy fail to arrange something like that?

Although I now had some rupees from changing the cash dollars, I needed to have a lot more, so I thought I'd try my luck in Darjeeling. I left my things in the hotel, and took a jeep for the drive to Darjeeling, with the bike loaded onto the roof. The drive was brilliant, leaving the tropical vegetation behind as we climbed a steep twisting road, with far-reaching views of Siliguri and the Indian plain.

Tea plantations covered the hillside, like fields of low privet bushes. We stopped at a little restaurant and I was able to enjoy the view before we carried on. There were dozens of Indian Mahindra jeeps going up and down the steep narrow road, crammed full of people. Ours had twelve onboard, plus two more hanging off the back. Amazingly, though, I only saw one other Westerner on the whole fifty-mile drive.

The road was lined at intervals with groups of houses made of wood and corrugated iron, all painted up and looking like the houses which Verena and I had seen in Chile. Here, they were often balanced on the edge of a steep slope, which dropped hundreds of metres. For most of the way, the road followed a narrow-gauge railway line; the "Toy Train" as it's known. Built by the British in 1889, it still runs, though there was no train today, and the railway line was acting as a children's playground.

We reached the cold mountain pass at about two thousand three hundred metres above sea level, having just climbed from a mere two hundred metres! The view opened out onto a spectacularly deep valley in the mountains, with a white Himalayan background and the town of Darjeeling clinging on to the valley sides, a far more dramatic setting than Kathmandu in Nepal, or Huaraz in Peru. Here the mountains were closer than I'd ever seen them, and the town, though not very pretty, was interesting in the way it was built onto such a slope. It was fairly clean, and I only saw a handful of travellers.

I couldn't hang around, though; I had to get back to Siliguri once I'd changed some travellers' cheques. A pile of Indian rupees three inches thick in my money-belt, I cycled back up to the mountain pass. The sun was starting to set on the mighty peaks, as it streaked through the mist on the lower ridge. Far below, the folds of valleys and gorges faded deeper and deeper to an indistinguishable grey distance.

Past the wandering people in the busy streets, past the Toy Train in its engine shed and on to the top of the pass, I left the mountains behind only half an hour after first seeing them. The sky was now red and the cold was coming in. I was wearing sandals and my feet felt the rush of the wind. I was still forty-five miles from Siliguri, and as the road swept around the broad curves I streamed past the children on the railway, the houses lining the road and an immensely sharp drop back down to the Indian plain.

Flying around the curves in the fading light was exhilarating, but I was worried about the amount of distance I'd have to do in the dark. The jeep ride had taken much longer than they'd said it would, and we'd spent an hour waiting for more passengers before we set off. Still, I had my bike lights with me and night cycling is something I enjoy.

At first it was okay because I was still able to see, and when it became really dark I put the lights on. But the back one suddenly decided it wasn't working anymore. The front one was next to useless because all the twists and turns meant that it was never actually lighting up the road. Another potential hazard was that both my tyres were worn through in a couple of places.

By far the biggest problem was the Toy Train's railway line; it was no doubt built long before the road, and they kept crossing each other, rather than remaining parallel. Sometimes I thought the road was straight ahead but actually it would suddenly cross the lines, then I had to slow right down and cross them at an obtuse angle so the tyres wouldn't slip on the rails.

Add to that the fact that the road was all jagged and stepped, the railway sleepers sometimes overlapped the edge of the road, and there was a sheer drop on the other side and nothing to warn you; I started to think that this was a bit mad! The traffic was much heavier than it had been during the daylight hours, big trucks with only one headlight working and the rest invisible in the pitch black. I had to get off the edge of the road, wherever that was, when something came, but I knew that the ride would take too long and my front light batteries would run out too soon.

The plan for the day had been very simple; go to the bank, take a jeep up the hill and ride back down again. But this was India, and everything takes twice as long as you think. There was another small worry; banditry on the road at night in this region. Luckily I found a truck that was going slowly down the hill, so I was able to follow him and see with his headlights. The road was very narrow in places and I had to watch for the telltale glint of the railway as it crossed the road every now and then.

Unfortunately the slow truck stopped in a village, so I went on, still at a high altitude and thirty-five miles from Siliguri, getting very cold and aware that my front light was fading. I was just thinking, "This is really dumb!" when the railway line crossed the road again and I didn't react quickly enough, because I was cold and tired. Sure enough, the front tyre slid along the rail and before I knew it, my elbow hit the road and I was off.

I picked myself up and kept going, far too slowly to make it back to Siliguri, but unable to go any faster. A jeep overtook me and when I came round the corner I found that the driver had stopped for a pee. I asked if he was going to Siliguri. He replied that they were, and that the fare was the same as on the way up; forty-seven rupees.

WEST BENGAL, INDIA '98.

The bike was roped onto the roof-rack and we set off down the hill. I was relieved, thinking about the huge plate of chicken curry I had at my hotel last night – I'd have the same again; it was still only six-thirty. The drama didn't stop there though - all that happened in the jeep was that the corners came up faster and we couldn't squeeze past the trucks! Several times we slammed to a stop when another vehicle came towards us around a tight bend, and the concrete edging on the drop-side of the road had been breached in several places.

Further down, we went through a place with some streetlights and I looked at the spare tyre bolted to the back door just next to me. It was quite literally a bald tyre with a wide strip of another tyre wound very crudely around it, like a marzipan edging around a cake. Remould tyres, Indian style! The jeep kept stalling every couple of minutes, and whenever the driver tried to bump-start it on the steep slope, the lights would go off so we could neither see the wall on one side nor the precipice on the other.

At the bottom of the hill we pulled up to a small garage which seemed to keep all the Mahindras on the Siliguri-to-Darjeeling route running. A couple of tweaks were made under the bonnet and to my relief the spare was swapped for a brand new tyre. We weren't stalling anymore and the mountains were behind us. But this only meant that we could go even faster, overtaking army trucks and passing by within inches of the pedestrians, forced to walk on the road because there was no pavement.

We reached the end, however, and I was still alive. A plate of chicken curry was placed in front of me and I pondered the next set of problems...

Chittagong, Bangladesh

I was heading south to visit the Chittagong Hill Tracts; a tribal region in Bangladesh which, only three months before, had been opened up to foreign travellers, without the need for a government permit. I only had a few days before I was due to fly to Myanmar (Burma) and the main problem in getting there was that everyone in Bangladesh was so friendly and hospitable...

I set off early to try and find an ancient Buddhist monastery called Mainamati. I rode along a low ridge looking for it, and watched the farmers working, wearing their wrap-around longhis. A couple of ancient tractors trundled past and the children ran after me, giggling. I gave up, but eventually happened upon a sign saying, "Mainamati Museum and Archaeological Remains."

I stopped in a small restaurant for breakfast before entering the museum. These places are much more pleasant than the ones in India; everything is brightly painted and clean, with simple wooden chairs and tables, and a refreshing breeze blowing through. It turned out that there was a Polytechnic nearby, and a few students came over for a chat. Outside there was commotion when a cycle rickshaw driver was getting beaten up by his passenger, but was then dragged off to safety by the villagers.

Outside the museum I stopped for a Sprite, at a little stall. Again I was surrounded by students and local kids, and sat talking with them under the coconut palms. After a few minutes I got up, and the students walked with me to the gates of the museum. One of them suddenly said, "Of course it's closed today, being Saturday." I wondered why they hadn't told me earlier!

Instead, we all went for a walk in the low hills, with acacia trees all around and small thatched huts dotted about. We passed through the site of the ancient Buddhist Temple, a set of low red brick walls with an indication of the one hundred and ten monastic cells that once stood there.

As we walked, the students said that the British often help Bangladesh with foreign aid. I asked who paid for the new three-mile long Jamuna Bridge, and they told me it was the Japanese. The students treated me to a young green coconut, which the seller gave to me with a straw after lopping off the top with his curved knife.

Just before I left, a Buddhist monk invited me to his monastery, but like the students I met earlier and the motorcyclist I met just after, I had to turn down his offer of hospitality or else I'd never make it to Feni! About an hour later a pick-up stopped and a German guy jumped out and invited me back to his place! He told me that he works for ABB and they're laying a new transmission line. I had to turn him down as well; I only had a few days left on my visa.

Getting the visa had been no easy matter. I should have been able to get it in Kathmandu, but the Embassy there told me I'd have to go to Calcutta, which was way off my route. Cycling down through West Bengal from Siliguri, certain things were impossible to do. I couldn't get through to Austria by phone or fax for two weeks, the map I had was very unclear as to where I could cross over to Bangladesh, and I had no way of knowing the state of the roads and bridges there after the recent floods. Village after village I passed through, looking for food, with nothing more than a couple of old bananas and a tiny packet of biscuits to choose from. Despite the friendliness of the people, I was finding it hard going in the tropical heat.

One night, in a mosquito-infested room, I woke with a terrible fever. I was aching all over, my eyes were popping out and I had nausea, sweating and an intense headache. I squatted at the toilet, wondering if I'd finally come down with malaria. When morning came, I awoke feeling half dead. Luckily I'd met a doctor in the restaurant the previous evening. I managed to find him and showed him the fever tablets which I'd been carrying with me. He said that these should tide me over till I got to Calcutta, but that I shouldn't hang about.

I had to cycle fifty miles to Malda for the sleepless, backbreaking overnight bus ride to Calcutta. Once there, I met a man who called himself John. He said he sleeps on the streets, and that he would help me find somewhere to stay, in return for baksheesh. I ended up in an airless, windowless room because most of the hotels wouldn't let me bring the bike in. Later on, I went to the Bangladesh Embassy and found that I was a special case, as I wanted to cross the border by bike. This would take more time to organise.

I managed to get through to Verena by phone at last, but I didn't tell her of my illness. I was too exhausted, though, after so much running around, to find a doctor. I went to bed in the afternoon and slept till morning. After another visit to the Embassy the next day, I found an internet café and sent an e-mail to Claudia in Bangladesh, a friend of Verena's who'd invited me to stay. While the message was sending, I came over all peculiar; sweating, headache and nausea again. Back in my room, I had three or four similar turns in half an hour. I tried walking down to reception but I kept blanking out, with my head buzzing and a strong feeling of wanting to throw up. Everything had become bright and colourless, as if the stairs and the reception desk had lost any definition, and were merged into the walls.

I made it to the desk and slumped over, my head in my hands. My shirt was soaked with sweat and I could barely talk. After all this time, it turned out that the doctor's was just on the other side of the road. I must have been in a terrible state because I was sent straight in to the consultation room. A blood test was taken, and I was clear for malaria. I was given some pills and spent the next week in bed, whilst waiting for the visa.

I put the illness down to bad water; my filter had stopped working in Nepal and I'd been relying on bottled water ever since. When this hadn't been available I'd had no choice but to put purifying tablets into the tap water. Eventually, the visa came through and I was just about well enough to take the overnight bus back up to Malda, to carry on where I'd left off, only to catch a cold from someone on the bus.

Three hundred and forty six miles of very weary pedalling later, I rode up to the gate of Claudia and Gianni's house in Dhaka, where I was welcomed into a world of luxury. They let me ring up Verena and my family back home; five different phone calls. This was timely as I had a policy of only phoning up when things were going well, as the news would inevitably be spread around and would keep everyone going for another couple of weeks. Claudia and Gianni's hospitality was the most generous that I've ever experienced, and I finally began to re-gain my strength.

Hello Verena!

How are you? You must be missing Tim a lot and having to be very patient. Never mind, you'll see him in January and that will be a wonderful re-union.

Could you let me have his fax number in Bangladesh? I've got some messages for him from the family – I've been saving them for six weeks as I've not had a fax number for him since Kathmandu! He left a message on my answer-phone this morning and I was glad to hear his voice again. He'd sounded very tired last time and I'd thought that he might not be very well. Anyway, typically he has bounced back up again and obviously needed that rest at your friend Claudia's.

All well here – Sally and I are doing lots of gigs and Janna is cheerful. Are you still busy at this time of year?
Take care –
Love, Berlie.

Two days south of Dhaka, I reached the town of Feni, where I accepted the invitation of a local doctor who led me to a guesthouse. First, however, he showed me a Hindu temple, dedicated to the goddess Kali. A man explained to me the significance of all the different elements of the temple, and the importance of the sun as the giver of energy.

Dear Berlie!
I hadn't heard from him much recently, which made it all harder. I always get so worried, which is probably silly, because I know he's looking very well after himself, but I can't help it. Luckily I had a long conversation with him the other day, despite the terrible connection.

He said that Claudia and Gianni have been brilliant hosts. He turned up at their house in Dhaka, covered in dirt from the road and the traffic pollution, and totally skinny because he'd been really ill for over a week in Calcutta. They fed him well and gave him some new clothes; he's so grateful to them! If we ever get married, we'll definitely invite them to the wedding!

He's now left Claudia's house, but he'll be back there in a few days, to stay for one or two nights before heading off to Burma. Oh! You wanted their fax number! I'll look it up this evening and send it to you!

Work doesn't seem to get any less and the busy Christmas period is approaching already. But the hardest bit of all is to come home to an empty house.
I did a pottery class the last few weeks and my things will be glazed next week. I'm really excited!
  A big hug to all of you
  - Verena

The doctor then took me to the local branch of the Sri Ram Krishna Mission, a movement which, he said, has been going for over a hundred years. There was a set of chairs outside and a meeting was about to start. For some bizarre reason, I was introduced as an important guest, and was made to sit in the centre at the front, on the only comfortable chair, facing the audience with the speakers on either side of me!

The purpose of the meeting was to decide on the final matters regarding the construction of a new Hindu temple here, starting on December 11th, only a week away. The farmers sat there with "Doctor Who" scarves wrapped around their heads as it was a winter evening, and the temperature was only in the twenties! The businessmen wore suits, and were busy answering their mobile phones.

All in all, about fifty people were present and I was made to stand up, introduce myself and wish them well for the building of the temple. I managed to do this, somehow, and was clapped at the end of my improvised speech! We were served half-way through with cake, Bombay mix and a banana. The doctor next to me, who'd asked me to do the speech, turned to me and said very sincerely, "I give you my banana."

The funding for the new temple was done without any help from the government. Most was donated by local benefactors while the community, both Hindu and Muslim, clubbed together for the rest, in traditional co-operation. After this we went for a Chinese meal which the doctor said he'd just arranged over his mobile phone, on my behalf. I was surprised at how many people were there, again about fifty, and a lot of them were freedom fighters from the 1971 struggle for Independence, when East Pakistan became Bangladesh.

The next morning the doctor picked me up from my guesthouse at six o'clock, and took me to see another temple and also the government resthouse, where he said I would be put up, were I to return with Verena. Next I was taken to meet the local MP, Mr Joynal Abedin Hazari. I was a little surprised because he seemed to know nothing at all about British politics. This was in complete contrast to all of the students I'd met so far in Bangladesh, and with many of the farmers and truck drivers in India. One time, I was slacking around on a charpois and an old man was sitting there looking very thoughtful, trying to think of a question. Then he turned, leant towards me and asked, "How many legislative councils are there in your country?"

The MP took his early morning walkabout, backwards and forwards across his badminton courts with two of his friends and me. He said that I was a very important guest because Britain helped Bangladesh so much in the 1971 struggle for Independence, whilst America sided with (then West) Pakistan. Also, he added, Britain helped Bangladesh during the recent floods and other crises. He said that Bangladesh is crying out for more foreign investment to help get the country on its feet, and that politics in Bangladesh is a strange affair as it doesn't really function democratically. Politicians, he told me, argue for the sake of contradicting each other, and occasionally get bumped off for saying the wrong thing.

The MP is a bachelor, devoting himself to his work and his community. He said that any British traveller should be treated with the utmost respect. The Doctor was late picking me up and the MP said jokingly that he would have him "severely punished" for making me late! He offered to put me up for a few days, saying it would be his pleasure, and that I could have anything I wanted, even asking if I wanted to ring home to England! I thanked him for his kind offer of hospitality, but said that I was keen to reach Rangamati. For me, that was important because it marked the end of the Indian Subcontinent, and on the other side of the hills was the start of South East Asia.

The doctor came back for me and we had a tasty Bengali breakfast, cooked by his sister in law; his entire family lives in one huge house. I showed my gratitude, but all this hospitality had made me late again and I only had until five o'clock before darkness fell. I left Feni in the mid-day heat and had to push it for nearly sixty miles to get to the next place which might have a guesthouse.

The many stinking trucks and buses kept forcing me off the road at regular intervals. In trying to find Shangmu guesthouse, I wasted my last precious hour of daylight in the office of a scuzz-bucket who buys and sells marine pump engines. He assured me that the guesthouse was just around the corner. After lots of persuasion, I was able to follow him as he drove to the guesthouse.

"This is it," he said, stopping the car and getting out.

"This is a joke isn't it!" I exclaimed.

We were standing outside a massive gas plantation, all shiny pipes and ladders, lit by sodium lights. A group of English and Scottish construction workers were standing behind the fence with their arms folded, wearing red boiler suits.

"Is there a guesthouse here?" I asked them, feeling like a complete donkey.

"There's no guesthouse here," they answered, bemused. "You'll have to go into Chittagong, mate!"

"What the hell were you talking about?" I shouted at the marine pumps man.

"Er, I thought there was one here!" He looked like he couldn't believe it.

"You'd better get a move on, pal!" the construction workers suggested.

"Yeah, cheers," I replied, setting off. "I'd have got there in the daylight if it wasn't for this clown!"

It was already starting to go dark and suddenly I was in trouble. I took off at speed to try and do the last six miles to Chittagong, Bangladesh's second city, as quickly as possible.

The road was extremely dangerous, and as I rode between the almost invisible potholes and deep patches of sand, the trucks and the maniac auto-rickshaws, I was cursing. The marine pumps man had wasted my last hour of daylight, and the doctor had stalled me for several hours in Feni.

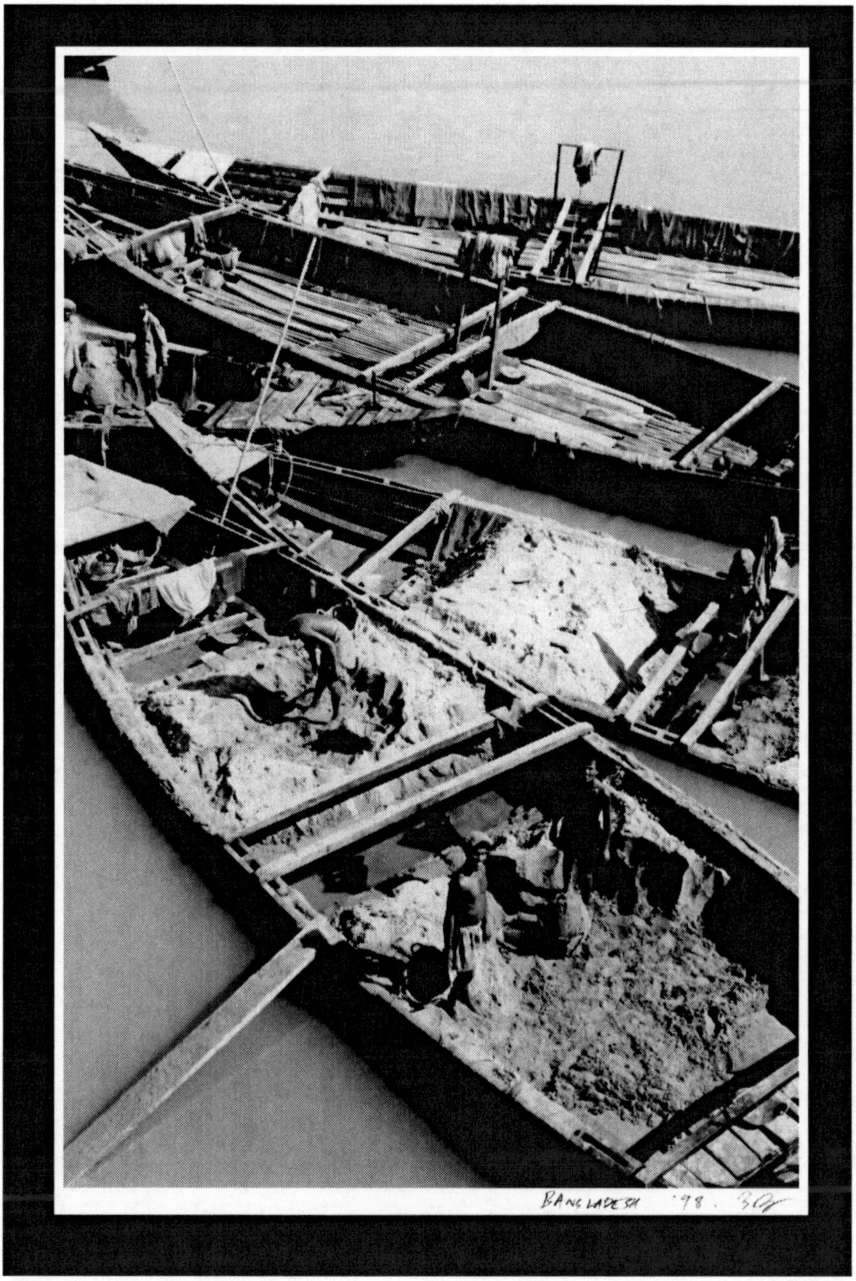
BANGLADESH '98.

CHITTAGONG HILL TRACTS, BANGLADESH, '98.

After a few miles of hair-raising traffic, a minibus overtook me and pulled over. The door flew open and somebody jumped out, waving at me to stop. It was one of the construction workers. He said I could follow the minibus and stay in their staff-house!

Suddenly, I was plunged into the ex-pat world of "Aufwiedersehen, Pet." Chips, eggs, ham and beans were followed by large quantities of smuggled beer, and songs about "Tatties and Herrin'." Then, later on; football, darts and dancing girls.

Mandalay, Myanmar (Burma)

Doing this sort of thing fully prepared on my expedition bike would be a bit mad, but forgivable. But on this dodgy bike and in this way it was definitely insane, but it beats riding across Germany! If I'd got a puncture, I'd have been stuffed. What could I do, wait for the next lazy oxen cart to amble along, or push the bike for thirty miles through the sand in the tropical heat?

There were practically no vehicles all day, and huge expanses of nothing; a semi-arid landscape with lots of hill climbs. The real problem was my map. I was on a road which wasn't even shown, but I knew that when I arrived in Myotha I would reach what the map told me was a primary road. That turned out to be a sand track too...

Getting to Mandalay from Bangladesh was a problem. The first thing is that you can't cross the border from Bangladesh to Myanmar, and you can't cross the border from Myanmar to Thailand. So you have to fly in and fly out. Having ridden to the Rangamati Hill Tracts, thereby completing the subcontinent, I'd returned to Claudia's in Dhaka to sort out a visa. In order to get one, I first had to buy the plane tickets, and only then would the Myanmar Embassy allow me to come for an interview, to see if I was suitable for visiting the country.

The next problem was that they told me I couldn't take the bike into the country, so I had to fly first to Bangkok in Thailand to store the bike at the airport, then get straight on a plane to Yangon (Rangoon). This turned out to be very expensive, but I wasn't going to miss this country out, as I'd already been forced to leave out Iran.

The third problem was that you have to change three hundred dollars on arrival in Myanmar, into a "Monopoly" type money called Foreign Exchange Certificates. Legally, you're not allowed to change them back again! So my first task in Yangon was to find a black-market moneychanger, so I could re-convert some dollars, and change some FECs for the local currency, kyat, because that was all that the small businesses would accept! The moneychanger man was

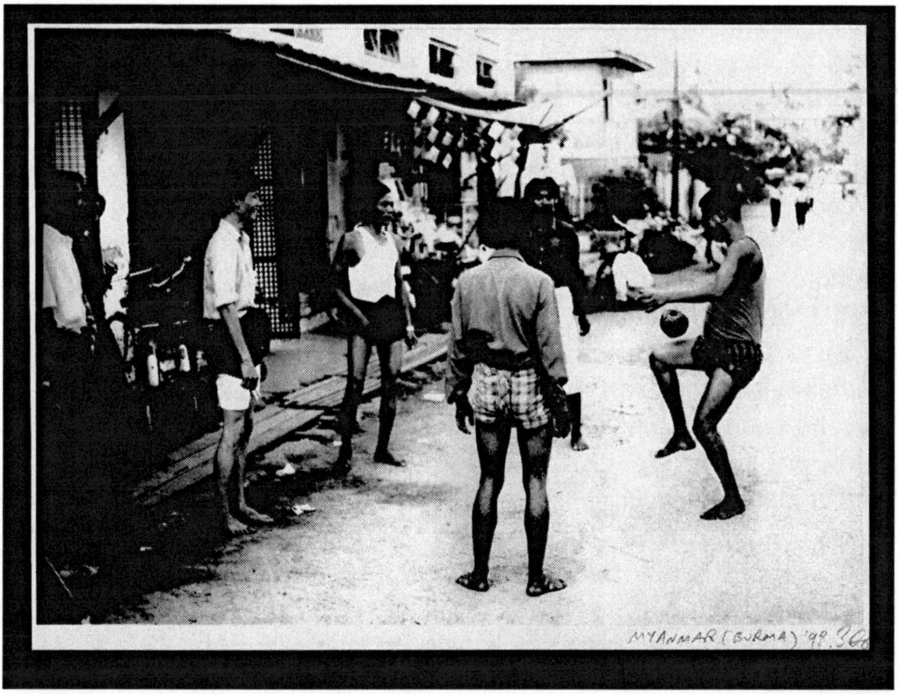
MYANMAR (BURMA) '98.

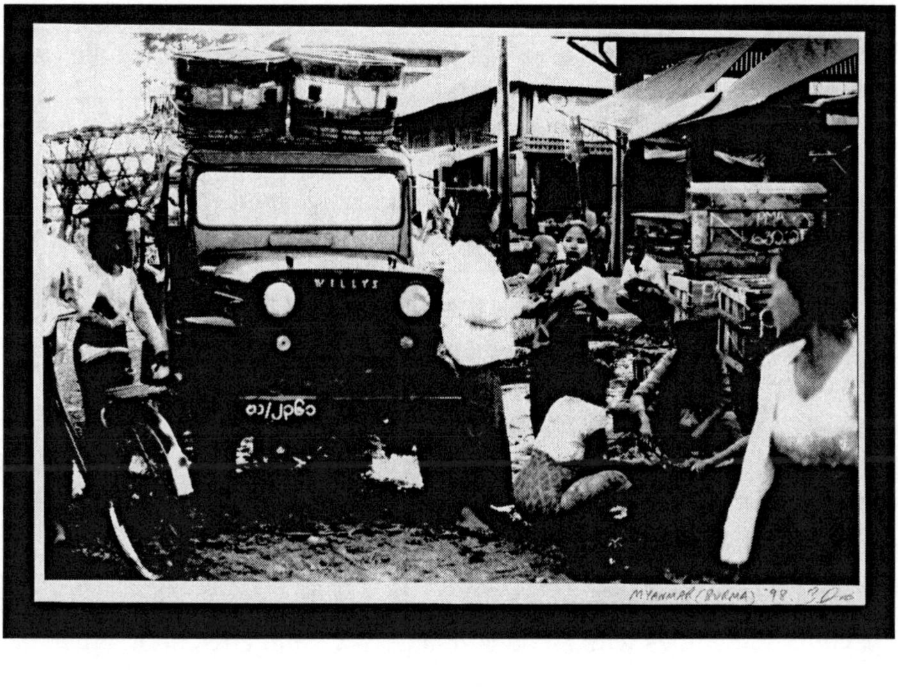
WILLYS
MYANMAR (BURMA) '98.

a star, and I told him I wanted to go to Mandalay, buy a bike and ride back to Yangon. He said that I could get a new one for fifty dollars, then he'd buy it from me for thirty dollars, nine days and nearly five hundred miles later.

I disembarked from the overnight Yangon to Mandalay bus, with a French couple I'd been talking to. They very kindly offered to share a room with me, so it was only three FECs for me instead of five. They went to look around but I had to crash out for a bit, then I went to find a bike shop.

I was keen on the idea of riding to Yangon on a single-speed Indian bike, as most of my baggage was stored in Bangkok. Buying a second-hand one proved impossible, however, and a new one was the same price as an eighteen-speed mountain bike, which I knew I could sell at the end.

So I chose a brand new mountain bike, the biggest in the shop, but still four inches too small for me! Optimistically named "Five Star Mountain," it was Chinese and absolutely rubbish, but for thirty-five quid I couldn't complain! The lads in the shop were a bit sloppy because they didn't seem bothered about tightening things up properly; everything was loose, but the more I pointed things out the more they realised I was serious about having a bike that worked.

I rode it for five miles around Mandalay Palace, and the saddle stem slipped right down. The gears stopped working as well, so I went back to the shop and the lads did their best, but they had Chinese technology against them; getting the lowest gear ratio just wasn't possible! Anyway, it was my bike now, and I rode to the theatre of the Mandalay Marionettes to buy a ticket for the evening's performance.

Back at the hotel, my French friends were asleep, so I took a walk up Mandalay Hill. I started up the steps leading to the Pagoda at the top of the hill. There was a fiery sunset, so I paused to sit on a rock next to a stupa. I sat there until after dark, gazing down at Mandalay's myriad pagodas, decorated by fairy lights.

Up the covered walkway in utter darkness I climbed, bare-foot on the stone steps, sandals in hand. One of those nervous but exciting experiences. The entire hill is a Buddhist monument, and all was quiet and dark. Once in a while, the path would open to reveal a pagoda, sometimes with Buddha images several metres high, other

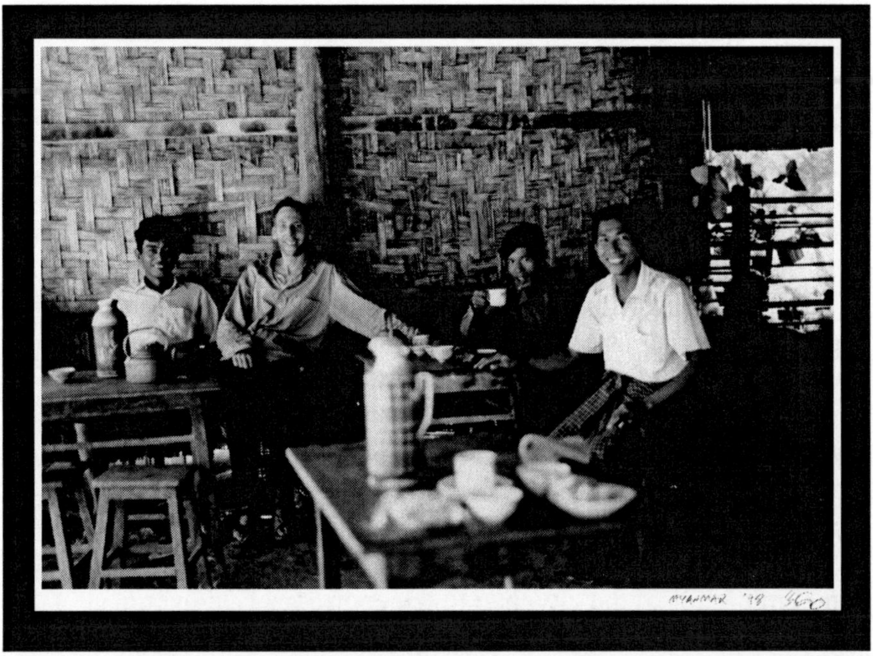
MYANMAR '98

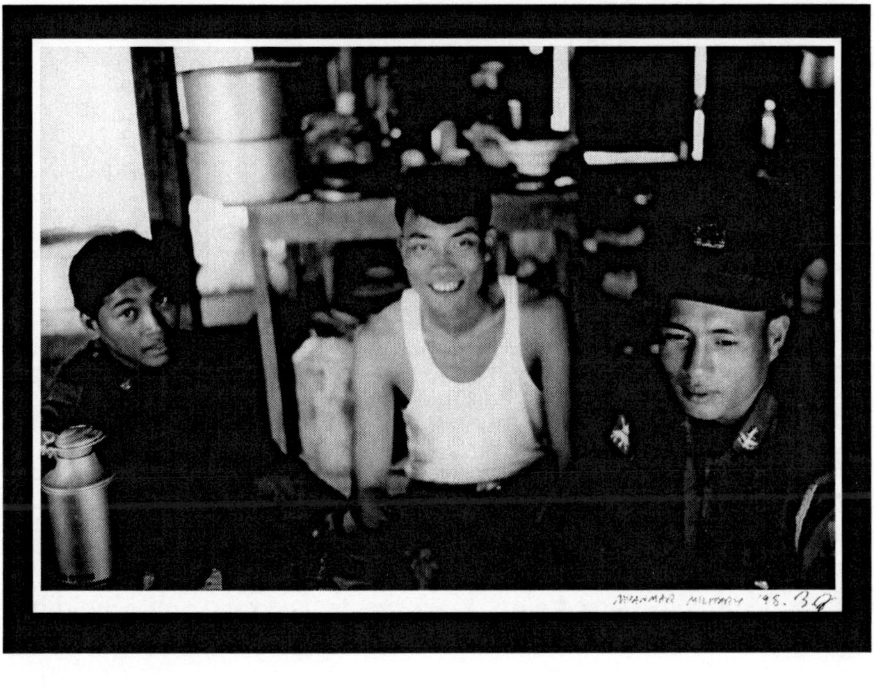
MYANMAR MILITARY '98.

times with small sitting Buddhas. The strange echoes of voices floated in the warm air, and each pagoda seemed to have a guardian family living within. On the walkway and in the surrounding woodland, not a soul stirred.

At a junction of two paths, I met a couple of local lads. They walked with me, saying that there are 1,796 steps in total. I told them that I'd been climbing for nearly an hour already. The higher we climbed, the more surreal it became. We passed yet more pagodas with people living there, in makeshift quarters, watching little black and white televisions or sleeping under mosquito nets. These are the people who sell souvenirs to the pilgrims and tourists, most of whom are Burmese.

Nearer the top there was a lot more action; a couple of cafes and a road coming up from the bottom! This is obviously how everybody else had got up, because on the top there were dozens of Burmese teenagers hanging out in groups, paying more attention to the panoramic view of the city than to the enormous Buddha image. I only just made it to the Manadalay Marionettes on time, and who should be in the seats next to me but the two French people from my hotel room.

"Oh, hello!" I said. "I knew you wanted to come, but I didn't know you had tickets!"

"Yes, we bought them this afternoon, when we woke up."

"There's hardly anybody here," I pointed out, "only us and five others!"

"We could have just turned up!" they laughed.

"I'm already glad I came. This place is a real find."

"This auditorium is very… intimate, I think!"

"And that basketwork panelling is nice," I added. "Is that what you call rattan?"

"Probably! Look at those puppets hanging up on the walls…"

The performance began, with a band sitting just in front of the stage. They played loud Chinese-sounding music with lots of clashing, high-pitched singing and a high-sounding instrument like a little clarinet. A lady came onto the stage, beautifully dressed in silk, singing to a swan-shaped harp. Then she danced for a while, holding a candle in the palm of each hand.

MYANMAR (BURMA) '98. 3. 6

The marionettes followed, with short acts from Hindu, Buddhist and folk stories. We were able to watch the puppeteers at work, sweetly singing along to the story, as they occasionally raised the curtain from its halfway position. Amusing and clever movements of the characters became even more fascinating and magical when the arms of the puppeteers were visible, deftly spinning and swinging the strings.

My favourite scene was one in which two green demons were fighting. Running and jumping across the stage they went, to kick each other up the bum! The whole stage was used, as the puppets whirled and flew around, especially the dancing horse, which could spin on one hoof. New characters appeared out of the blue to surprise the audience, such as the two-metre long snake.

The most extraordinary set involved a puppet holding a red stick in both hands, above his head. The puppet master, a man with forty-five years' experience and a gold medal to his name, managed with ease to make the puppet do what he wanted. The marionette held the stick in one hand, then the other. He swung it around his head, made it dangle on the floor, and then, with the stick standing vertically, flew around the top of it on the palm of his hand. Finally, the puppet stood up straight again, holding the stick in both hands!

I said goodbye to my French friends in the morning, and started riding on my new bike. The saddle was too hard and low, even though it was raised as much as possible. The handlebar grips hurt like hell, especially when twisting them to change gear, and everything was generally cheap and nasty. It looked I had a comical week ahead of me.

After only five miles, I lost my forward motion; when I pedalled, nothing happened! I examined the chain-set, a cheap swaged one, and found that it had failed already. Luckily there was a mechanic nearby and, with an unbelievably basic set of tools, he removed the chain-set and bashed the bottom end of the crank with a hammer and a length of iron, to make the joint fast. It didn't work, so we went round the corner to see his friend the welder. The welding didn't work either, because of the thick paint on the crank. They tried bashing it with a hammer again, using a six-inch length of railway line as an anvil. This time, it did the trick. They laughed their heads off when I said, "You know I've got to cycle to Rangoon on this thing!"

They were squatting on the floor as they worked, and the welder's wife sat giggling in a wicker chair in front of the basketwork house. Also, the saddle kept going down at the back when I sat on it, no matter how tightly it was done up. So I got them to weld it up, bringing the bill to a staggering thirty English pence.

I was on the road again, not even out of Mandalay, but winging it big-time. I was asking for trouble using a bike like this, but I thought, "What the hell!" I didn't even have any tools, spares, puncture kit, pump or anything, just the clothes I was wearing, a map, some water and a camera! The rest was in storage at Bangkok Airport.

First stop was a deserted ancient capital, Innwa, which cost four dollars to visit and wasn't worth it. It was clearly part of the government's cream-the-tourists-to-fund-the-oppressive-regime trick. I avoided the tourist sites after that.

At least the ferry to Innwa was an experience, and definitely not government-run. It was full of locals in their Chinese-style hats, the women's cheeks covered with yellow sun-cream, made from natural ingredients and worn by nearly everybody, including some of the fashionable women in the capital. The boat was a tiny wooden thing, creaky and dusty, but somehow they managed to get a pick-up truck on board, as well as the people, bikes and scooters. On the way across, I saw another boat, jam-packed with oxen.

From Innwa there was a railway marked on my map, going to a town called Myotha, which was on my way. After lots of difficulty trying to explain myself, the locals told me that yes, this dirt track did go to Myotha, vaguely following the railway. To go via the main-road would have meant another forty miles. The rest of the day was spent on the dirt track...

I was constantly worried about the bike breaking down, or not being able to find anywhere to stay, or even getting hopelessly lost, since my track and all the other adjoining ones weren't on the map! I had to rely totally on the people, but there were hardly any around and my pronunciation of the place names baffled them.

In spite of my worries, the ride was stunningly beautiful. There was no traffic, only the occasional ambling ox cart. It was dry grassland, almost like a savannah, where I'd expected jungle or rainforest. A huge open space, it felt relaxing, after the incessant hustle and bustle of the Indian subcontinent. A few local cyclists were about and they tried out their English on me, but they find it very hard to get the pronunciations right, unlike people in India who are much more easy to understand.

At one point, the right-hand pedal body came clean off the spindle! I stood there looking at it, thinking, "Is this some kind of joke?" A metal spindle is not very easy to pedal on, but it is possible, and it had to do until I got to Myingyan the next day, thirty miles away.

I was still out in the middle of nowhere when darkness fell. Even though I'd been going hell for leather through the sand on my too-small bike with one pedal, there was no way I could get to Myingyan. I came to a river with a wide ford and a little bridge at its narrow end, like a piece of fencing laid down just above the water. Coming the other way were two lads on a moped. They said that there was a village around the corner, and a man whose house I could stay in. But all this was so difficult to understand because of their pronunciation, and my total lack of their language, that I felt sure I'd never find this man.

What I did find was a teahouse, very simple but well stocked, the first place like it I'd seen all day. I was pretty stuck and I felt sure that if I hung around long enough, the people would allow me to find a quiet corner to sleep in. Riding on in the dark was out of the question; the sand only had a narrow, meandering path from the bikes that had passed over it, and the soft sand on either side was treacherous. Also, there would be no one around to give me directions at the junctions.

A few of the villagers were there, and the teahouse had a generator, some strip lights and a black and white television. I ordered some instant noodles and eggs, and sat there drinking glass after glass of the complimentary Chinese tea. A few people joined me at my table and made me feel welcome, but when the man started closing up the shop I still had a problem.

I pointed to a bench outside the shop, and asked if I could kip there. He'd obviously been thinking about this, because he led me through the shop to the back. He proudly pointed out that there was a bigger bench, with some cardboard on it for comfort! A tall bamboo fence surrounded the bench, so I knew that I'd be safe. The man and

151

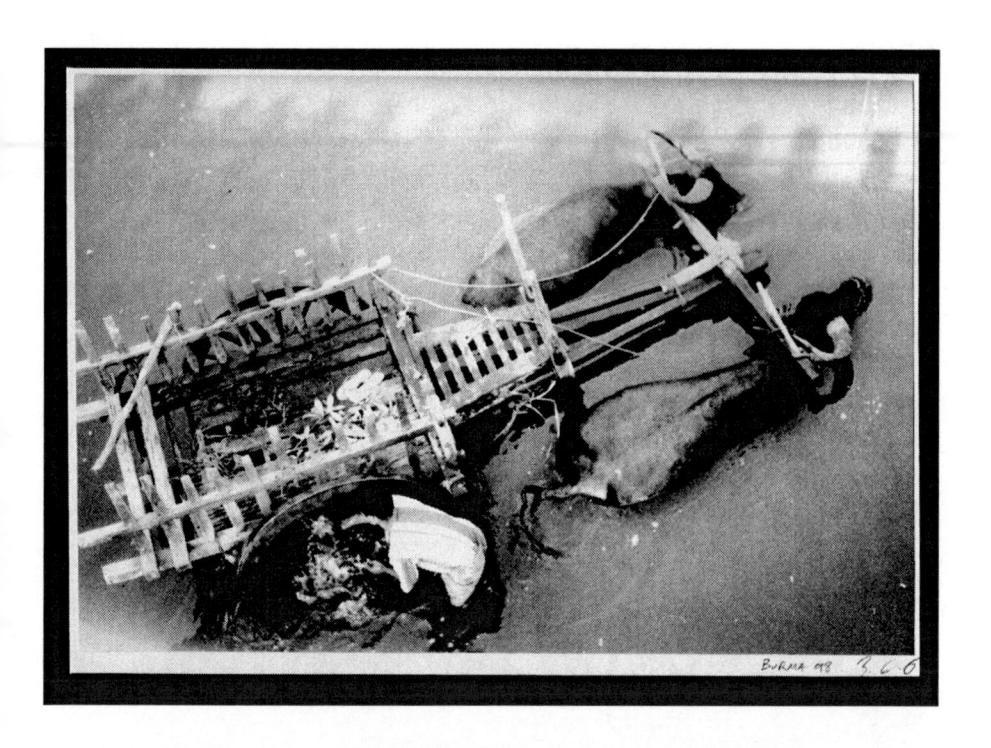

his wife fussed around bringing me some blankets, and the bike was locked inside the shop. I thanked them profusely, and I think they enjoyed the novelty of it all.

It wasn't the best night, but I've had much worse. The mosquitoes made me paranoid, even though I knew that there was no malaria in this region. Every time a mossie buzzed up I hid under the blanket, but that was full of dust so I got asthma! I kept switching my torch on and off to try and catch the mosquitoes, and to see what the creatures were that were scurrying around under the bench. Fortunately, I never managed to spot them. I was convinced that they were rats.

I woke up in the middle of the night, feeling very cold. I had that horrible feeling that diarrhoea was on its way. Luckily I'd already sussed out which corner of the yard the family used as a toilet...

Chiang Mai To Bangkok, Thailand

After eight superb days, I made it to Yangon and sold the Chinese bike for thirty dollars, as planned. I took my flight to Bangkok the next day, picked up my expedition bike and caught the overnight bus north to Chiang Mai. There I spent Christmas Day, before setting off to cycle straight back down to Bangkok, with an initial detour through the stunning mountains to the west. All this trouble and confusion was just to get around the fact that Myanmar's land crossings were closed.

I was hoping to spend New Year's Eve in Bangkok, both for the celebrations and because my travel insurance would expire at midnight. It wasn't to be, though. Despite lots of problems, I managed to stick to eighty miles a day. I was now carrying my tent, though I'd left the sleeping bag in Bangkok to save weight. Since there were so few guesthouses on the way, it was a case of putting the tent up wherever I was when darkness fell. I discovered that the people at the petrol stations were happy to let me camp for the night; comfortable grass, toilets, showers, a restaurant and plenty of amiable people to talk to...

I woke up at six o'clock and packed the tent away. I'd had a good night's sleep because the petrol station manager said I could camp on his little manicured lawn, next to a Buddhist shrine. This was much better than the night before, when I'd had the choice of the car park or a thick, dry mattress of cut grass under some trees. There, the petrol station man had condemned me to an uncomfortable night but had quite possibly saved my skin. He'd come out just as I was finishing putting the tent up on the thick grass.

"No, No, No!" he shouted. "You don't sleep there! Very many snake...COBRA!"

I set off, passing the "243 km to Bangkok" marker almost immediately. I ended up having sweet and sour pork with rice five times during the day, and just as the "83 km" marker came up, half an hour before sunset, there was another petrol station. As I'd hoped, the ride was exactly one hundred miles, and I'd consumed no less than eight litres of mineral water. I was confident now that I should make it to Bangkok the next day, New Year's Day (with no travel insurance!), in time for my pre-booked flight to Austria.

"Do you mind if I camp here for the night," I asked the first person I found.

"No problem!" said the man.

"Are there any snakes?" I ventured.

"No, not here!" he laughed.

I pitched the tent and went for a shower, then went over to sit with the man. He had a little stall selling eggs outside the restaurant.

"You must be the Egg-man," I joked.

"Ha! Yes, you are right. I am the Egg-man!"

At the next stall was a woman selling little round sausages, with bags of salad.

"And you are the Sausage-lady!" I told her.

"Of course!" she laughed.

"Pleased to meet you! My name is Tim. I am crazy-English-cycling-man!"

"You must be hungry," said the Egg-man, "You like hard-boiled eggs?"

"Yes, please. I'll have four, please!" My eyes lit up.

"We give you some sausages also!"

"Thank you very much!" I said, my mouth already watering.

"Tell me where you are going," asked the Egg-man, handing me a plate of mango.

"Oh, Thank you! How much?"

"Nothing," he said.

"But, all this food," I protested, "I must pay you!"

"No No No No! You are welcome!"

"Are you sure? You are very kind!"

"Yes, very sure!" he insisted, waving his hand, "Where are you going?"

"Oh, well, I'm going to Bangkok. In two days I must fly to Vienna to see my lady!"

"Vientiane!" he corrected me.

"No, Vienna. In Austria! My lady is Austrian. I haven't seen her for four months!"

Anyone who came to buy hard-boiled eggs was told all about this sunburnt Englishman sitting there, stuffing his face. One of the customers was a spoilt girl from Bangkok, who decided she liked me. Her dad was sleeping in the car and she was bored, so she tried to teach me some Thai words, but her arrogance put me off.

She kept saying, "Blah blah blah -you speak Thai - blah blah blah," as in "Repeat after me". She then said I could have a lift to Bangkok.

"Thank you, but I'd rather cycle there," I said.

"You won't be my friend," she complained. "I know it and you know it!"

"Show me picture of your lady!" asked the Egg-man, mischievously.

"Lady." I said, taking out Verena's photo to show him.

The girl saw it, tutted and rolled her eyes, then went off in a huff and slammed the car door shut.

"Lady, beautiful!" said the Egg-man, looking at the photo and laughing at the girl's reaction.

The only other strange person I met was the mechanic. He kept threatening me with the Egg-man's knife. It was obviously just his way of having a joke, as all the others were laughing their heads off, but I still thought he was an idiot. His wife seemed intent on getting me drunk; she kept bringing over glasses of whisky and soda, saying, "Soda!"

The Egg-man's wife came out of her little restaurant to join us. Their three-year old daughter was there, along with a few other kids, trying to kill each other in various different ways.

At half-past ten, the Egg-man loaded his beaten up, twenty-five year-old pick-up truck, while his wife stayed in the restaurant. Everything was piled into the back of the truck, including the Sausage-lady and the hyperactive kids. He said he was just dropping everyone off, before coming back. He said I could come for the ride, so I sat in the passenger seat and closed the door. The door lock had broken, and in its place was a sliding lock from a toilet door!

"Safety lock!" he said.

After doing the rounds, we went back to the petrol station and into their little restaurant. Thai boxing was on the television, so I sat there with the two of them, eating popcorn, followed by sweet and sour pork with rice. I told them I'd already had five meals today, plus loads of other snacks. They were chuffed to bits when I fitted it all in, and they refused my money.

The Egg-man said he used to practise Thai boxing, and he demonstrated the moves. The women's Thai boxing came on the TV, but then I noticed that my watch said 11:59:50. I counted down the last ten seconds, thinking that this was much more cool than spending New Year with a load of drunken travellers in Bangkok. We hit 1999, shook hands and jumped around, then went out to watch the fireworks. I thought it was wacky that England still had another six hours of 1998!

The next morning I packed up and went back into the restaurant because the Egg-man and his wife had invited me for breakfast. They were such kind people and so much fun to be with that I felt sorry to leave them. I could have kicked around there a lot longer, but I had a plane to catch!

Thirty miles later, I was on the approach to Bangkok, though still twenty miles from the centre; the city is one massive concrete sprawl. From that point on, my road was a sixteen-lane monster; an elevated motorway with another six lanes underneath, and a dual frontage road on either side. The danger and confusion were exacerbated by the phenomenal heat, so I put my helmet on and just got on with it.

The frontage road was two lanes with a hard shoulder, and that's where I was, sealed off from most of the traffic. The many junctions had me worried though, the cars feeding in from both sides at seventy miles per hour. Scooters and motorbikes rode up the hard shoulder against the flow of traffic, heading straight at me, and I'd have to guess as to which side of me they would pass.

I got past the airport, where the next day I would return for the long flight back to Verena. I carried on pedalling for another hour before I saw a sign for Victory Monument. Looking at the map, I saw that I was only a couple of miles from Democracy Monument, near to the guesthouse where I'd stored my stuff.

I turned off from the sixteen-lane monster and the city streets seemed amazingly quiet on this New Year's Day. I made my way to Democracy Monument, saying in my Irish "Commitments" impression, "Hey Look, Jimmy, we've made it!" I turned the last corner and slammed to a stop outside the guesthouse, after five hundred and thirteen miles in the last seven days from Chiang Mai. In fact, the miles were really starting to clock up now. Since leaving

Mumbai four months before, I'd cycled 4,830 miles. The total since Sheffield now stood at 10,200. Cycling Round the World seemed to be a distinct possibility; all I had to do was keep plodding along. After a five-week break with Verena, I would return to Bangkok to continue south. I couldn't wait to see her again; four months is a long, long time to be apart. Too long. Keeping in touch had been difficult at times, and I was lucky that she hadn't decided that enough is enough. It might so easily have happened.

I still had enough time to see the Grand Palace and the sacred Emerald Buddha within, but I wanted to get hold of a book first, so that I could read up on them. I found a copy of the "Rough Guide to Thailand" in a second-hand bookshop, and did my sightseeing the following morning, before the flight.

I walked through the gateway of the Grand Palace and instantly fell in love with the place; a crazy world of wild ornamentation, with a distinctive aesthetic quality. Thirty-foot high demons towered over the visitors, elephants stood to attention on the terraces, and gold was abundant in the statues of fantastic mythical monsters.

157

GRAND PALACE, BANGKOK, THAILAND '99

Grand Palace, Bangkok, Thailand '99

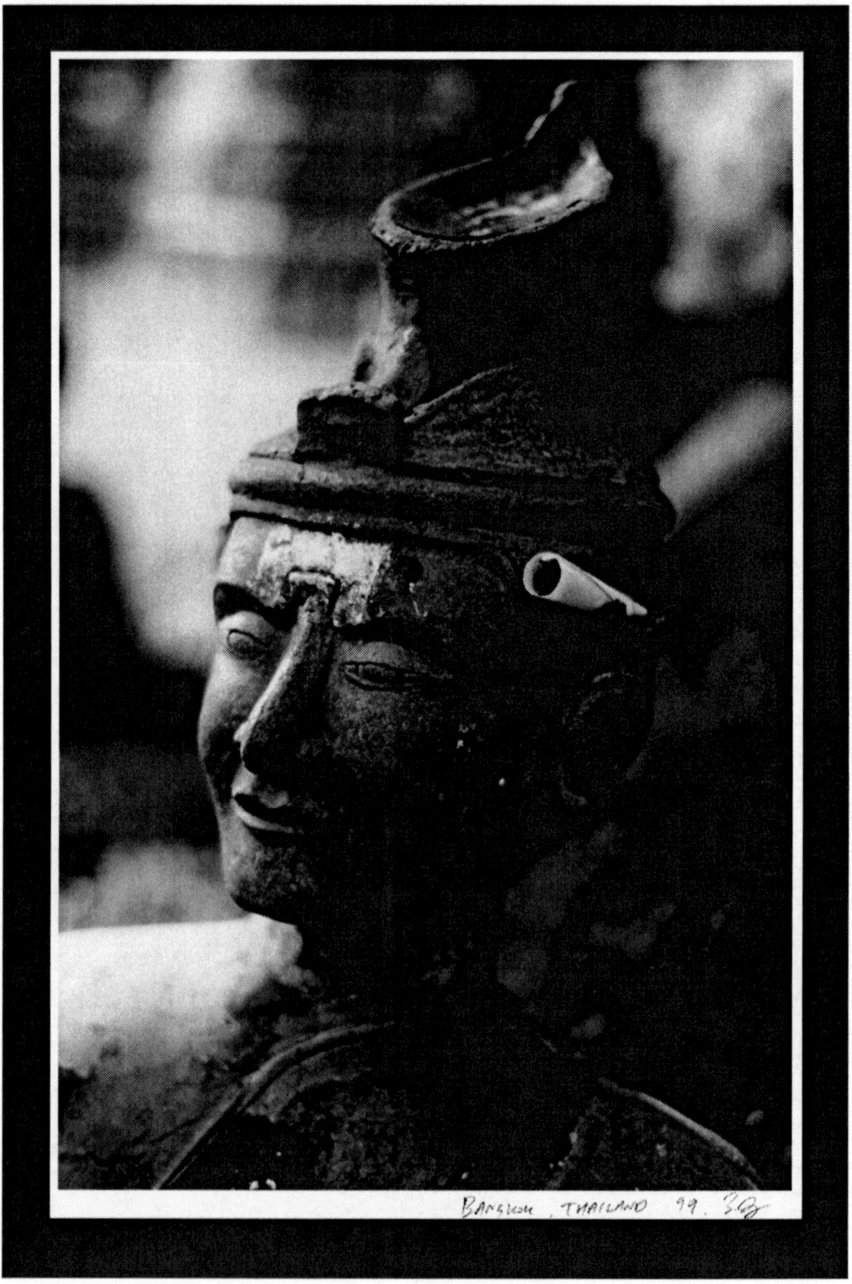
BANGKOK, THAILAND 99.

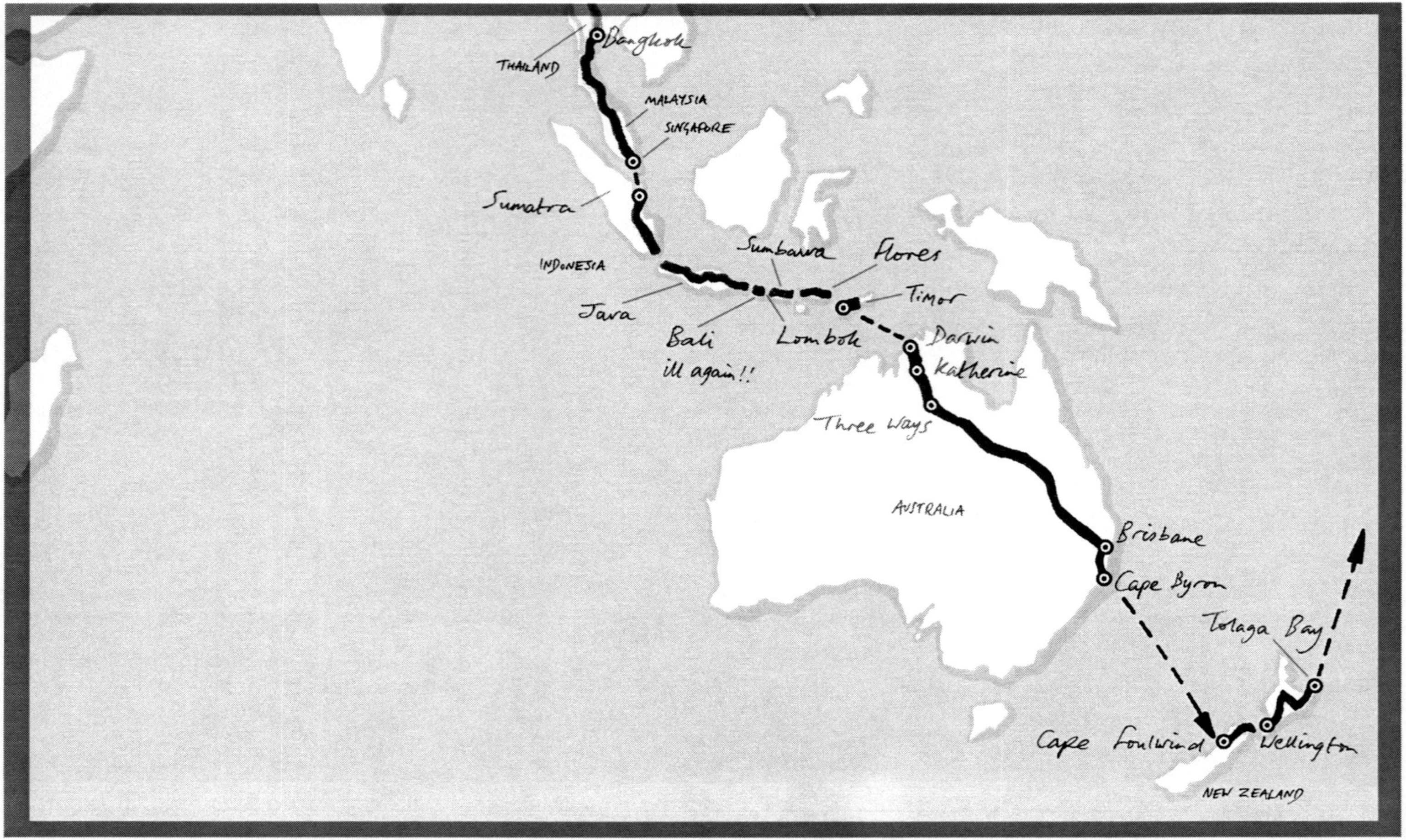
Bangkok
THAILAND
MALAYSIA
SINGAPORE
Sumatra
INDONESIA
Java
Bali
ill again!!
Lombok
Sumbawa
Flores
Timor
Darwin
Katherine
Three Ways
AUSTRALIA
Brisbane
Cape Byron
Tolaga Bay
Cape Foulwind
Wellington
NEW ZEALAND

Four

Thailand to New Zealand
February to June 1999

The first I saw of this posse was the torchlight shining along the barrel of a gun. I switched on my torch to show them I was there, my heart thumping out of control. By now they were only a few metres away from me; a group of about ten people, most of whom had big knives. I folded away the blade of my sad Swiss army knife and put my hands up in surrender...

To Pattalung, Thailand

After a revitalising break in the crystal-frozen winter of Austria, I took my flight back to Bangkok, without having cured one of the problems I'd been putting up with since my illness in Calcutta. What I was suffering from was an itchy bum, thought at first to be worms or haemorrhoids. In spite of an intensive treatment programme, expensive doctors' fees and squirty-up-your-bum potions, it was still very painful to walk, even on the very day that Verena took me to Vienna Airport.

A few days before my departure, I'd been to see yet another specialist, who charged me 1,200 Schillings (£60). He stuffed his hand up my bum and then said, "You have not haemorrhoids, zis is eczem!" He said that, to treat this eczema, I should throw away all of the potions and lotions and just use a tiny bit of E45 cream after each visit to the loo, having first made sure that the area in question was absolutely clean and dry. On reaching Bangkok I'd have to get straight back on the saddle (OUCH!!) to cycle nearly seven thousand miles to New Zealand!

Verena and I were quite good at doing tearful goodbyes by now, but we decided that another four months without seeing each other would be too much. We planned to meet up at the halfway point, on Bali. She seemed much happier with this arrangement, saying, "It's only two months; that's nothing!"

I got to Bangkok to find that the bike was still in the guesthouse, and two days later I cycled out (on the wrong road!) and started the exhausting process of re-gaining my fitness and getting used to the tropical heat.

I had four punctures in the first two hundred miles, but at least the skin specialist's treatment kept my bum problems to an almost bearable level. I headed directly south on the only available road, through the tacky tourist resorts where sad and boring Europeans hang out with their Thai "girlfriends."

In Southern Thailand I was able to escape the main road. The dust, debris and pollution were left behind in a flash. The air cleared and the mountains came into focus, covered in a froth of effervescent trees. Tall palms lined the winding lane, and the sun floated high in a perfect sky.

I crossed a bridge over a quiet river and noticed a shape like a young crocodile. I stopped to have a look and there he lay, a Siamese croc, sticking his head out of the water and looking straight at me. He dived under and disappeared, and two minutes later a kingfisher flew by.

When the sun was setting I found a little petrol station. It was one of those ancient ones where the petrol is hand-pumped from a barrel. A group of men were sitting around on a sheltered wooden table. I sat with them and had a Fanta. I asked if I could camp there and they said, "No prom-plem!" One of them gave me a couple of cakes, then they brought the beers out.

There was an old man who looked at me suspiciously at first, but then started smiling. One of the men went off and came back with some salad and a delicious but almost unbearably hot curry. They were laughing at my "Exploding head" mimes, giving me some cooling beer to wash the curry down.

"Curry – Hot!" I gasped.

"No, no! Not hot!" said the man with the cakes. He had a shiny grin, wide eyes and an incredulous look.

"For me, very hot!" I said, "But I like it!"

"You like Thailand?" he asked.

"Yes, I love Thailand!" I beamed. "Thailand... beautiful!"

"Amayssing Thailand!" he laughed, repeating the year's tourism slogan.

"Thailand, Land of Smiles!"

"Amayssing Thailand!"

"Number One!" I said, my thumbs up. This was a favourite catch-phrase in Thailand, and it always made people smile.

"Laos; Vientiane!" said my friend, introducing his neighbour, who started pretending to beat him up, while everyone else fell about laughing.

"Ahh, he comes from the capital of Laos!" I said. Again, everyone fell about in stitches.

The neighbour's features were very different, and one of his friends, a farmer, said that he was actually from the far Thai north, near the Laos border. From now on, however, his name was Laos Vientiane.

The farmer asked if I liked snooker, then we all piled off to the local snooker joint. I went on the bike, the wind rushing round my drunken head, whilst behind me was the deafening roar of three motorbikes loaded with the six jabbering Thais, their headlights lighting up the road for me.

The snooker table was on a concrete patch in the open air, under a canopy. The elements had taken their toll on the ragged and dusty table, and a couple of chickens were scratching around underneath. An old ghetto-blaster wobbled out a string of Thai tunes, and when the game finished it was my turn to play in a three-sided game against the farmer and Laos Vientiane. I never got the hang of the unusual scoring system, but I was always losing! The table only had only five red balls instead of fifteen, and most of them seemed to be alive, jumping off the table and narrowly missing the scrabbling chickens.

I gave them some money for a beer run, and another curry was also brought back. This time it was a beautiful, mild pork dish called "La muu." For most of my time in Thailand, I'd been eating a dish called "Moo cow pat," the name of which had turned my stomach for a while! It turned out that it was actually "Muu khao Pat," meaning "Pork fried rice."

One restaurant had "Noodle soup with crap" on the menu, and as a man, I'm supposed to say "crap" at the end of a greeting, e.g. "Sawat dii Khrap."

I ended up spending that night in the spare room of a teacher's house. In the morning I was lying in bed with a terrible hangover. The teacher lined up the school kids outside, all shouting "Hello!" to get me up. After a team photo I set off in the blistering heat, but by the following night I was climbing up into the cool of the hills.

I found a nice stretch of woodland to camp in, and rode up the path when the coast was clear. As soon as I got the tent out, the mosquitoes attacked me. I hastily donned some extra clothes to cover my arms and legs but they were still getting me through my shirt and socks. Putting the tent up was a panic, and as soon as I was safely inside, the sweat came streaming out. I had to take all my clothes off

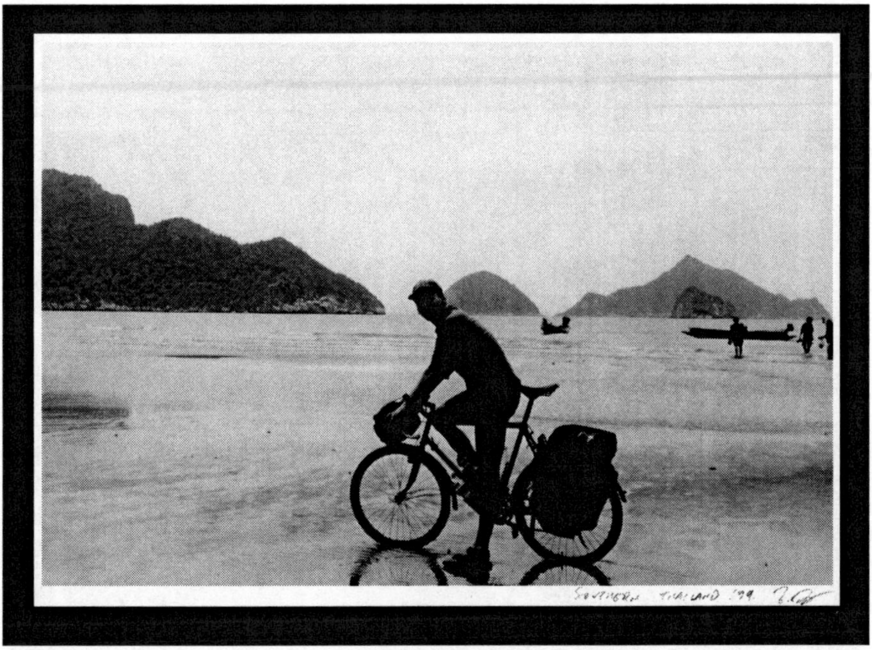
SOUTHERN THAILAND '99.

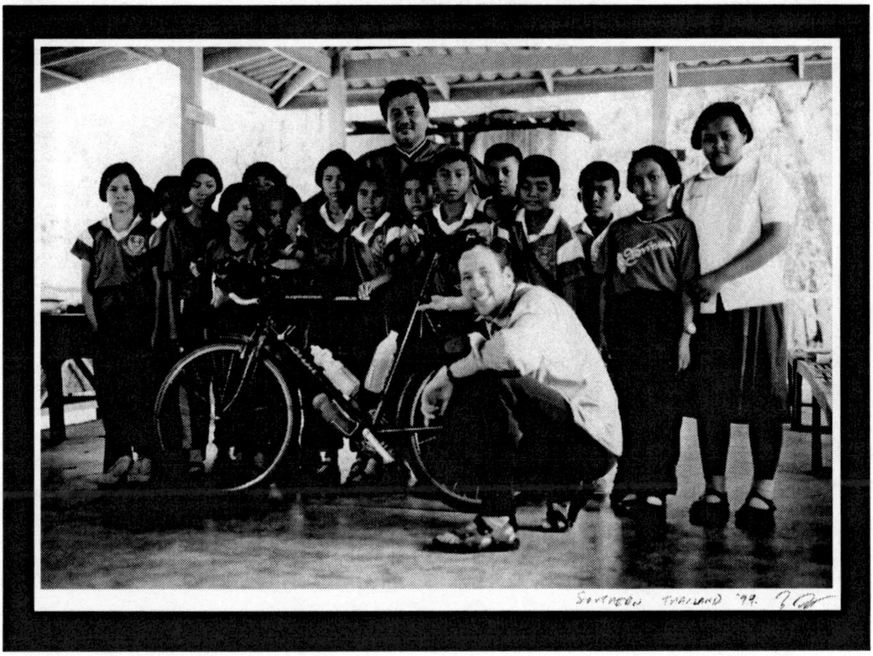
SOUTHERN THAILAND '99.

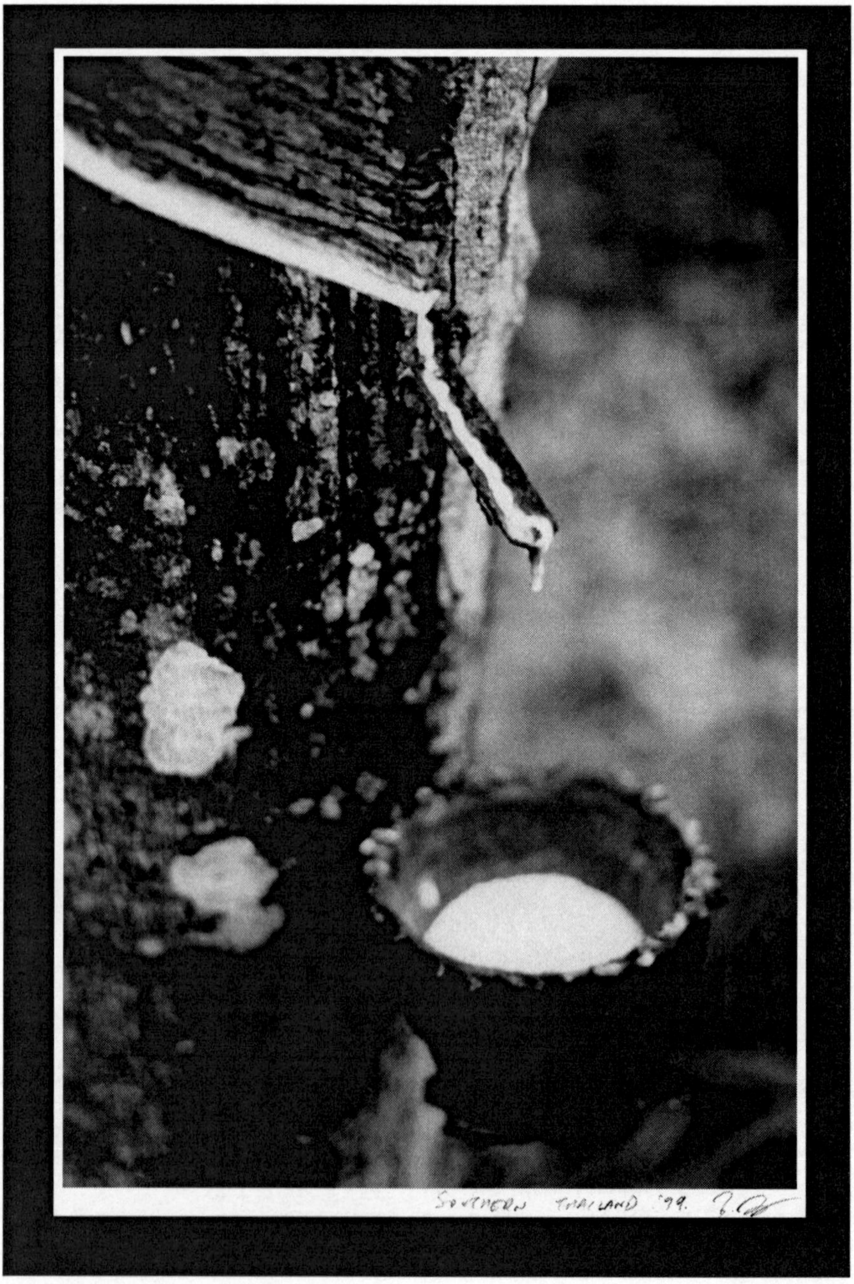
SOUTHERN THAILAND '99.

to try and cool down, while outside the mozzies were on the prowl, buzzing their way around the tent.

I'd just drifted off to sleep when I woke up with a start. A blinding light pierced the wafer-thin wall of the tent, and the thunderous noise of an engine shattered the stillness. Terrified, I peered out of the tent to see an off-road motorbike towering above me, the rider and passenger silhouetted against the night sky. The passenger was wearing a head torch and they were looking at me as they went past. They turned around a tree and came back, the torch shining right into my eyes. They didn't stop, but roared back to the road and off into the night. I didn't know if they'd be coming back but, on balance, I decided I'd be better off staying put.

The next thing was that I desperately needed a pee, but I knew that if I went outside I'd be eaten alive by potentially malarial mosquitoes; not a nice thought. I had an empty mineral water bottle, and thought it would be a cool idea to try to pee into it, inside my tiny one-man tent. This sounds like an easy operation, but unfortunately I failed, big time! To put it in simple terms: a back-fire!

I looked at the mess and couldn't believe what had happened, thinking, "What the heck do I do now?" Worried that the attackers on the motorbike might return, I started off by chucking the bottle out of the tent, along with the soaked sleeping bag and boxer shorts. Using soap, water and toilet roll I managed to clean my legs and the floor of the tent.

So, all was well again. I thought I'd better get some clothes on before they came back, and was fumbling with my sandals when I heard the sound of engines. I got out of the tent as the headlight shone down the path. I'd managed to grasp my Swiss army knife and torch, but was shaking like a leaf. The motorbike engines were switched off, and as the voices came down the path I chucked the stinking sleeping bag, boxer shorts and bottle behind the tent and into the bushes. Then I started walking towards the voices.

"I'm English," I said in a shaky voice, seeing the posse with their gun and big knives. "I'm just a cyclist. That's all! I'm going to Singapore."

They didn't seem to understand, so I dragged the bike out of the bushes to show them. They went "Oh!" The man with the gun nodded his head towards the woman next to him and mimed

"Collecting rubber from the tree." So, this was the Sap-lady and these were her trees.

They could see that I was as nervous as hell, so it was a relief when they all started giggling when I asked, "No problem?"

"No prom-plem!" they replied. This is another one of the Thai / English catchphrases, mispronounced just like on the pop song they know it from.

So it was cool, and I was allowed to stay. Even so, I couldn't sleep, and at a quarter to four I could see a light through the back of the tent. I heard a scratching noise followed by silence, footsteps through the undergrowth, then scratching again. Presently, the light was right outside my tent. I could see a tall man with a long, curved knife. I guessed he was the Sap-lady's son, the Sapling.

"They said I could stay!" I called out.

"No prom-plem!" he replied.

He carried on working, cutting a thin strip of bark from around the tree trunk, in a downward spiral. The rubber started to flow along this groove, forming a white line, winding down the tree. It reached a small spout at the end of the groove, and dripped into a collecting bowl. Made from a half coconut shell, the bowl rested on a piece of wire twisted round the tree trunk. I wondered how many tourists get to see this in the middle of the night.

At 7:15 I was awake again and packing everything away. The stinky sleeping bag and boxer shorts went in a bin bag in one pannier, along with the emptied and washed out bottle. All the clean stuff went in the other pannier. I was just about to take down the tent when the Sap-lady and the Sapling turned up again. They waved and said hello, and the Sapling came over, saying, "Your tent – beautiful!" He showed me what he was doing; he had a big bucket and a scraper made from a piece of coconut shell. He took down the half-coconut from the tree that I'd watched him cutting, only four hours before. It was almost full of pure white rubber. He scraped the liquid into the bucket, which must have had about ten litres in it.

Before leaving, I showed him my map and my route. We said goodbye and I cycled off down the road, past rubber plantation after rubber plantation, scooters zooming about with pillion passengers carrying heavy black buckets, just like the Sapling's. A few miles down the road I saw two latex processing plants.

I cycled all day in the heat, as usual. When I reached a hotel and took out my sleeping bag and boxer shorts, they reeked! There was hot water on tap, and the hotel man gave me a bucket and some washing powder, as I'd said I needed to do some washing.

The hotel was well funny. Just as I'd been told when I'd asked for directions, it was "a special kind of hotel, where people bring their mistresses." There were no windows, so people couldn't see in. It was all concrete, so the noise wouldn't carry. There wasn't even a blanket on the bed, as most people don't stay long enough to need one. Best of all, each room had its own curtained-off garage to hide the car!

Melaka, Malaysia

The dragons threw back their heads, their ferocious mouths only inches away from the screaming crowd. Arching their backs, they towered above, poised, before swiftly lowering their heads to the ground; streaks of red, black and white following on in a blurred display of authority and power...

A fortnight after leaving Bangkok I crossed the Malaysian border. No visa was required, just a stamp allowing me to stay for sixty days; four times the number of days needed to reach Singapore. The road instantly became immaculate, with well-tended grass verges and flowers in the central reservation. The downside was the lack of a scooter or cycle lane, despite the greater popularity of bicycles and rickshaws, so I was back to looking over my shoulder to keep checking the traffic behind me.

Melaka, in Southern Malaysia, has had a very interesting history involving the Chinese, the Portuguese, the Dutch and the British. The streets in the Chinese part of town were lined with old stone houses painted in pastel shades. The first floor, supported by stone pillars, overhangs the pavement. Outside every front door was a little shrine, smoking with the burning of incense.

Round, red Chinese lanterns were hung in rows along the houses and bridges. Many of the streets also had rows of yellow cylindrical lanterns, elegant and simple, giving out a soft glow. Earlier on, a woman had told me mysteriously; "Come back to this street at 8 o'clock!"

"You must come with me!" said a man, as I was taking some photos. "There will be a dragon dance at eight o'clock, with 118 dancing dragons!"

His three children seemed to be excited about it. We made our way to the square, where a gathering crowd was waiting. Over our heads were three enormous rabbits as this was now the year of the rabbit. A troupe of men in T-shirts and dragon trousers walked past, each carrying the head and trailing body of a dragon. The father told me that at the end of the dance, the World Champion dragon dancer

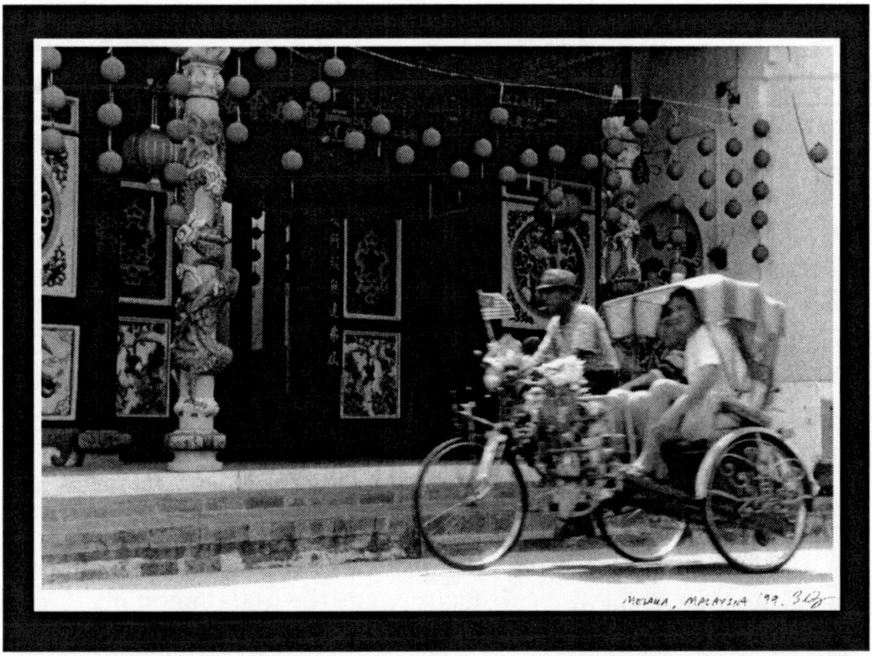
MELAKA, MALAYSIA '99.

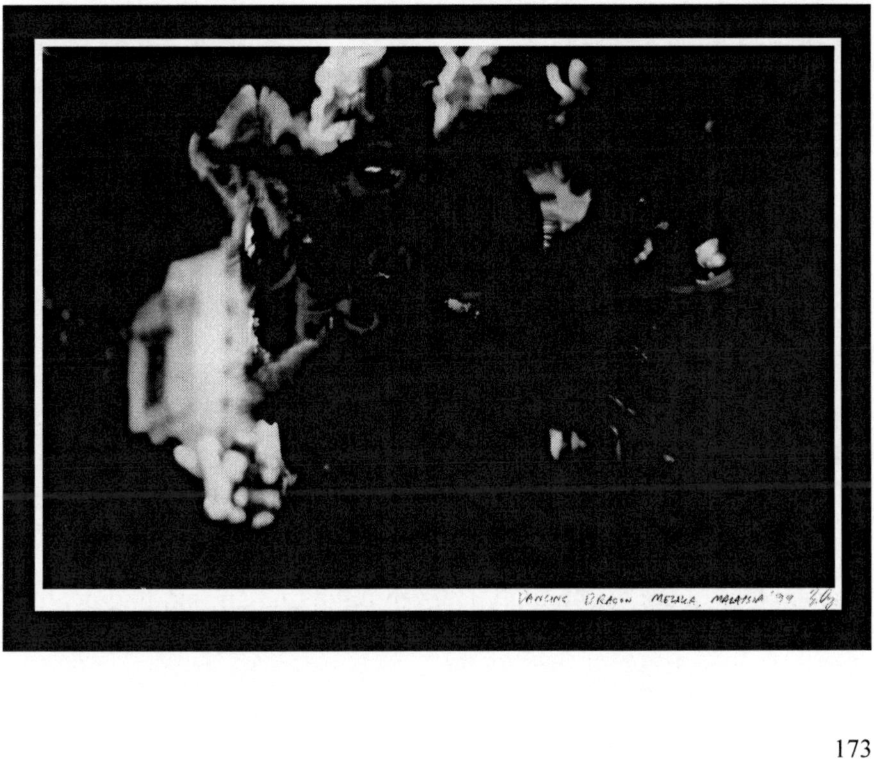
DANCING DRAGON MELAKA, MALAYSIA '99

would perform. He actually comes from Melaka, though the championships are held in Beijing.

I decided to get something to eat from one of the hawker stalls. I had to wait a long time for my pancake with crushed peanuts, but watching the woman working was interesting. She had five pancakes on the go constantly, each one on a little hotplate under a tin lid, on her pancake cart. When one was ready, she'd scrape it out, fold it up and pass it to her husband, then get a new ladle full of mixture and dollop it on, spread it around at put the lid over the top. She was sweating away as she worked, lifting up each lid in turn to see what was going on underneath, and spreading crushed peanuts, sweet-corn or both on to the pancakes at the right moment. Needless to say, my pancake was delicious, and before long it was time for the dragon dance.

By this time, the square was jam-packed with people standing on tiptoes to see what was happening. First came the sound of crashing drums and then, right in the distance, came the first dragon, its enormous head dancing to the sound of the drums. The other dragons were following behind, though I didn't bother to count them.

They danced their way right along in front of us, and at the back was a truck with a four-legged dragon dancing on it, standing on tall steel pillars. The procession disappeared around the block for about twenty minutes, then congregated while the judges announced the best dancers. They were let into the central area in the little square, where they had to shin up enormous poles to perform their dances, high above our heads.

The remaining dragons wandered about among the crowd, their googly eyes lit up. Their favourite trick seemed to be to come face to face with little kids sat on their dads' shoulders.

The dragons up the poles were sensational, rising up and dropping their heads down, twisting and turning to the beat of the drums. An announcement was made, followed by enormous cheers and laughter; time for the star attraction, the World Champion.

This was the four-legged dragon from the float at the back of the procession, nodding its head from side to side. When the float reached the square, it suddenly leapt through thin air, landing neatly on a set of tall, thin pillars.

Resplendent in glistening white, the dragon glared down at the crowd, twisting his body and swinging two of his legs around. He moved in sharp, fast bursts before leaping into the air again, landing this time on an even higher set of pillars. Standing on his hind legs, he reared up towards the sky, then down again as the drums crashed. He stroked the air with his front leg, spun around to face the other direction and leapt effortlessly around above our heads.

For five energetic minutes he danced, and I was thinking, "Wow! This is the best thing I've ever seen!" When he finished, the crowd went wild with cheering, and the two men appeared from beneath the costume; bowing, beaming and pouring with sweat.

Sumatra, Indonesia

From Melaka it was only a short distance to Singapore, where Chinatown has changed in the last thirty years from squalid ghetto to yuppie bars and karaoke joints. I took the ferry from Singapore to Sumatra via Batam, Indonesia on the very morning that I thought I would, when I'd planned this stage six weeks earlier.

We passed the islands of the beautiful Riau Archipelago. Golden beaches lined the coast, and out of the water, only twenty metres away, jumped a huge manta ray. It soared clean out of the sea, clapped its wings together under its body and dropped back into the water. Later on, we crossed the equator and approached Sumatra…

We arrived at Kuala Tungkal, a tiny fishing village made of ramshackle houses on stilts. To disembark, I had to climb through another boat, as the baggage handlers passed the bags along to the floating jetty. The bike was the last thing to be brought out, and as I waited, the jetty suddenly tipped its corner under the water and I had to dive for my bags to stop them rolling from in.

Dozens of people were clammering around me, trying to get me to their hotel, taxi or bus, as I walked along the jetty. My first job was to find a new bike tyre. This proved unsuccessful, as all of the tyres I was shown were even more knackered than the ones on my bike!

A man invited me into his teashop for a free drink. He said I should avoid camping, or cycling at night, because of the tigers. The next town was Jambi, supposedly ninety miles away on a road which wasn't on the map. I had three hours of daylight left and a slow puncture. I bought a bag full of food from a shop where everyone was laughing their heads off, and set off in the direction of Jambi.

The traffic wasn't a problem, and people greeted me as I rode past. I noticed the logging tracks going into the jungle, with logs laid down so that the trucks could drive over them without getting stuck in the mud. Either side of the road were narrow waterways, where men slowly paddled in canoes, presumably fishing. I didn't expect to see any tigers but I was warned that the danger from bandits was far

SUMATRA '99

greater; armed robberies are a common occurrence on Sumatra, particularly at night.

The darkness came much earlier than it should have done. At five o'clock a thunderstorm rolled in, blotting out the sky, and there I was, riding alone on a little road through the jungle, my first day in a very strange country. An hour later I came to a village and rolled up to a restaurant. The door opened and the owner came straight out, saying, "You stay here!" He said it in Indonesian but his meaning was obvious. He told me that to carry on now would be extremely dangerous, drawing his finger across his throat like a knife, and miming gunshots.

I ate chicken and rice in the restaurant, followed by several cups of tea. They said I could wash myself, and I was led to a well out the back, with a couple of barrels full of dirty water and mosquito larvae. I stripped off and bucketed the water over my head. I could hear them, giggling inside the wooden restaurant; they were obviously spying on the strange white man through the gaps in the wall.

When I'd almost finished, I could make out someone hovering outside the doorway. I dried myself off with my T-shirt and he came out from his hiding place and straight up to the barrel of water that I'd just used for washing. He was holding a plastic bag and he took out four massive fish and dropped them in the water, obviously destined for the restaurant!

I sat back at my table and the proprietor came over for a chat. I started off not knowing a single word of Bahasa Indonesia, yet after only four hours with the family and their guests, I'd learned the basics. I couldn't believe their patience, not to mention their contagious sense of humour. We started off by pointing at things in the restaurant, so I could write down the translations phonetically. Who needs a dictionary? The family's cat walked past and I pointed at it. They said "Kuching!"

When we'd run out of things to point at, I started drawing pictures on my map of Indonesia, on the blue bits between the islands. This was cool! I drew sharks, trucks, palm trees, dogs, and cars, learning the word for each in turn. My big nose was pointed out as usual, and in explaining about it and my Irish surname, I ended up explaining, with the help of some drawing, about the Irish potato famine and the influx of the Irish into England. And they understood me, or at least they appeared to!

I was made to sleep in the restaurant on a wooden table with a mosquito coil burning. The only way to turn the lights off was by unscrewing the bulbs. As today was my first of sixty days in Indonesia, I was carrying all the money I'd need in my money-belt; four million Rupiah in a three-inch thick wad. I couldn't get to sleep, as I was worried about having all this money on my person. As I was trying to get to sleep, something brushed my arm. I thought at first it was a rat, until it said, "Miaow!"

This turned out to be my only incident with a cat on Sumatra, the danger from tigers having been exaggerated by wide-eyed villagers. The danger from bandits remained a big threat, however, and I wasn't calmed when I asked a policeman one evening.

"Is the road from Jambi to Pelambang dangerous?"

"Indonesia; safe!" he replied, shaking his head.

This went against the advice of another restaurant owner who'd put me up for the night.

"Please; you must not cycle from Jambi to Pelambang....very very dangerous...please tell me you will take the bus!"

Nobody else I met seemed quite so worried. They all said it would be okay in the daytime, but as that stretch would take nearly three days, I must stay overnight in police stations on the way, in return for treating the police to a meal. I was told exactly where the police stations were, but I was still worried at times when the road was empty, passing through what would be perfect ambush territory. I made up a few rules when going through these stretches, such as not even stopping for a pee, but the words "sitting" and "duck" kept springing to mind.

Even so, this was one of those uniquely special places, where the tiny, broken road climbed up to reveal views over the jungle, spreading out over thousands of square miles. As with the Amazon, much of this jungle is still to be explored. It's possible that there are ancient communities still surviving there, having never been in contact with the outside world.

I found the people on Sumatra to be even more friendly and humorous than in any of the places I'd visited since Burma. Every day, the cycling was hard work. But every evening was a classic, be it in a restaurant or in a police station.

One big problem was the sheer distance. I'd actually made huge errors in my estimation of how far I'd have to ride, to reach the ferry for Java. I was out by well over two hundred miles, and though the landscape looked flat on the map, it was actually a never-ending series of steep undulations which had me changing from top to bottom gear and back again, every few minutes.

I lost count of how many chickens died for me to eat, to get the energy I needed! I couldn't risk being out after dark but even so, two days in a row were one hundred miles each, with literally nowhere to stay in between. The other days were around the eighty-five to ninety mile mark. It really was too hard to do this in the tropical heat on this kind of terrain, but because of Indonesia's sixty-day visa policy, I had to get the ferry on the same day I'd planned to. If not, the whole thing would start to slip and I would have to leave the country before I'd finished.

I was in luck when I got past Palembang, to be told that the next place I was heading for was a hotbed of violence. They said that on no account should I go there. Instead I should take a different road, which wasn't even shown on my map! Incredibly, this road saved me about one hundred miles, although I didn't know where on earth I was. I went along it for two days, going non-stop. When I thought I might be approaching the place at which it re-joined the main road, I asked some people how far it was to that point. The first person said, "Sixty km." The next said, "Two hundred km." The third person I asked said, "Thirty km." This almost killed my enthusiasm for trying to make the ferry, but luckily the third person was right.

I reached the main road two hours later, and the following night I rolled onto the ferry for Java, exactly on time! Well, to say I rolled on is not quite true. While standing by the ferry and waiting for the door of the car deck to open, I was chatting to some people. I turned the pedal back while I leaned against the bike, when the rear derailleur exploded! A total of eleven little pieces sproinged off the main body, and I had no choice but to put all the bits into a plastic bag and walk the bike onto the ferry. I cleaned and re-assembled all of the parts with an audience watching, as we crossed to Java, and rode off the ferry at the other side!

Java, Indonesia

The numb feeling began to take over my whole body, my legs turning to jelly and my vision becoming blurred. All I knew was that I must try to run. Get away from this man. Must try to run. Get some adrenalin going. Reach the main road before I fall unconscious...

Having made it to Java on time, I got up the next morning and mended a couple of slow punctures I'd been trying to ignore. There was now a new challenge, to get to Bali on time!

Java basically has two kinds of roads. One is the "far-too-narrow-with-five-times-too-many-crazy-buses-and-trucks" type of road. The other is of the "climb-vertically-up-the-side-of-a-volcano-in-the-unbearable-heat-and-take-three-times-as-long" variety.

I ended up switching from one to the other and back again. Somehow I made it across this over-congested and politically volatile island in just two weeks, where even a month wouldn't have done it justice, as there were so many wonderful things I had to ride past without stopping. I didn't meet any tourists in Indonesia until I reached Bali, and they all said the same thing;

"Why are we only allowed to stay for sixty days? There are so many islands, all completely different, and the economy here is in a desperate state, surely our being here can only help...blah blah blah"

A lot happened during those two weeks on Java, but one incident has had me pondering ever since.

After an evening of stomach-ache, I woke up feeling queasy and set off up a very hot and sweaty fifteen-mile ascent. After half an hour the nausea passed off and I ended up having the best ride for a long time, around a volcano called Mt. Tang-Kubanperahu. Never straight and never flat, the road flew up and down the many hills and valleys radiating out from the mountain, hidden in cloud from halfway up its rugged flanks.

I was back into a region of rubber plantations at first, followed by tea plantations. The landscape was a patchwork of paddy fields when I finally dropped down from the mountainside, and all of the fields were in different stages of growth. On the roadside, men carried loads in baskets hung from lengths of bamboo across their shoulders. Their houses were built of stone, whitewashed and with tiled roofs, which overhung at the front to create some shade.

I was passed by two groups of motorcyclists riding the other way, flying the green flags of the Islamic political parties. All had stern looks on their faces, getting ready for the general election in six weeks. I didn't know whether to be worried or not, but they were practically the only people not to greet me all day. I saw more groups later, and in the villages were the same green flags, both the PPP and the PNU.

For the last hour I was cycling in torrential rain, the road covered in dancing raindrops. When it cleared, the palm trees stood in milky swirls of mist, and I cruised down the last few miles into Sumedang. A man on a moped showed me to a losmen, costing twelve thousand Rupiah for the night, less than a pound but not really a bargain.

"So, you stay here?" said the moped man.

"I think so. Thank you for your help."

"I own a video and DVD rental shop here in Sumedang," he told me. "Maybe you come later for a cup of tea?"

"Yes, I'll do that. There's nothing going on here!"

He drew a map of the local streets, showing my losmen and his shop, and when I got there we chatted about travelling. He said his name was Rusty, and he claimed to have travelled extensively in forty-two different countries, and married a Dutch woman. He gave me tea and some useful information about the eastern islands, where I would be going after Bali. He also told me about the up-coming election on June the seventh; fortunately for me I would be in Australia by then.

"Do you think President Habibi should go?" I asked him.

"Oh, yes!" he said. "The new leader should be Megawati Sukarnoputri."

"I think that this will happen," I ventured. "She seems to have great popularity."

"Depending on which of our islands you are on. We have so many islands! But she is the daughter of Indonesia's first president."

"I know. Do you think that the election will happen democratically?"

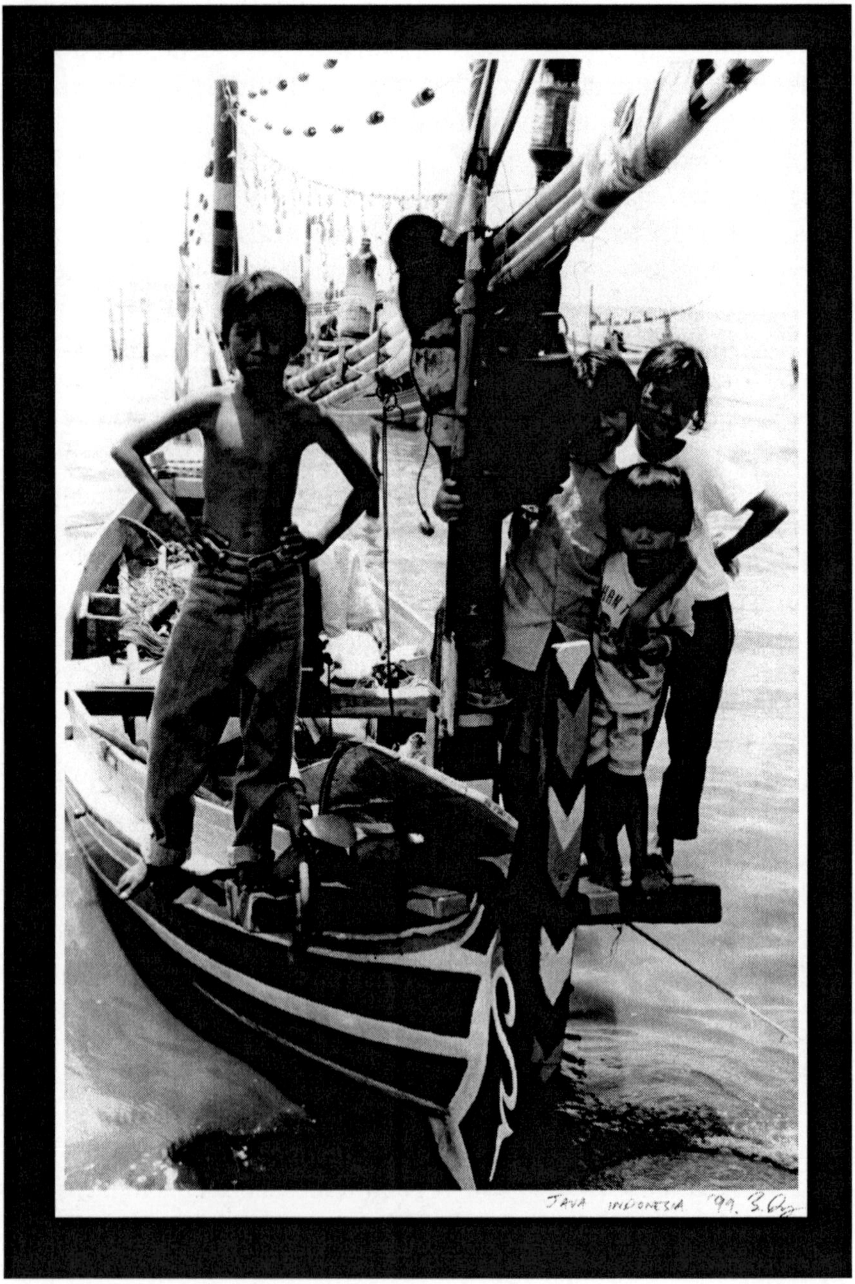
JAVA INDONESIA '99.

"I doubt it," Rusty said, raising his arms as if in surrender. "There is much corruption."

"What about violence? Some of the Fundamentalist groups seem quite intimidating."

"Possibly some violence, yes. But you have no need to worry."

Rusty and I went to a hawker to get some satay chicken, which we ate in the video shop. I had a third and last cup of tea and then he said it was time to go.

Rusty insisted on walking me home, but started walking up the road instead of down. He said that this way was parallel to the main road but much quieter. It was also very dark, and I didn't like it. After about two hundred metres I started to get a dry throat, then my head felt funny, like it was going numb. I walked on for a few more steps and it became worse. I suddenly got a deep suspicion about what was in the last cup of tea, and why he was so adamant that we should be on this dark road.

"My head feels funny! I'm going back to the hotel." I said in a blurred, distant voice.

I turned around and started running back down the road. As if in a dream, I could hear Rusty calling after me. I got to the main road and started asking people, "Kantor Polisi?"

Nobody could give me a clear answer and I was swaying like a drunk. I decided I didn't have time to find the police station, I had to have water immediately. I stumbled my way across the road and into a shop. Picking up a big bottle of mineral water, I drank the whole lot while sitting on a chair, with a few concerned people around.

I gradually regained myself, but still felt incredibly weak, so I ate some bars of chocolate. I told the people what had happened, but didn't tell them where the guy was or that he owned a video shop. After all, I wasn't totally sure that I'd been drugged. I could have been suffering from the effects of the sun and dehydration. Worse still, I thought that I might be coming down with malaria or dengue fever. When I got back to the hotel half an hour later, there was a note from Rusty...

Dear Mr Tim!
   I am really not understood: what hapened with you? I am not a bad man; you run from me, when we walk together.

I really confushed; please trust me; I am not a bad man! and hopely you can give me some reason.
If I maked mistake, tell me what hapened or you don't want to talk with me.
I need your explanation of that

Rusty Muchfree.

Quite possibly a man with a made up name, but then I'd met plenty of people in Indonesia with such names. In the morning I felt off colour, but I didn't have malaria or dengue fever, and I suppose I'll never know what was in the third cup of tea.

Bali, Indonesia

Still alive in Eastern Java, I was playing slalom with a string of volcanoes that would lead me all the way to the Bali ferry. I'd only had two rest days in seven weeks and nearly three thousand miles since Bangkok, and Bali was the place that Verena had chosen to come and see me for a week's holiday. But the week before, just by coincidence, my mum Berlie and her partner Alan were to be on Bali on a stop-over from Australia back to England. This was part of the reason for my rush to get to Bali and I rolled straight onto the ferry, two days ahead of schedule, giving us five days together.

I can sum up the things I don't like about Bali in one sentence... It's very, very, very touristy! Enough said. Other than that, once you look beneath it all and see just how genuine the village culture still is, it's an awesome island and a good place for a rest. It had also remained free of trouble. Even within the last month, there were violent conflicts in the region of eastern Java where I caught the ferry from, but at that time the ferry wasn't running, in order to stop the violence spreading onto Bali.

As Hindus, the Balinese worship a huge pantheon of gods, including the trio of Brahma, Wisnu (Vishnu) and Shiva. Here on Bali, they are all aspects of one god; Sanghyang Widi. Every morning the islanders put out their offerings, delicately prepared and placed in the many shrines within each family compound. Offerings also line the streets, outside every shop and office. We happened to catch Bali at a special time, a once in ten year festival at the Mother Temple; Pura Besakih. Balinese festivals are happening all the time, but this one is especially important, and every single Hindu on the island is expected to visit the temple during this festival.

As we climbed the hill to the temple, we could see the devotees dressed in finely woven sarongs, with a kain around the waist. The women also wore the kemban, woven with gold and silver threads. Being well turned out for a festival is of great importance to the Balinese, as that's how the gods will see them. The offerings carried on their heads can be anything from simple but stylishly arranged affairs, to huge piles of fruit, carried effortlessly up the hill.

Everything that is traditional on the island is beautiful; the terraced landscape, the people and the way they dress, the family compounds with their numerous shrines, the temples, carvings and every other art-form that seems to crop up no matter where you are. It seems that every single Balinese person was born with innate artistic skill, and the notion of being well presented for the gods even goes as far as the women's teeth, which are filed to form a smooth line, so as not to resemble the teeth of the evil spirits.

"They're all so beautiful, aren't they!" my mum said.

"I know," I replied. "Imagine what it must have been like before all us Westerners came!"

"Before the concrete houses and the cars," she added, "and the tourists!"

"Yeah, look at us in our nasty shorts and T-shirts!"

"Speak for yourself!" joked Alan, pointing at the holes in my shorts.

"I know, it's embarrassing, isn't it!" I laughed. "But we have to hire some sarongs before we get into the temple, anyway!"

"You'll have to get some new clothes before Verena comes next week," he pointed out.

"Five dollars ought to do it! It's a shame she couldn't come this week, but it's Easter so they're dead busy in the hotel."

"She must be missing you so much," my mum put in. "She's a good one, that girl!"

An enthralling scene of commotion and banter greeted us as we entered the temple. Groups of exquisitely dressed people carried lovingly prepared gifts. All around them were the meru, shrines with thatched roofs stacked up to eleven high. The highest was dedicated to the supreme god, who uses it to descend to earth to enjoy the festival from an elevated throne.

Gunung Agung, the sacred mountain, keeps watch over all, while below lies southern Bali and the ocean. The colours of the festival brought the temple to life like a market, with huge statues of the gods made from coloured rice or fresh vegetables. The temple itself was built on a series of ancient steps made from black volcanic rock, where the dogs fight each other, just like the pariah dogs of India.

Within the main compound were twenty-three smaller temples, each with its own meru and its devotees, filing from one to another. Either side of every gateway, and on all of Bali's bridges, were the Dwarpala, or Dwarf-fella as I called them. These monster-like stone guardians protect the doorways, preventing evil spirits from passing through. During times of festival, the Dwarf-fellas wear black and white checked sarongs, symbolising good and evil.

The following week, my mum and Alan had returned to England, and I was at the airport to meet Verena. I didn't sleep well that night because my nose kept running. Next morning, I woke up feeling distinctly dodgy, and after taking my malaria pills I went back to bed. Verena was tired from the flight, and we both slept on and off until two p.m. Every time I woke up, I felt sick and had a killer of a headache, my nose still running, aching back and joints and a high fever. I'd had two weeks of feeling fine since my evening with Rusty, so this was something new.

We found a doctor, who concluded that I'd either got malaria or tonsilo-pharingitis. She said I didn't have dengue fever, a mosquito-born virus, and my symptoms didn't quite fit malaria, because there was no heavy sweating. She gave me an injection to bring my fever down, then gave me some tablets in packets which she labelled "Stop rainning nose," "Anti headache," "Down-fever" and "Antibiotics".

An hour later we were in a restaurant, and after eating I took my tablets. I was still feeling very weird. I told Verena that I was going to the toilet. I never made it across the room though, because everything went white, my head closed in and my legs gave way. I managed to slump into a chair and within seconds I was soaked with sweat. I could hear Verena saying something, but she sounded as if she was miles away. She told me to put my feet up. Slowly, the pain in my head started going down and I was able to see again.

"Lady, I feel really bad!" I drawled.

"Are you thinking what I'm thinking?" she asked, her hand on my forehead.

"What, do you reckon it's malaria?"

"Well, it must be! The doctor said you had all the symptoms except the heavy sweating, but now you've got that, too."

"Oh, no, I hope not!" I said in defeat. "I've got to keep cycling!"

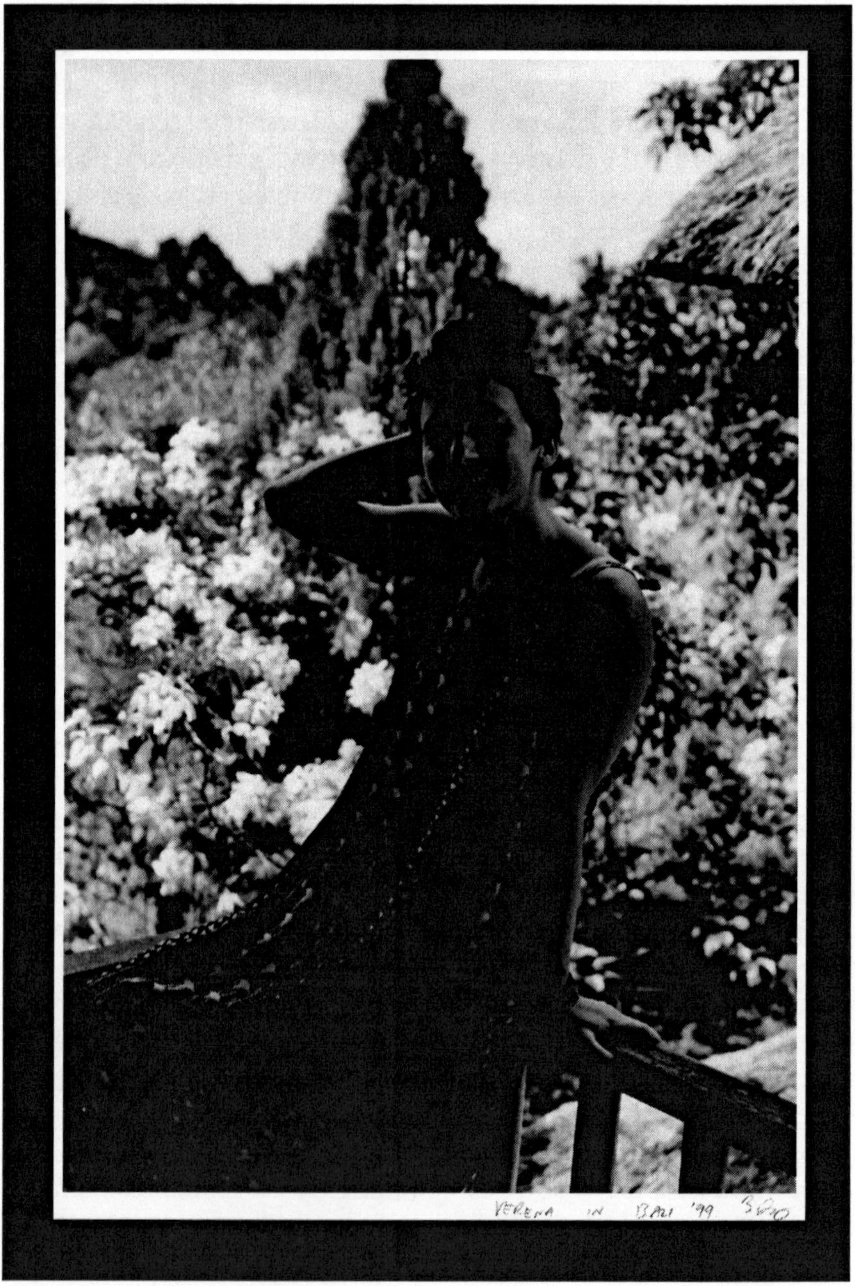
VERENA IN BALI '99

"Well, you've got a week's rest with me first, then we'll see."

"Well, it gets you off the hook, anyway. We won't be doing any trekking!"

"Good," she smiled. "I don't have to climb that Gunung-thingy volcano!"

I was very ill for the next three days, but on the fourth day I woke up with a sore throat. It appeared, then, that the doctor's other possible diagnosis was the one; tonsilo-pharingitis. I had yet again escaped malaria. It was several weeks before I felt better, though that didn't stop me from completing this, the most intensive stage of cycling.

I continued to have odd spells over the next nine months and, back in Sheffield after completing the whole trip, I had a relapse. I spent a few days in an isolation room in the tropical diseases ward, coming out on New Year's Eve, the turn of the new millennium. After numerous urine, blood and stool tests, it was discovered that I had in fact had dengue fever at some point, and was still suffering the after-effects. I was worn out after cycling round the world, my body completely exhausted, and other stomach and intestinal problems had manifested themselves along the way. For several years afterwards, I continued to suffer from minor daily symptoms, and had to think very hard before going back-packing with Verena in Tanzania in 2001.

After four days of sitting in the shade on our Balinese beach, Verena was saying, "Pleeeeease can we take a bus to another town so we can stay somewhere else?" We went to Ubud, which seemed like a major trip for me in that condition, even though it was only forty-five minutes by bus.

On a cool, fresh morning I felt up to taking her to see the Mother Temple. The festival was still going on, but by the time we arrived there was a torrential downpour. Instead of a festival, it looked more like the aftermath of a football match. Thousands of people were traipsing around in the mud or hiding under whatever shelter they could find. Those still climbing the hill to make their offerings pitted themselves against a fast river of rainwater, with plastic bags to cover their gifts. We splashed our way back down the hill after an hour, the islanders laughing at us as we tripped over our sarongs, but like them, we just didn't care!

That evening we went to a performance of the Wayang Kulit, the shadow play using leather puppets. Verena and I didn't really know what to expect, but we'd read that this was one of the traditional ways of presenting stories from the Ramayana and the Mahabarata. It's also a form which keeps alive old Javanese literature, so the puppet master must be able to speak in the old Javanese tongue, amongst his many other talents.

Hidden behind a screen with a "blincung" lamp to cast the shadows, the puppet man began his performance. The dark silhouettes and the soft glow were the only tones on the screen. Strange music played throughout, the puppet man singing along to it or changing his voice to suit the many different characters he presented.

Each puppet was finely detailed and extremely beautiful, with patterns all over them in the form of tiny holes to let the light through. The story followed the usual theme of good winning over evil, with many fast action battle scenes, the puppets flying around behind the screen, coming and going in quick succession.

The characters flickered in a nightmarish way as he drew them away from the screen, close to the lamp, reeling them round and round in a blurred, tormented image. Arrows struck their targets and brought instant death, as army after army was defeated in this high-speed excerpt from the Mahabarata.

We were captivated by the magic of this ancient art form. The crazy screeching of the voices, the mad music; the swirling shadows swooping and diving to and fro behind the screen, crashing violently against the lamp, sending the sparks flying as the puppeteer became lost in his whirling world of heroes, gods and demons.

Hello Berlie!
Thanks for the fax. I only got it today, I've just got back from Bali. Tim had fever for a few days, but he's recovering now!
We really had a great time and I was terribly sad to leave him. Tim gave me the book "Skellig." I'll send it back to you, along with a few of his films.
Bye, Verena

MOTHER TEMPLE, BALI, INDONESIA '99

Sumbawa, Indonesia

After Bali was the little island of Lombok, which I crossed in one day. Here the horses wear pom-poms but many of the children wear nothing. Tourists were already thin on the ground and the busy roads of Sumatra, Java and Bali were behind me. The landscape changes as well, once you reach this, the first island of the Nusa Tengarra archipelago.

Lombok and neighbouring Sumbawa are predominantly Muslim islands and are still very traditional. The town of Sumbawa Besar has a strange local custom; bull racing. This takes place just before rice planting and the twist is that a magician uses a spell, to stop the bulls reaching the field. If they fail, the magician wins all the prizes! Over the period of a few days I rode across Sumbawa and approached the ferry for Flores...

The last hill climb went on for about ten miles, made worse by the fact I was still recovering from my illness, and I'd also had diarrhoea just after the start, in the middle of nowhere, in the rain! When I pulled into Sape, near the ferry, I had to go again. At a Warung Makan (restaurant), the lady showed me the loo, a low bamboo hut with a corrugated roof in the middle of a muddy yard. As I went in it started raining yet again.

Luckily there was a Losmen over the road, but the next ferry wasn't until the following afternoon. In the morning I went down to the ferry because it seemed like a good place to hang around. There was no ferry terminal as such, just a ticket office and a few restaurants. I went inside a little Warung Makan and ordered the usual Mie Goreng, or fried noodles, and sat there watching "Tom and Jerry."

I got chatting with some friendly Sumbawans, then went to the cash desk to pay. The roof was so low that I had to stoop to reach the desk. I left the bike locked up and went for a walk to take some photos. I had no problem at all. It seemed that everybody wanted to be photographed, from the laughing kids in their scruffy shorts and

T-shirts, to the man building a fishing boat, drilling holes for the wooden pegs which hold it together. Families stood proudly in the doorways of their wooden houses on stilts, surrounded by seawater. The drivers of the colourful cidomos, the horse-drawn taxis, pulled up to let me get some photos, and the shop owners called out to me, surrounded by piles of biscuits and bottles of Sprite.

I went back to the restaurant to load a new film, and after ten minutes I noticed a puddle on the floor. A couple of minutes later I was puzzled by the fact that it had grown. I was trying to work out what the hell was going on, then I realised that the tide was coming in! After a few minutes, the waitresses were wading ankle-deep through the water, laughing their heads off while I took their photo! Guests were served while sitting with their feet up on plastic chairs, and it became obvious why the television was fixed so high in the beams! This ramshackle, home-made restaurant looked like it might float away to the nearby island of Komodo.

One of the guests needed to leave, so the waitresses set up a row of plastic chairs in the water as a bridge over the water, which was now six inches deep. Finally the tide turned, the giggling subsided, the floor was swept with the retreating water and life went back to normal.

When the ferry set off for Flores, we passed by an island which was literally a volcanic cone rising, straight up out of the water, to a height of about two thousand metres. Its name is Sangan and nobody lives there. Behind it was a dramatic sunset, whilst over the other side of the ferry was a place where cycling was definitely not the thing to do; Komodo Island. I wanted to go there, but the ferry schedules had just been changed. Some people told me that the dragons really are impressive, whilst other people told me that the experience is spoiled by the fact that you have to walk in a group, complete with guides in-front and behind.

"Have you been there?" I asked the man next to me on the boat.

"I have been!" he grinned.

"And what is it like?" I asked. "Are the dragons as dangerous as people say?"

"Yes. But we only call them komodo, not dragons!"

"But you saw these komodo?"

"I saw many. One of them came into the room of my bungalow!"

"No way!" I gasped. "But they can kill you!"

"Yes. The komodo, he bit me!" He showed me the scar on his knee.

"So how did you find a doctor?" I asked.

"The poison make me sick. I had to take a boat to Flores. There a doctor help me."

Luckily for him, it was only a young komodo. Had it been fully-grown, the poison could have killed him. I heard other stories about tourists being killed by dragons. As for the people who live on the island, they don't have a problem because they respect the komodo who are, in fact, their ancestors.

Flores, Indonesia

Flores was my favourite Indonesian island. Yet, on the very first day, it looked like it might be the one to stop me in my tracks. The Trans-Flores Highway is a grand title for a little road that runs for four hundred and fifty roller-coaster miles, from ferry to ferry. After the first twelve miles I was soaked in sweat, still thirty miles from the next town, with most of my water gone and a road that went up from sea level towards the heavens...

The beauty of the island was truly breathtaking. Folding volcanic mountains dropped away under a blanket of lush, tropical vegetation. The road tumbled and dived its way around deep ravines with wild rivers, steeply terraced paddy fields and ominous peaks, towering above the clouds. Its name translates as "Flowers" and was left behind by the Portuguese, along with Christianity, now the dominant religion.

When the sun went down at the end of my first day, I was in the middle of nowhere, still going uphill. After dark, I carried on because it was cool and there was no traffic. It seemed that the string of houses along the side of the road would never end, and I had to find somewhere to pitch the tent. I stood outside one house and shouted, "Hello! Tourist!" I decided that these are two words that everyone must know, since that was how people had been calling out their greetings to me all day!

The owner of the house came out and said I could camp there, but I should keep away from the road and put my tent right in front of his house! He, his wife and five little kids helped me to pitch the tent by shining their oil lamp and my torch wherever I needed the light.

I'd just bought ten oranges, so I gave them to the family and thanked them for letting me camp there. They were very excited about what was happening, and after they went back inside I was able to lie in the tent with the door open; there were no mosquitoes because of the altitude. I was watching the clear night sky and the wacky upside-down moon until a couple of dogs discovered the tent and started barking their heads off.

FLORES INDONESIA 99. 3.06

FLORES INDONESIA 99. 3.06

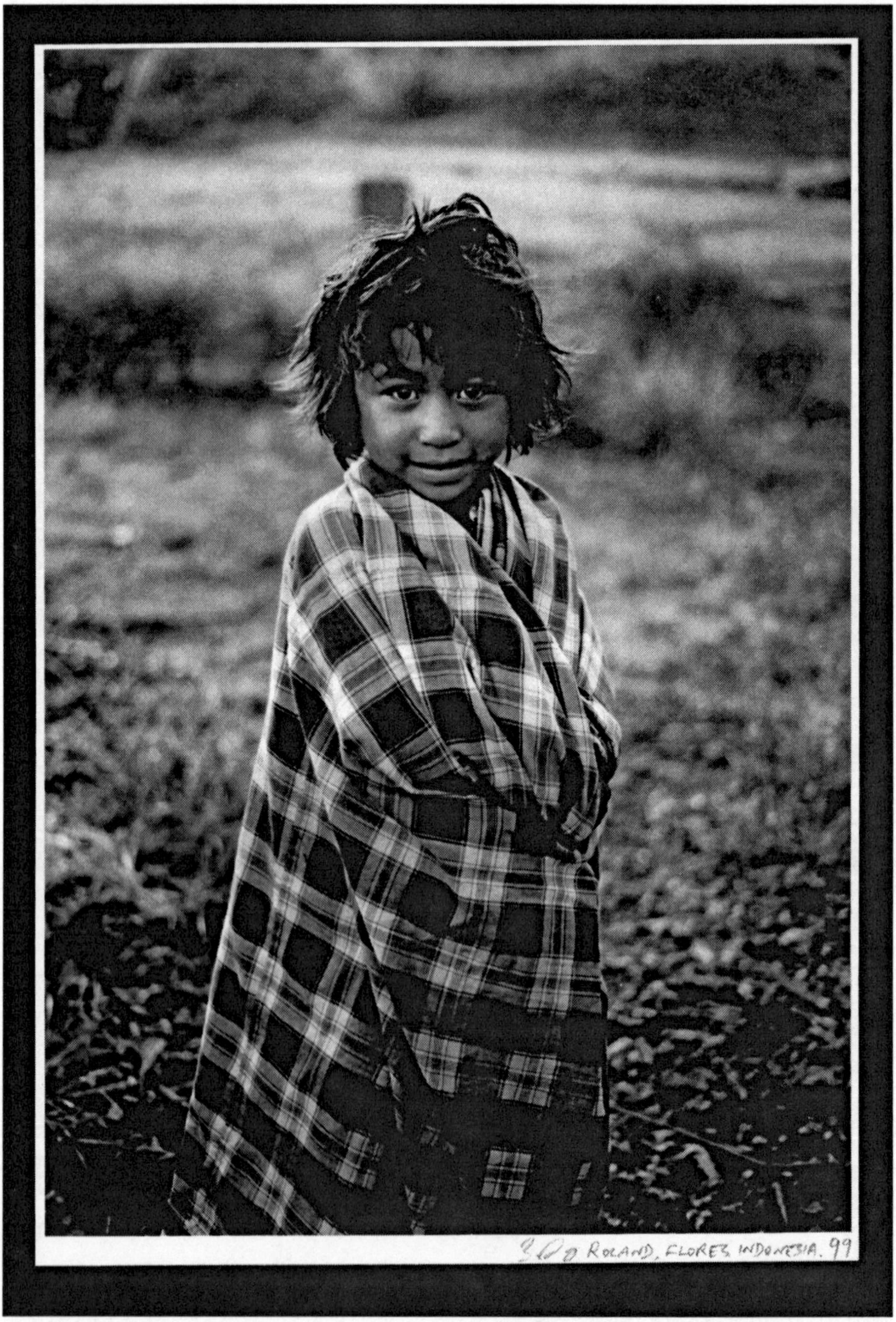
ROLAND, FLORES INDONESIA. 99

A woman came out of one of the neighbouring houses. She obviously didn't know what the hell my tent was, because she started yelling at it and throwing stones! The man who'd let me camp came out to calm her down, but within a couple of minutes my tent was surrounded by people. I'd already zipped the door shut and was sitting inside, my hands covering my ears, thinking, "I want to go to sleep; I'm knackered!"

Everyone was going mad with laughter and shouting, "WAKE UP, TOURIST!" and "HELLO MRS!" and "WHAT IS YOUR NAME?" I decided that camping on Flores was not such a great idea. A tent obviously looks too much like something from outer space! After half an hour, everyone calmed down and went back to bed, but in the cold of the early morning I could tell that they were all back again, though much quieter this time. I figured that the best thing to do would be to pack everything away into the pannier bags, get out of the tent and quickly take it down.

I got ready to open the door and... zzzip! Suddenly I found myself saying out loud, "Ooh 'eck!" I was faced with about thirty people, most of them kids with snotty noses and ancient clothes. They were all a bit bemused but I managed to entertain them by taking photos of everyone standing by the tent, and they were all smiling like it was the best thing since Christmas. Then I miraculously packed the tent and the huge long pole away to a tiny bundle and stuffed it into one of the panniers.

I loaded the bike, and one of the women invited me in for Kopi, or coffee. Smoke filled the house, the low doorway forming the only opening, along with a few gaps in the wooden walls. Two pictures of Jesus hung on the wall, the only decoration in the dark room. The family sat on a bare wooden bed, laughing, while I chatted to them in basic Indonesian.

In the room was a little boy with matted hair and an old chequered sarong. For some reason I liked him in particular, probably because he was quiet. I asked him what his name was, and he looked at me shyly. His mother laughed affectionately, and told me he was called Roland. She encouraged him to say a few words, and invited me to take his portrait. We went out into the daylight and he was unsure of how to react in front of the camera. He stood still, with an innocent look on his face, until it was all over.

When the time came for the older children to leave for school, they were reluctant to go. They kept running back to have one last look at the strange "Mrs" who had come to visit them. In return for the coffee, I gave them the rest of my food, and said goodbye to Roland. Then I shook hands with everyone except those with their arms full of babies. I started riding up the road, with jaw-dropping views all around, in the early morning light. The school kids were waiting for me, along with their friends, and they ran alongside, till we reached their school, where they waved me off with shouts of "Hello Mrs!"

The Trans-Flores Highway is the only main road on the island. Built by the Dutch about seventy-five years ago, it's only recently that the last of it has been surfaced. Luckily it carries very little traffic, as much of the road is in a terrible state of repair. The never-ending hills were worth it for the awesome descents, up to thirty miles long, from half-way up a volcano, right down to sea level.

Cycling fast downhill on Flores demands a lot of concentration. Coming around a corner, there's a chance that the road will be blocked by a truck. It's also possible that there'll be an excavator clearing the latest landslide, or a wooden bridge with half of the planks missing. Even a group of water buffalo, a horse or some goats, chickens or dogs. A huge hole in the road wasn't out of the question, or even no road at all, when it's dropped down the side of the volcano!

By the fourth day I was half-way across the island. Dropping down towards the village of Moni, I came round a corner and saw an enormous black snake in the middle of the road. It was five feet

long and I thought it was dead, but as I watched, it slowly meandered in tight curves across the road.

Just a hundred metres further on, I found a restaurant. I stopped and ordered some food because I was about to ride to the top of the most famous volcano on the island. Gunung Kelimutu has three coloured lakes which change colour with time. In the restaurant were the two wardens in charge of the volcano. They said that camping is not allowed because it's too dangerous, due to the evil spirits, and I would have to wait till morning to go up.

203

In the past, two Dutch tourists were warned by their guide not to go near the edge. They ignored him, saying, "We do this all the time in Europe." The ground didn't support them, though; they tumbled down the cliff and into the water and their bodies were never found. Another tourist, also Dutch, went up on foot in the evening and was never seen again.

These lakes have local keepers, who use magic to prevent the spirits from becoming angry and causing floods. Only respectful conversation is allowed up there. Too much banal conversation, or talk about sex, will upset the spirits.

A lady in the restaurant told me that the green lake is for magic, the brown lake for young people, the black lake for grandfather and grandmother, and the point in the middle for boyfriend and girlfriend. On the restaurant wall was an aerial photograph of the lakes and all were different from the present colours, and also different from those shown on the picture on the five thousand Rupiah note.

Since I couldn't go up the volcano until the morning, I stayed in the restaurant chatting with the locals. I told them about the black snake I'd seen. They said that it might bite, but it's not venomous. Suddenly, something that looked like an earthworm dropped down from the thatched roof and landed on the wooden floor, only six feet away from where I was sitting. Everyone jumped back in fright and said, "Keep away, keep away!"

The worm turned out to be a snake, and as it disappeared through a small crack in the floorboards, they told me that it is deadly. Only two weeks ago, they said, a farmer in this same village died after he was bitten by one of these. Two lads were playing badminton outside, with an improvised shuttlecock. They ran under the restaurant, retrieved the snake and brought it out to the front for execution-by-badminton-racket. The first racket was used to hold the snake down, while the other lad hit the snake on the head. One of the men told me that these snakes are very clever. If they aren't held down they wrap themselves around the racket or stick, and when you draw your arm up they drop down onto your face or neck and BITE!

I stayed in a little hotel by the restaurant and got up at four in the morning. First I ate my "mie goreng ayam Kelimutu." This was a joke I'd had with them the night before, because it was to be the fried noodles and chicken that I'd eat before cycling up volcano Kelimutu.

Riding up the mountain in the cool moonlight was made even better as I'd left my bags in the hotel. I didn't have any lights with me, but I only met one truck and I could see perfectly well. After a few miles it started to get light, and by the time I reached the wardens' hut the sun was rising. The early morning light filled the valley and the quiet seascape below.

The villagers started coming out of their bamboo and thatched houses. I passed two men, one with a big knife and one with a bow and five arrows. They stayed squatting at the roadside, greeting me with "Selamat pagi!" I climbed slowly but surely in first gear all the way, just drinking it all in. With two miles to go, the anticipation was building and when the tarmac ended I was mountain biking along a stony track.

The broken, contorted and jagged summit came into view, and I had to carry the bike on my shoulders to get up there. My back to the lakes, I reached the very top, with not a soul in sight. I took a deep breath and turned around to see the lakes for the first time. I almost fell over with excitement!

Vertical walls of torn and twisted rock, in shades of gold and brown, towered above the lakes, each cradled in its own crater. In vivid, unearthly colours, the lakes appeared viscous, not like water. A deep black lake lay behind me. To my right was a lake the colour of Coca-Cola; a black-ish, reddish brown. In front of me was the most peculiar of all. An impossibly rich green colour with a swirl of cream, it appeared to have been photo-retouched.

Shadows retreated as the sun climbed high over the green lake, its colours becoming ever more vibrant. Alone on the mountain for two hours, I saw landslides of rocks and debris crashing into the strange water.

I carried the bike back down to the track, and inspected the back tyre. It was bald after fifteen hundred miles since the bike-shop on Java. Not bad for a tyre costing $2.50! Zooming back down the narrow, overgrown road, I met no cars but did have a few surprises; a horse, a big group of villagers with bows and arrows, and a metre-long brown snake with a green underbelly. I nearly crashed into him, and had to slam the brakes on and swerve to avoid him.

I got back to the restaurant where I'd been the previous evening. I told a guy about the snake, and he said I'd been very lucky.

"This snake very very dangerous," he scowled.

"Have you ever been bitten by one?"

"No, but you keep away from them!" he warned. "My friend, he died."

"Oh, dear," I said, "that's not so good."

"Yes, this snake called Ularr Naga. It bit my friend when he cut bamboo in forest."

"Couldn't they get it off?"

"No, the snake bit, then locked his jaws, so!" He demonstrated with his hand.

"So it bit him on the arm like that?"

"On his leg. They cut off snake with a knife, but poison already in. His legs turn black."

"And, did he die straight away?"

"No, after two days. He died after two days."

It was time for me to get moving, not because of the snakes but because of the ferry. I booked out of my hotel with a special promise to the owner; to deliver a letter to his brother in Soe, on the island of Timor. I would get there next week, two weeks ahead of the post!

Soon after leaving the hotel I had another puncture. I was having big problems because I couldn't get inner tubes with the right valve to fit the hole in the wheel rim. I wasn't going to risk the wheels by filing the holes out, either. In total, I had four inner tubes with presta valves; two had been with me since Bangkok, the other two since India and all had been bought in Austria. Despite cracks caused by the spare tubes becoming dried out, old repair patches bursting open again and the glue failing because of the heat, somehow or other these tubes had to get me through Indonesia.

One old repair burst in such style that I had to take it to a mechanic, to get a mega-patch put on. His young brother was eager to do the job for me. Much to my relief, the crude repair actually worked.

The day after leaving Kelimutu, I almost got a couple of fang-shaped punctures. Riding up a mountain pass in the full moon, I came upon a brown and green snake. It was another deadly Ularr Naga. I wanted to go around him, but couldn't because a bemo, or minibus taxi, was coming up behind me. I therefore had to go inside him, on a

PUNCTURE REPAIR, FLORES, INDONESIA '99.

very narrow strip of road, only two inches from the edge. I cleared his tail, but by now the bemo was starting to overtake me. The snake suddenly changed direction, to avoid the noisy taxi. My front tyre was now in direct collision course. There was only one thing I could do; pull a wheelie over his head! Then I closed my eyes, as my back wheel missed him by a whisker. Yikes!

Timor, Indonesia

He pulled the sheath from the blade and stood there swaying, the sheath in one hand and the knife in the other...

I made it to the Timor ferry with leaking inner tubes, but no snakebites. Just after that snake incident, I'd met a man and his girlfriend on the top of the mountain pass. They insisted on holding a conversation with me, all the way to the bottom, lighting up the way with their headlight. As we rolled into a town, there was a volcano in the background, spewing a dust cloud two thousand metres into the moonlit sky.

I reached the ferry with my bike seemingly on its last legs. I'd already had to glue a bit of old inner tube onto the inside of a rip in the tyre. I had slow punctures on both wheels, with repair patches already overlapping each other, and the wheel bearings were making hideous noises.

The fourteen-hour ferry journey to Timor was an adventure in itself. The car deck was empty of cars, but full of boxes, piles of bananas, enormous pigs, sleeping passengers and lots of colour and commotion. I spent the journey chatting to a couple of young nuns, one local and the other Puerto Rican. I then met the Captain, dressed in jeans and a T-shirt. He apologised for the fact that there were no videos, but said he might be able to organise some karaoke. Luckily this never happened!

Once I reached Kupang in Timor, I still had a few days to kill before my flight to Australia; enough time to deliver the letter to the Kelimutu man's brother, as promised. The town of Soe was two days' easy cycling away, along the road that leads to the desperately troubled eastern half of the island. I followed the sketch map, drawn for me by the hotel man, and found his brother's school. Unfortunately, it was closed, and whilst trying to find his house I got into an adventure. I asked a man called Domi if he knew where the house was, and since we couldn't find it I decided to leave it for a couple of days till the school opened again.

Domi invited me to his house in the Soe village of Sentosa. It was down a steep track, which destroyed my now ancient cycling sandals.

Sentosa Village, West Timor, Indonesia 99

We met a small path that wound between the streams, past a communal water tank, where people bath and wash their clothes.

Domi's house was very simple. Built of bamboo with a thatched roof, it was actually two small buildings a few metres apart. One was the cooking room, the other was the bedroom, while the space in between was where the daytime was spent. I locked my bike to an upright post in the cooking room and the bags were put in the bedroom, probably the least secure place they'd ever been. The bamboo door had no lock of any kind.

A group of villagers gathered around and I took some photos while they giggled shyly. One man was chewing betel nut, so his teeth were all red. He invited me to take his portrait, and in return I bought him some whisky. After coffee at an uncle's house, we walked back into Soe and turned down a side street to visit Domi's friend.

I had to walk behind a man who was tying his shoelaces. He stepped backwards and trod on my toe. The next thing I knew was that his foot was swinging up to kick me and I had to turn around and catch his leg. Then he punched me in the face. I couldn't believe what was happening, and when I backed off up the road, he started on Domi.

Domi ran down the road and the man, who was in his twenties, was swinging around in a drunken stupor, pulling a knife from his jacket. I started running back to the main road and Domi got there by cutting through a garden. He was so scared, he held my hand as we ran up the road.

We went to see a different friend instead, and on the bemo on the way there Domi told the other passengers about what had just happened. They were all shocked, and it turned out that Domi actually knew the guy from school. His name was Jimy Hala and he was known as a trouble-maker. We reached the village of Neonmat, and Domi's friend Nicol Selan turned up. We were invited to have dinner with the family, and Domi was asking me if I wanted to eat a traditional Timorese dish.

"I'll eat anything!" I said, very grateful to have been invited.
"This dish very good!" said Domi. "Rice and mice."
"Err!" I stalled. "I'm not so sure..."
"Very very good!" he insisted. "Rice and mice!"

"Erm. I don't want to offend Nicol. Can I have just a little! More rice than mice!"

"Maybe you don't like mice!" laughed Domi. "We eat every day!"

He could see that was I wasn't keen, so we had rice and chicken instead. Later I discovered that he'd meant "rice and maize!"

In the full moon, we walked up the empty cobbled road from Nicol's house, "to see the dead." Each of us had an ikat-woven blanket wrapped around the waist, in the traditional style. I thought we were going to a cemetery, but it turned out we were to see a local man who had just died. He was a cousin of Nicol's and was only twenty-six.

We came upon a scene from the nativity, with a dead man in the place of the baby. His friends and relatives were there, gathered around in the open-fronted bamboo house. We walked up to shake hands with them and exchange solemn looks. I felt out of place but also very moved, especially because the man was so young. I could hardly look at him; death didn't fit so young a face. His body, legs and feet were wrapped in colourful blankets, and the candles cast quiet shadows onto the walls.

Three young girls, probably his sisters, were crying and bowing in a strange, repetitive rhythm. All around them, their friends were quietly singing hymns in Timorese. Nobody seemed to know why he'd died, though some had guessed that asthma might have been the cause. Nicol told me that many people die at a young age from asthma, drink or drugs.

I didn't feel that I should be there, yet nobody objected. I was welcomed in the same way as always in Indonesia. In fact, it was Nicol's father who'd said that I should go. He is actually a king; "Raja Selan" in Indonesian or "Meo Selan" in Timorese. He's a very humble king and you would never guess. When we were eating, he kept putting his hands together to coax me into eating more rice. An old man in a small house with laughing grandchildren and some small puppies, he became King the previous year, when his father died. Every village has a king and this region, Timor Tenga Selatan, has its big King as well; Raja Nope.

WEST TIMOR, INDONESIA '99.

Domi told Raja Selan about the madman with the knife. With a concerned look in his quiet eyes, the Raja assured us that he'd report the incident to the government.

The following day, Domi and I visited his father and stepmother in Babin, thirty miles away. His real mother, he said, "is a crazy-man." We went to the top of the village where people were washing in a stream, set up with channels made from bamboo. This was better than any shower I've ever had, and of course I was the centre of attention, though I'd been given a sarong to cover up my bits and bobs.

Afterwards, we walked around the village with my camera to photograph the people and their traditional domed houses, called "Ume Kbubu." Everybody burst out laughing as soon as they saw the camera. Like the pied piper, I had a long caravan of hyperactive kids behind, screaming and running away whenever I turned round.

That night, just like the night before, I suffered from terrible asthma, the worst I'd had in months. The houses in these villages are choked with dust and the smoke from the oil lamps, which are kept burning all night. My inhaler, which I'd carried for two years but only used a couple of times, had dried up completely. The people in the village don't even have that to help them. It's hardly surprising that so many people die of asthma, like Nicol's cousin, despite everybody's awareness of the problem. I thought about the money I'd raised for Intermediate Technology before leaving Sheffield. I hoped the project that the money was for, in Kenya, had been successful.

It was getting close to the date of my flight to Australia, so Domi and I returned to Soe. My bike was still there in Domi's house, and I said goodbye to him, thanking him for the adventure. Before returning to Kupang for the flight, however, I had business to attend to. I rode up the path of the school that I'd reached two days before.

"Excuse me, do you know a man called Mr. Simon?" I asked a couple of teachers.

"Yes! He is a teacher here. Why do you want to see him?"

"I have a letter for him," I replied.

They told me that he was in a meeting, but that they'd take it for him. Just then, a man came round the corner and they said, "Here he is!"

"Mr Simon," I told him. "I've come to bring you a letter from your brother on Flores!"

"Addi!" he beamed.

"There you go! Faster than the post office!" I joked, passing him the letter.

"Thank you!" he smiled, reaching into his pockets. "I haven't got anything to give you!"

"Your smile is enough!" I said.

"But… won't you come to stay in my house?"

"I can't stop," I said. "I'm flying to Australia!"

Darwin to Brisbane, Australia

An hour and ten minutes after taking off from Kupang, the plane landed in Darwin. The smiling world of kings, horse-drawn cidomos, jukung fishing boats and Rumah Makan was left behind in the blink of an eye. I'd fallen in love with Indonesia, but felt a big sense of relief and achievement when we flew out of Kupang. I'd reached a major milestone, made it across Asia and had no more worries about malaria, bandits and mad bus drivers...

Getting onto the plane was something I did by the skin of my teeth, however. I was detained at Kupang airport for not having an immigration card! Apparently it's not unusual for people to pass through immigration without being given a card, but the guards here suddenly turned nasty when I said I was never given one. I had a stamp in my passport, proving that I had indeed entered from Singapore, fifty-seven days before. This wasn't enough though, and things looked ugly, just an hour before take-off!

An Australian man tapped me on the shoulder, saying he'd overheard my conversation with the guards, and that I was in deep trouble. His companion was an Indonesian lady, and he said that she could help me. She was a passenger on my plane, and I later found out that her uncle owns Merpati Airlines.... jammy or what! She took a guard and me into an office and told him, "All you need to do is phone Bali, where the immigration records are kept." He would then be able to find out my immigration number, while I'd be on the plane to Australia, as long as I gave him some baksheesh...

Touchdown in Darwin! Relief!
Darwin was cool. I stayed with my cousin Pauline, who entertained me in first class style. We went out for a beer and tried to work out what to do the next day.
"I know... I'll give you the best view of Darwin!" she exclaimed.
"How are you going to do that?" I asked.

"I've just got my pilot's license! We'll go to the flying school and I'll take you up in a Piper."

The next morning, we took off in a little plane, Pauline in the pilot's seat and me the gob-smacked passenger....

"Wow!" I shouted over the noise. "Look at that!"

"That's the marina down there!" she said.

"Look at the outback," I cried. "I've got to cycle that!"

"Goes on for ever, doesn't it!"

"Wow! What about the ocean, as well. That's absolutely stunning!"

"Yeah! It's beautiful. Sorry about the wind, by the way!" she explained as we drifted sideways. "We've got twenty-five knots today!"

"Is that a lot, then?" I joked. "It's dead windy anyway!"

"Yeah. Oops! Better be careful. We've got traffic ahead," she warned.

"What do you mean, traffic? That's another plane!"

"You're taking the mickey, aren't you...."

After a bumpy landing in the strong wind, she took me up to the RAAF control tower where she works, guiding in everything from little planes with two people on-board, to international flights with three hundred passengers. That evening, we went with her future husband Murray to the Mindle Beach night market, with every type of food you can think of, as the sun set over the ocean.

Weeee-He! He made it!
Dear Verena –
Tim has just arrived in Australia – no probs! He sounds really happy and it was great to hear from him.
Love, Berlie x

Pauline had to go to work the following morning in the control tower, quarter of a mile away. I had to cycle to Brisbane to stay with Auntie Jean and Uncle Denis, 2157 miles away across the outback. My rear hub had nearly packed up during the last week in Indonesia, and Mr Misery-guts at the Darwin bike shop sold me the wrong parts. I had to go back to the shop, strip the bike down outside, fit new axle, cones and bearings to the back wheel and new bearings to the front wheel. When I'd finished, Mr Misery-guts checked my work and said, "You've done a good job there!" And he smiled!

I put the bike back together, loaded it up with three spare Indonesian tyres and all the gear, and set off into the scorching sun, down the Stuart Highway in a ferocious headwind. Eight days later I turned off the Stuart Highway, already six hundred miles from Darwin. I sat at the Three Ways Roadhouse, remembering the time last year when Verena and I were here in the car on our backpacking trip, waiting for the floods to die down. This time I sat on a bench in the shade, mending punctures.

I'd had two tyre blow outs in the first three days from Darwin, brand new tyres ripping their walls apart in style, causing massive punctures. The second one happened three miles before the town of Katherine, which had the last bike shop for eight hundred miles! I fitted some kevlar tyres and bought some new cleated cycling sandals. I needed all the help I could get to fight the headwind, on a fully loaded bike with up to ten litres of water and food for up to five days!

"This wind is a killer!" I told the lady in the bike shop.

"You're meant to ride the other way at this time of year!" she said.

"Well, it would be better!"

"We do a ride to Darwin every year at this time," she explained, "320 km with a tailwind!"

I'd picked this time of year to hit Australia because of the winter. It's only thirty-five degrees instead of forty-five! Also, it's much drier than when Verena and I were here, none of that killer humidity.

Reaching the Three Ways Roadhouse was a very significant moment. Last time I was there, with Verena, I'd taken my cheap old Australian bike off the roof of the car and gone for a little spin to stretch my legs:

I went for a bike ride and came to a sign that read "K 640"; six hundred and forty kilometres to Katherine. I turned back towards the roadhouse, depressed that this was actually part of my intended round the world cycle route, and that, on a bike, it seemed utterly boring.

Little had I known that just over a year later I would be back there again, having resumed the Round the World ride. And, what's more, I'd be loving it.

A red pick-up pulled up to the roadhouse, country music blaring out of the windows. A guy in cowboy hat and boots, black jeans and T-shirt got out. He came over and said, "Blow me mate! You wouldn't catch me ridin' across this country on a push-bike... you're ravin' mad!"

The typical distance between towns was sixty miles, but on leaving the Three Ways Roadhouse that would change. From there to Mt Isa, for example, I'd have to cycle over four hundred miles with nothing but one roadhouse and one small town on the way. I left the Three Ways after a couple of hours, with the sun setting and the wind dropping. By now, I was developing a daily pattern. I'd get up before sunrise, making use of the cool and calm of early morning. I'd keep riding all day, maintaining a fairly slow speed so as not to tire myself out against the relentless sun and wind. Then, when the sun had set at about six o'clock, the wind would drop and I could leg it for an hour before it became too dark to see. I'd then slow down again, and keep riding till the little 10 km road signs told me I'd done 130 or 140 km, or whatever target I'd set for the day.

I'd then lock the bike to the road sign, throw the tent up by chucking a heavy bag into each corner, since the ground was too sandy for tent pegs, and lie there looking at the stars. I decided that, to keep going at this pace and not have any days off, was the best way. I was cycling quite gently but putting in about twelve hours a day on the saddle, plus a couple of hours' rest.

The semi-desert landscape changes constantly but subtly. Reaching the top of a rise, the only man-made thing I'd see was the road I was on, stretching endlessly over a red plain. The awe-inspiring sense of space blows away the loneliness and fatigue.

There are colours and more colours in the Outback. Always different, changing with the light of day. Wedge-tailed eagles soar overhead, termite towers stretch away to the horizon. The dryness of the earth can be heard, and the hours drift away in the wind.

Everything about the place is vast; up to one hundred and sixty miles between one roadhouse and the next. No water for one hundred and eighteen miles after crossing the Queensland border from the Northern Territory. In the N.T., unlike Outback Queensland, they believe in maintaining the water-bores, which draw foul-tasting water out of the ground, every fifty miles or so.

As long as I was in the N.T., once a windmill-like pump came into view, everything would be okay. Time to take a break from the energy-sapping wind, sit there on a bench swatting flies, and welcome the arrival of the Australian couples with their touring caravans. They would ask me such easily answered questions as, "Would you like some cake?" or, "Would you like some sandwiches and an apple?" Or the most frequently asked question of all, "Would you like a cup of tea?"

The other good places to meet and eat were the roadhouses. I reached one almost everyday, and there I would break my staple diet of peanuts and tinned tuna and blow a few dollars on a plate of bacon and eggs. With no accommodation costs to worry about, I could afford this little luxury! I only stayed on one campsite the whole time between Darwin and Brisbane, and only had three showers. Incredibly, my skin remained completely clear of eczema, and I never had any asthma, despite the truckloads of junk food I had to eat to fuel my passage across the Outback! The weather was near perfect, save for the headwind, and the night cycling was sublime. I'd find myself almost dropping off to sleep, as the warm temperature and the darkness would trick me into thinking I was in bed. Everything I could see was in a deep shade of purple, my sleepy eyes trying to follow the faint white line at the edge of the road, the bike gliding along as if on silk.

Night cycling brought with it two dangers. One was, of course, road-trains. The only way to survive these inter-state monsters was to get off the road and wait till they'd gone past. Even if the driver sees you and clears you, the turbulence from the first trailer will drag you into the second or third trailer, something that nearly caught me out everyday as they'd pass me silently, streaming into the headwind. Forget snakes, spiders, crocs and dehydration; trucks are the single most dangerous thing, in every country from Turkey to Australia.

The other dangerous things at night were...kangaroos! I'd ride with my flashing back light on, but the front light was saved for those rare occasions when a bit of traffic came along. One night I was taken by surprise as a 'roo stirred from the gravel shoulder and bounced off into the bush, completely invisible in the night. The next time it happened, there was a loud slap-slapping of feet on the road right across the front of the bike!

I quickly took the light out of my handlebar bag and, still coasting, switched it on and swung it around. There he was, a massive kangaroo about my height. He legged it off the other side of the road and I cut my speed down a bit. Kangaroo carcasses lined the highway, in all states of decay from a freshly hit 'roo to a cracked and crunched spread of old bones, eventually to disappear to dust.

Once I was past half way to Brisbane, the moon started staying up in the sky for longer. Rather than being a thin crescent, setting two hours after sunset, it gradually turned full and stayed up till midnight.

This made life much easier and I was casting a shadow on the road at night, so bright was the moon.

The wind changed its habits too; not only did it blow straight into my face in the daytime, it carried on in the night as well! No matter, I was happy as Larry, meeting wacky characters every day, even in the smallest towns. In one place in the Outback, I stopped outside a shop, next to a fifty-year old woman with a funny trailer, its sides covered in cuddly toys.

AUSTRALIAN OUTBACK - SELF-PORTRAIT WHILST CYCLING '99.

"Where are you going?" she inquired.

"Brisbane," I answered. Then, looking at her trailer, "Are you selling things?"

"No!" she retorted. "I'm walking around the world!"

"Like Ffyona Campbell!"

"THAT girl. That's all I hear about! Anyway, I've got no support vehicle. It's just me, on my own!"

"So where did you start from?"

"Perth. That was two years ago. I walked across the Nullarbor, along the highway."

"And how long will it take altogether?" I ventured, still thinking she was mad.

"Oh, about sixteen years, but I'll just walk till I drop…"

Another time, I was riding in the sunset, a hundred miles from the last roadhouse, when a red Ford Falcon came towards me. It was exactly like the car that Petra, Verena and I had bought in Sydney the previous year!

Then it stopped! I thought, "Blimey, my car remembers me!" It was the first time in Australia that someone had simply stopped like that. In the car was an aboriginal family. They were great! They wanted to know everything about my trip, then the driver said;

"Us, we're born here. We wander round these tracks, and then we die!"

223

He had a broad grin, as if to say, "Simple!" He offered me some water, and told me it was only thirty kilometres to the next roadhouse. Before driving off, he said;

"Nice talkin' to you mate! Good luck!"

Heading into southern Queensland, I decided that the wind wouldn't get me, so I cranked up the pace. I covered seven hundred miles in a week, biting the bullet a few days before the end by ringing Uncle Denis and Auntie Jean, to tell them I'd be arriving a few days earlier than expected. Sometimes I had to tell myself to stop riding at the end of each day; the wide open space just gives you the impression that you can go on forever, and as I wasn't getting tired, there seemed to be no reason to stop.

Eventually, the mountains of the Great Dividing Range came into view. Nearly there now! The great rolling plains were almost at an end. From Toowoomba the road started its drop into coastal Queensland. Almost immediately, there was a sign saying "VERY STEEP DESCENT." This stretch was a tightly twisting dual carriageway. I was riding at night again, but didn't want to go slowly in case of traffic coming up behind me. I came round a corner to be faced by dozens of little orange lights, a road-train, going down the hill at walking pace! I slammed the brakes on and cast a quick glance over my shoulder. There were three cars about to overtake me, so I couldn't get past the road-train. I managed to avoid piling into the back of him, but this stretch of road was a bit hairy to say the least, after all that flat ground.

Half an hour later, my nerves back to normal, I found a safe place to rest for a while and write my diary;

"...I'm writing this by moonlight again. Right next to me is a huge Eucalyptus tree, its white limbs stretching upwards, as if it's holding up the night sky..."

I wasn't yet finished for the day, though. I got back on the bike, singing, "Keep on runnin' man, keep on hidin' man!" in a Geordie accent, as I had been for the last couple of weeks. I had a few more scary moments with road-trains, and after a late meal at a service station I at last found the sign I'd been waiting for; "Brisbane 80 km." I went down into a field and stuck the tent up.

The next morning, I woke up and had instant diarrhoea, just like every other morning. Luckily I always had time to get out of the tent.

Once I entered Brisbane, things became complicated because the road suddenly turned into a motorway. I asked a Greek man in a shop, and he explained the back-roads way. The road became a series of rolling hills, which put me in racing-bike mode, legging it away from each set of traffic lights to beat the cars.

The tall buildings of central Brisbane came into view at the end of the road, but this wasn't my destination. I had to find my way out through the suburbs and down to Cleveland, on the coast. I rode past sun-drenched golf courses, so perfect that they resembled computer images.

I reached Cleveland, and went first to the place where Verena and I had taken the ferry to Stradbroke Island a year before. I sat there for a while, just thinking and watching the calm sea. As the sun began to set, I cycled back through the town and managed to remember the way to Mergowie Drive, then coasted down the road; Number 3,.. Number 5... Number 7! So, I'd made it, door to door from Pauline's in Darwin: 2,157 miles in 25 days!

"There's a bike outside!" I heard Denis say, just before the door opened.

"Quick, let's take a photo before the sun goes!" I was so excited I forgot to shake hands.

"Have you spoken to Pauline?" I asked, setting up one of my special worm's eye-view, self-timer pictures.

"Yes. She rang yesterday," said Jean. "I told her you'd be here today, and she said "Mum, what's he like?" or something!"

"I had a cool time in Darwin! It's a shame Verena and I didn't get there last year!"

"You were close, though, weren't you; Kakadu. Anyway, how is Verena?"

"Oh, she's a superstar. She's mega-busy with work, but she came to see me in Bali!"

"Didn't you get ill there?" asked Denis.

"Yeah, something tropical. It lingered on for ages. Oh, and I hit a big stone in the night last week. It dented the wheel rim…"

"Oh well! We should be able to tap it out with a hammer..."

Staying with Jean, Denis and Foster the dog again was a very welcome break. Pauline rang up and couldn't believe I'd got there on May 31st, having only left her flat on May 7th! In fact, I was so early that I did another four-day ride, to Cape Byron (Australia's most Easterly point) and back.

Nevertheless, I had five relaxing days with them, eating fantastic food, sleeping in a bed, catching up on the gossip, sending e-mails and getting ready for New Zealand...

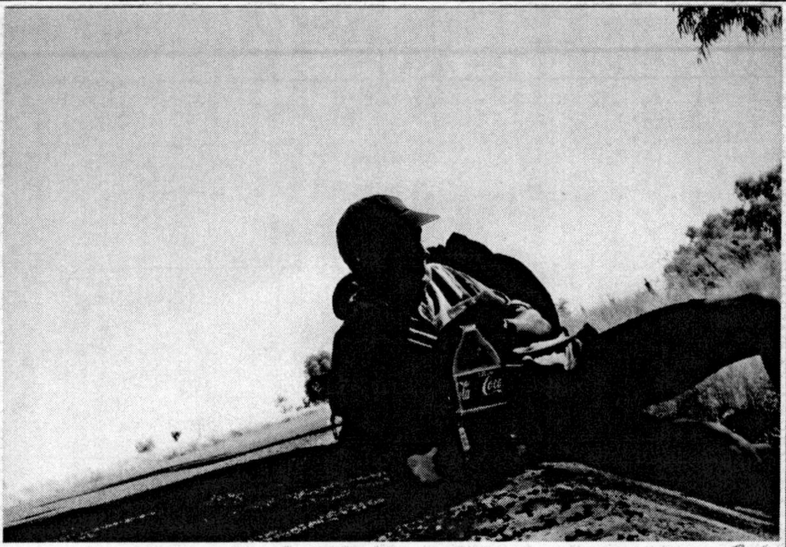

AUSTRALIAN OUTBACK '99.

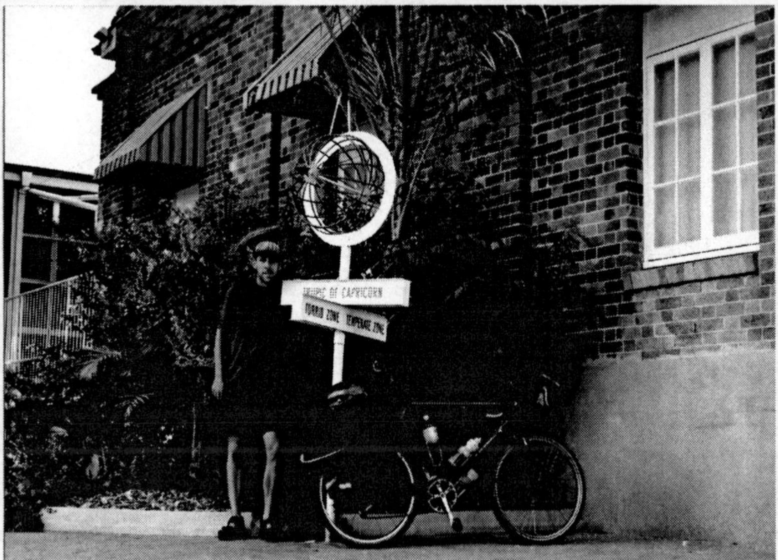

QUEENSLAND. AUSTRALIA '99.

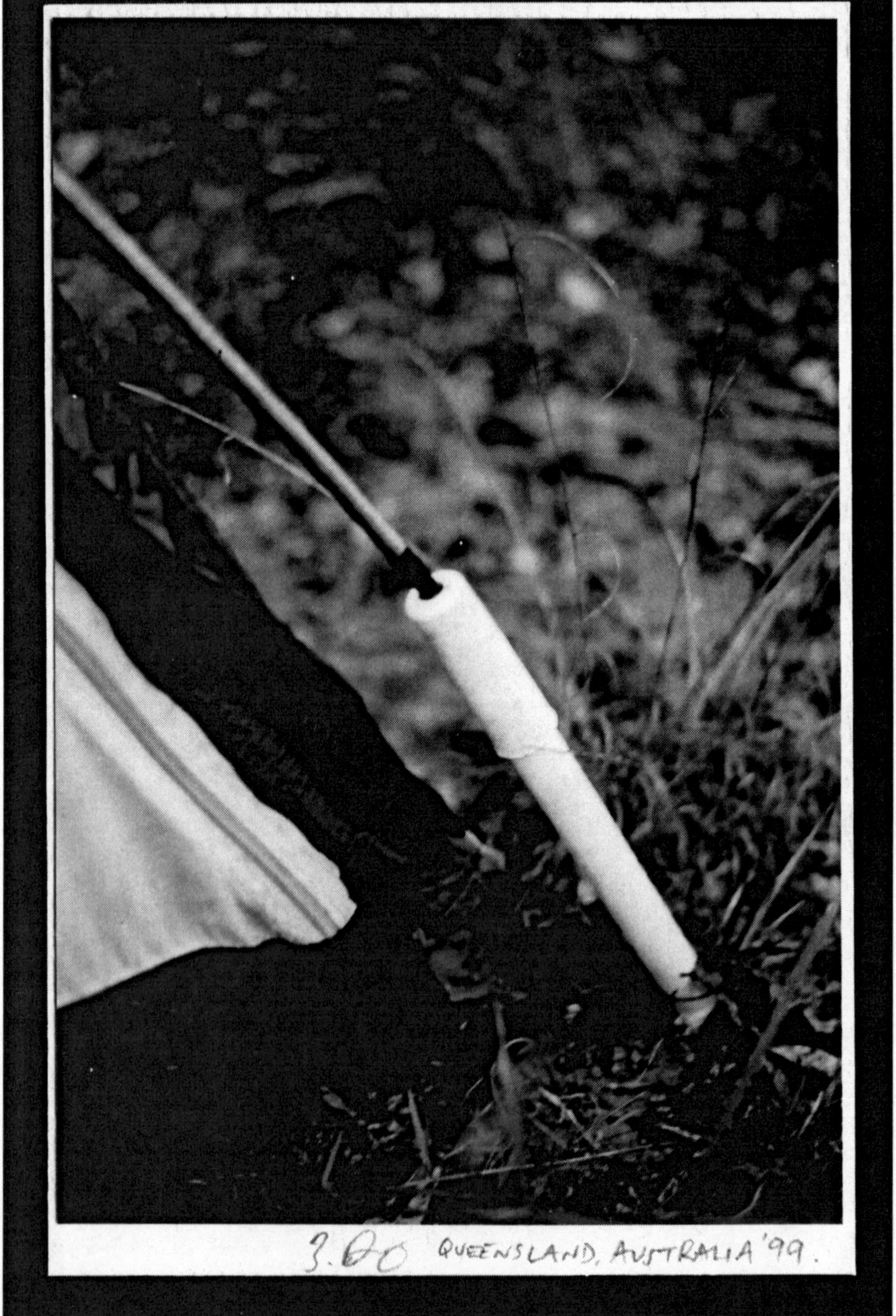
QUEENSLAND, AUSTRALIA '99.

Cape Foulwind to Tolaga Bay, New Zealand

Shivering uncontrollably, I was getting worried. I had nearly all my clothes on inside the sleeping bag, with the old sleeping bag underneath as a mattress. I could feel that my body heat was fighting against a constant stream of freezing cold water, both within and underneath the poorly pitched tent. I had visions of waking up at three o'clock in the morning with hypothermia or, worse still, not waking up at all...

Winter.

"They don't call it Cape Foulwind for nothing!" said the lady in the Westport chip shop. "It rains and it rains and it rains and it rains!"

I finished my chips and rode the seven miles to Cape Foulwind. I couldn't believe how mild it was, and I could hear the crashing waves and the seagulls. I pitched the tent near the lighthouse, under a shelter in case the rain came; using the bike pump as a tent pole was only effective to a point!

I woke up at half past six in the morning and had to leg it out of the tent before the diarrhoea came; I must be allergic to camping or something! It had rained during the night and the tent had got a bit wet, despite the shelter. It was quite mild but the sky was grey and it looked like something was brewing. Never mind. In less than two weeks I'd be back with Verena.

With a strange feeling that I must actually be in Scotland, I packed up and rode up the track to the lighthouse and along a footpath. I came to a stile, where I left the bike and clambered down to the crashing waves. Stepping down onto the wet rocks, I stared across the sea, back towards Australia. I noticed something stirring, just a couple of metres away. It was a seal, clambering over the rocks before disappearing into the water. I thought it was a special way to mark the start of my journey in New Zealand. But, in retrospect, it seems that he was trying to tell me something else; "You're gonna get wet, boy!"

As soon as I started cycling, the rain started. For the first couple of hours it was okay, because my fleece was holding out. The valleys in the distance were black with clouds, and I was heading straight for them.

Gradually, I had to don more and more clothes, until I was wearing everything I had, most of which had been sent by my mum to Uncle Denis'. On my feet were two pairs of skiing socks, a pair of Gore-Tex socks, a couple of plastic bags to keep out the wind, and a pair of boots. Then I had cycling shorts, two pairs of tracksuit trousers, and a pair of waterproof trousers. On my upper body were three T-shirts, a thick shirt, a fleece, a wind-shell and a waterproof kagoul. Over the hood of the kagoul sat a cap and my cycling helmet. Finally, on my hands I had a pair of thermal gloves, and some woolly mittens.

I took a photo of myself like this, but it was the only photo I took on the South Island, because I had to keep the camera dry! As the afternoon drew in, the rain found itself into every single nook and cranny. I was heading for the mountains and the temperature was dropping. For the first fifty miles, there were impressive deer and gushing rivers to look at, but nowhere to stop, so I kept going until I found a sheltered corner in Reefton.

"Are you waiting for the shower to clear?" asked a pedestrian. "It'll clear on Wednesday!"

I stood there, huddled up against a wall as I ate some sandwiches, then set off again, up the road leading to the Lewis Pass. The next town would be Springs Junction, but I didn't know if I'd get there. It was getting dark and very cold, and the rain went on and on.

The hill-climb was obviously going to be a very long one, but eventually the rain turned to drizzle and I could see clearly because of the shiny, wet road. All day, there had been no kilometre markers, and it turned out that it's possible to cycle for hours in New Zealand without having a clue how far it is to the next town.

In spite of the cold and the wet, there was something magical about riding into the mountains in the dark. The road drifted slowly around sweeping curves in the eerie quiet. A ceiling of icy stars drifted overhead, and the forest was filled with the green "eyes" of hundreds of glow-worms. I didn't know how far it was to Springs Junction and the cold was getting to me. I decided to camp, even though there was no shelter. Once I'd found a natural "quarry" the rain came back, so I had to throw the tent up quickly. The ground was made up of small stones so I didn't stand a chance of pitching it properly, even if I'd had the full set of poles.

I'd brought two sleeping bags with me to New Zealand, a clever bit of forethought that ended up doing me no good at all. Within ten minutes, both sleeping bags were soaked through. The water seemed to be coming from everywhere; through the walls of the inner tent, through the ground sheet, running off the soaked pannier bags, and from my already sopping wet clothes.

WINTER '99 – NEW ZEALAND'S SOUTH ISLAND

I managed to stop shivering for long enough to look at my watch. It was only eight p.m. I was annoyed at how quickly a £250 tent could leak, and I later discovered that this tent was made right here on New Zealand's South Island! Well, okay, I was using a bike pump as a tent pole section, but that was because the pole had snapped one night in Australia. I'd mended it cunningly at a roadhouse, but in order to do so I'd had to cut the elastic that runs through the ten sections of the pole. That was how I was able to leave one of the sections behind by mistake, one dark morning! I couldn't get hold of a replacement section in Australia, hence the bike pump!

The shivering and cursing didn't warm me up, so I had to spring into action and go for the next town, even though I had no idea how far it was. I jumped out of the tent, into the torrential rain. I chucked everything into the panniers and made a run for it, painfully slowly because of the gradient. I was riding for an hour and a half, so it was about ten miles and just about the worst ten miles ever. Down the ditches at the edges of the road were two fast flowing rivers, which had probably been dry the day before.

My front light was useless, getting more and more dim, even though the batteries were new. The last bit was downhill and as I could hardly see I had to slow right down, my hands almost too cold to operate the brakes. The brakes themselves weren't up to much either, as the wheel rims were filthy and the new cables were stretching. I had to resort to the "foot-on-the-road" braking technique to stop, when I finally found a bed and breakfast.

I knocked on the door, but there was no answer. All the lights were off, the owners obviously staying somewhere with a more hospitable climate. I'd obviously put on a fair bit of altitude today; the difference from last night's balmy air at Cape Foulwind was incredible.

Just down the road was a motel. It was now ten o'clock and there was no one around; this tiny town was dead. Nobody answered the motel door either, and I was hopping around with my teeth chattering. I went to a house over the road and knocked on the door. A lad answered, and told me where I could find the owner of the motel.

He turned out to be a big-fat-cheerful-slap-you-on-the-back-have-a-laugh type of bloke, coming out with a string of one-liners;

"Good job the man at the bed and breakfast wasn't in – he's an idiot!"

"I didn't care where I stayed, just somewhere dry!" I shivered.

"It looks like it might rain tonight, what do you reckon?" he laughed.

"Probably. It's been doing it for the last fifteen hours!"

"Round here it's all rainforest. You know why, don't you!" he said, letting me in to the office. "We measure our rain in metres here!"

"I've gathered that much," I groaned, trying to write my name in the book.

"This is just a drizzle! You're lucky it didn't snow when you were camping; you'd have been stuck then!"

The motel room cost $55; about £18.50, the most I've ever paid for accommodation, and something I couldn't afford to do very much on my dwindling funds.

"Go and have a hot shower before you die!" said the owner, as he opened the door to my room.

Even before taking a shower though, I turned on the television and saw some old footage of Edmund Hillary being carried down in a stretcher from some Himalayan peak, his voice-over saying something like;

"It was time I spent some time with my family, instead of risking my life in the wild."

I understood what he meant. While I was watching, I tried to dry out my stuff in front of the little heater, but it didn't do much. It took me ages to get warm in bed, even after a hot shower. My feet looked like prunes and I drank so much coffee that I couldn't sleep till three o'clock, the rain still hammering down outside.

In the morning I put on all of my cold, wet clothes and went outside to sort out the brakes. There would be no camping again in New Zealand, though I actually managed to get the tent pole sorted on my last day in N.Z. From now on, it would be Youth Hostels, backpackers and cabins on campsites. The rain had stopped, but when I tilted the bike up to unlock it, a cupful of water came out of each end of the handlebars! I noticed that the brake blocks were nearly worn out, as was the tyre. I fitted the spare tyre but punctured the inner tube in the process!

Two days later, I reached the town of Nelson, still soaking wet and freezing cold. Another puncture the following morning led me to ride back into town, and I ended up spending the morning in the bike shop. I told the bike shop lady about my flat tyre and broken tent pole.

"You're having a rough time of it!" she said.
"Well, it'll be alright!" I replied. "D'you mind if I sort the bike out, outside the shop?"
"Be my guest!" she offered. "Would you like a cup of coffee?"
"Oh, that'd be great!"
Before long I'd fitted a new inner tube, four new brake blocks and a new rear light. She was chatting to me for most of the time, telling me about her six thousand-mile tour of Europe with her husband. She never had a single puncture and never changed her tyres! Ireland was her favourite place, and she regretted having to miss out Turkey.
"Who's this, then?" asked a customer.
"He's cycling round the world!" she told him.
"You LUCKY man!" he said, shaking my hand. "I'm off soon, to ride from Vancouver to Calgary."
"Oh, right. Canada's my next place, too! But I'm going to Austria first for a month, to see my girlfriend."
"Looks like we'll miss each other. I'll be back here by then!"
"Never mind. I hope the Canadian bike shops are as good as this one!" I laughed.
"This is the friendliest shop in Nelson, but the mechanics are absolutely useless!" He cast a glance over at the mechanics, who stood there beaming.
This was obviously a real adventure-cookie town. The guy I'd stopped the previous night to ask for a hostel had said, "There's truck-loads of em!" He was grinning as he walked with me to show me the way, quite tickled that I was touring in this weather. He told me that he'd spent a year cycling in India, Thailand, Laos, Vietnam, Cambodia, Malaysia and Indonesia.
That night, I was huddled in front of a heater in a cabin, on a campsite in Havelock, the Youth Hostel having closed for the winter. I woke up to find a pleasant surprise. It was Wednesday, and just as the man in Reefton had predicted on Saturday, the rain had stopped, the sky was clear and the sun was out! Also, the road I was on was the virtually traffic-free Queen Charlotte Drive; all of the cars and the hefty logging trucks use the main road to go to Picton.
My clothes were still wet and there was a two hundred-mile exclusion zone around my boots because of the smell. I took it slowly

Gisborne, North Island, N.Z. '99

from Havelock, my handlebar bag full of food from the baker; two date scones, a baguette pizza, a bacon and egg slice and an apple pie!

The road wound behind the little harbour and up over the headland, soaring and diving its way along the coast like a seagull in the wind. Snow-capped mountains, once in cloud, now stood tall and proud in the morning blue. Islands and yachts were scattered on the crystal green waters and the air was cold, crisp and invigorating. After a few hours of leisurely riding, I dropped down a final descent, with a breathtaking panorama of the Milford Sounds and Picton, and rode straight onto the ferry, bound for Wellington, North Island.

Over the following three days I worked my way across the North Island in fantastic weather. Up the West coast I went, through the dramatic Manuwatu gorge and over to the East coast at Napier. I rolled into town, thinking about how far I'd come, when a little girl on the pavement asked me, "Are you the paperboy?"

Art-deco buildings and painted wooden houses lined the seafront, and the Youth Hostel was a welcoming place. After a shower I went out to find the festival that my Scottish room-mate had told me about. I soon found it, down on the beach; a huge bonfire with the crowd huddled around, dancing to the drummers.

This was the mid-winter festival, and as the drumming became more intense and energetic and the huge timbers of the bonfire became engulfed in flames, I looked at the dark sea. I walked down the pebbles to the edge, and the Pacific rushed up to me, as if to draw me in.

The morning brought my thirtieth birthday, and I continued to follow the coast north for another three days, all the way to Tolaga Bay on the East Cape. Due now for a whole month's rest in Austria with the ever-patient Verena, I'd once again added up the miles recorded in my diary. In the four months since riding out of Bangkok, I'd cycled 6,895 of the most testing miles of my life. The total since Sheffield now stood at 17,095.

Even so, as I stood on the beach at Tolaga Bay, standing right up on my tip-toes, and jumping up and squinting, I still couldn't see across the Pacific to the place where my ride would resume...

CANADA!

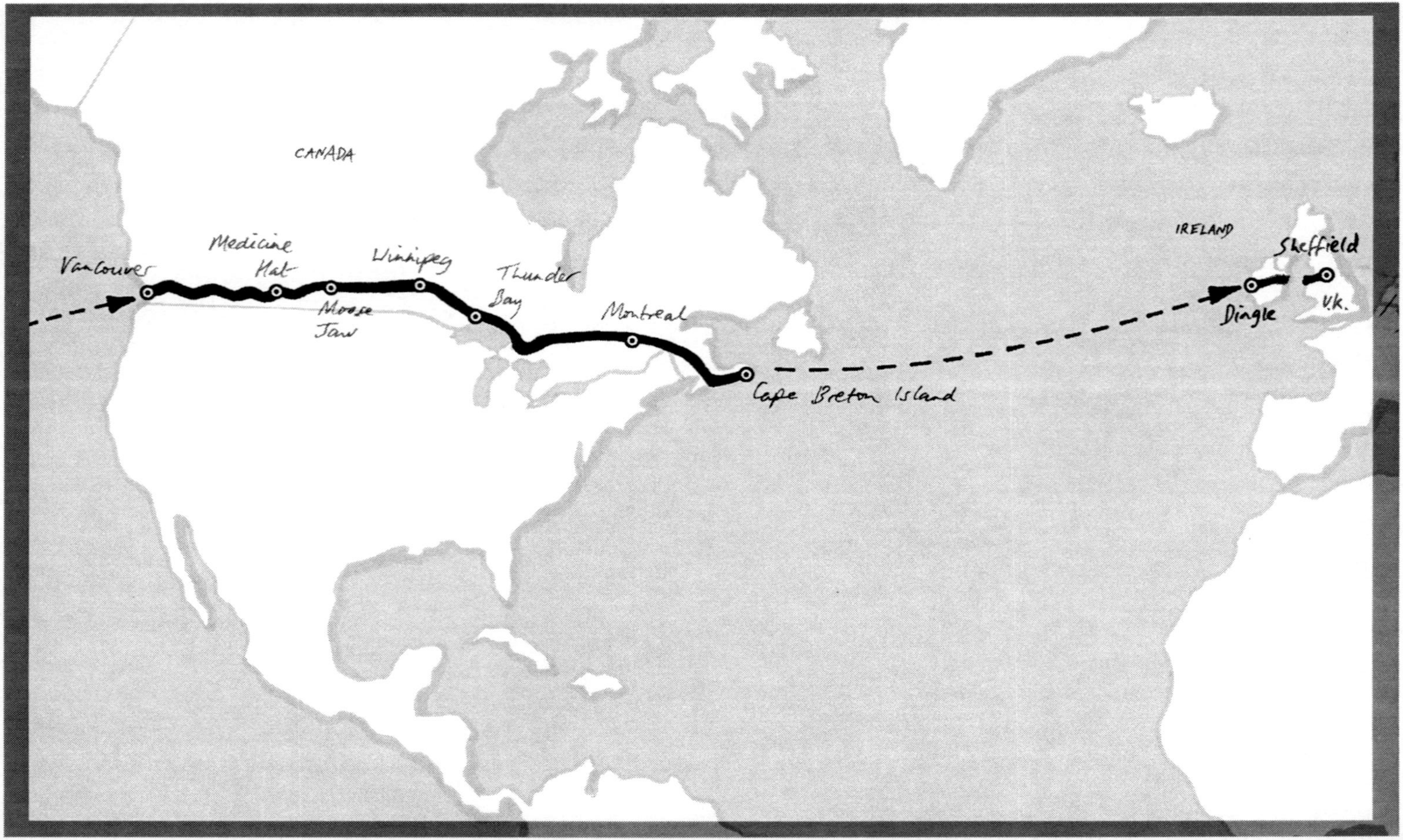
CANADA
Vancouver
Medicine Hat
Moose Jaw
Winnipeg
Thunder Bay
Montreal
Cape Breton Island
IRELAND
Dingle
Sheffield
U.K.

Five

Canada, Ireland, home
July to October 1999

I left the Youth Hostel in Vancouver, on Canada's West coast, for the longest single stretch of the whole trip. I'd flown out of New Zealand thinking, "I've cracked it!" But now, after a break with Verena, I realised that I still had a long, long way to go.

There was only one thing for it; don't stop! I only had two days off, all of the other days being spent pedalling. The other reason for getting on with it was that autumn was coming, and I didn't want to be on the road in the winter...

Canada, coast to coast

4133 miles in seven and a half weeks…

I did the ceremonial dipping-of-the-toes into the Pacific, just as I had done in New Zealand. The next ocean I would see would be the Atlantic, at Cape Breton Island, Nova Scotia.

I fitted some new bits to the bike; a chain and sprockets, two chain-rings, and two tyres. Reluctantly at first, I was now ready to hit the road again. It was July the thirtieth, but the summer was lagging behind.

I was eased back into the cycling, fortunately, as I had company for the first few miles. A guy called Mike showed me the way through the centre of Vancouver, with its boats and skyscrapers. He was off to catch a ferry, and he wished me luck, pointing out my road and telling me to follow my nose. Gradually, I left the city behind as I headed for the mountains, along an immense river with the smell of redwood in the air.

The next day I met an American cyclist called Davey, on a week's escape from Seattle. We rode together to a town called Hope and he booked us into a motel, saying that he didn't mind paying for the two of us as he'd already paid off his mortgage. Before going out to eat, we slacked around, swapping stories.

"The scariest I ever had was in Serbia last year," he said, sipping a bottle of beer.

"Were you there on your own?"

"There were three of us. We thought we'd just go and cycle round the country."

"Fair enough!" I said, cracking open another bottle.

"Anyway, these guys offered to put us up for the night, two of us in one room, and my friend Tommy on the couch. Just after we went to bed, we heard Tommy shouting…"

"No way," I said, trying to guess what might be coming.

"It was very fast, but there was suddenly this shouting and… BAM!"

"What!"

"A gunshot. We just jumped out of the window and ran for it, thinking, "Man! Tommy's dead!""

"So, was he?" I asked, hooked.

"No, he was lucky. He'd managed to push the gun away, just as the guy pulled the trigger, then he ran out of the house."

"He must have been scared out of his wits!"

"You bet. Anyway, we went to the police station, all three of us totally naked!"

"Did you get your stuff back?"

"Yep, we were lucky. They went in to the house and brought everything back to us…"

Davey headed north the next morning, while I continued east. I rode out of Hope and up the Allison Pass, surrounded by mountains draped in pine trees, laced with huge rivers of crystal clear water. I saw my very first bear, running across the road in front of me, almost too close for comfort.

Free-camping was fun in British Columbia. As soon as the sun went down, the temperature would plummet, the stars coming out to sparkle above the tall black pines. I had to hang up my food away

INN
SALOON
RESTAURANT
The Harbor
HOTEL
LICENCED
BRITISH COLUMBIA, CANADA '99.

from the tent, in case the bears came along. Then I'd wake up in the crisp early morning cold and take my food down, for an idyllic breakfast by the river.

Beyond the 1283 metre high Sunday Summit, the road dropped into an arid valley and through two Indian reserves. Here the Similkameen River passed through a dry valley with steep crags and screes, lit up like gold by the sun as it dropped below the brewing thunder clouds. Here I camped under some trees, just beyond the sign saying, "You are now entering Chuchuwayha Indian Reserve number 2, Upper Similkameen Indian Band."

In Keremeos I entered a valley rich in fruits and wineries. The Richter Pass took me over to Canada's only desert, and in the searing heat I rolled into the town of Osoyoos. I had to go into an air-conditioned restaurant to eat, but I wasn't complaining. In fact these places turned out to be so cheap that I stopped using my camping stove, and ended up posting it home again. "The Anarchist" was the threatening name of the mountain pass out of Osoyoos, taking me right from the desert right up to a high plateau, with much of the forest cleared for grazing. On the plateau were some picturesque old-style ranches, simple wooden houses, some with stone-built corners and dark wooden walls.

A storm brewed up across the valley as I pitched the tent next to the summit sign of The Anarchist. One bolt of lightning actually struck the far hills of the valley I'd just cycled across, and the storm was centred directly over the American / Canadian border. After an audible explosion on the hillside I could make out a bush fire, glowing but gradually fading. Darkness fell, adding to my feeling of anxiety. I couldn't tell whether or not the storm was heading my way, but I knew that I wasn't in a good place, in a tent at the very top of the mountain pass, underneath some power lines.

I remembered what this Canadian girl in Peru had told me, about people being found dead, on top of Canadian mountains, their cameras yielding photos of them with their hair standing up in the electrically charged air.

When I decided that the storm was actually coming my way, I closed the tent, locked the bike, took my valuables and tried to hitch a ride back down to Osoyoos for the night. Amazingly, I failed!

Nobody would even stop! Fate had decided that I would sleep on the mountain, and I was too tired to stand by the road any longer. Even the horses on the ranches were going mad, sensing the encroaching storm, and I got into the tent to watch the lightning.

I survived the night, but it wasn't the last storm or the last pass. The highest one I came across was the 1774 metre Kootenay Pass, which started as dense pine forest with a sparkling river, and ended up as bare rock and snow. It was just over a week since I'd left Vancouver, and I was regaining my fitness, so I was able to go for it on the climb.

A cold wind swept down as I approached the summit at eight o'clock. I'd been in the shadows for a couple of hours, yet I passed several cars which had given up through over-heating, and the cars coming down were burning their brakes out. I had the last rays of the sun on me as I pedalled the final few hundred metres to the summit. I pitched the tent next to a small lake with the pines behind and fish jumping out for the flies. I thought that I'd have a tranquil night here, if a little cold.

Tranquil it was not! Those huge trucks chose the bit of road right next to my tent to stop and leave their engines running all night. This was worse than India, the diesel engines hammering away and shattering the peace.

Trucks excluded, the sense of wilderness in British Columbia was profound, and amongst the varied wildlife I saw were elk, chipmunks, beavers and a coyote. On the last day in British Colombia, I crossed the Rocky Mountains, which are the most curiously shaped mountains imaginable. Some resemble vast broken ice-sheets, while others are craggy, with coloured vertical bands and hundreds of pinnacles on top. Crowsnest Mountain, just before the border with Alberta, was weird, looking like something from Monument Valley in the States, its jagged faces and soaring cliffs rising straight out of the landscape.

Ahead of me now lay an endless arid plain; the end of the mountains and the start of the Prairies. Despite the heat, I was told that there was a big storm coming down from Calgary. At the next place, a couple of truckers also warned me about it, so I decided I had to find somewhere to hide. It soon became apparent that there was nothing; not a single tree, shelter or bridge.

I entered the Peigan Reserve, a confederacy of the Blackfoot tribe. I saw two Indian kids sit down to watch the sunset on the Oldman River, as it curved its golden way through a verdant valley. The reddening plain of windswept grass lay beyond; a scene of timeless beauty.

In the gas station in Brocket, I met a friendly Red Indian, who said that, yes, there are such things as hailstones as big as golf balls. This particular storm, of which there was still no sign, could be one like that. He gave me a brooch for luck and wished me a good trip.

I pedalled out to find that a strong headwind had blown up out of nowhere. It was starting to go dark and the next place, Fort Macleod, was twenty miles away. I knew that getting caught in such a hailstorm would be no joke. I passed by the farms and homesteads of the Indian Reserve, many of which had old tee-pees in the garden.

Darkness fell and I was still battling against the headwind. Heavy black clouds rolled in from all sides, and I pulled over to put on my helmet and switch on the bike lights. I was thankful for the hard shoulder, which kept me clear of the trucks, as I was finding it hard to keep a straight line. I could see streetlights on the horizon, and two exhausting hours after leaving Brocket, I made it into Fort Macleod and straight onto a campsite.

As soon as I'd pitched the tent, the storm hit. The rain came lashing down, and the thunder and lightning scared me to death, sounding like a series of explosions in a quarry. In the morning, I met the campsite lady.

"I'm glad we didn't have to deal with *your* charred remains!" she joked.

"It was a close one! I considered hiding in the shower block all night!"

"You're lucky the hailstones didn't get here last night!"

"So there were some?"

"Oh, yes! I was driving back from Lethbridge with my husband…"

"Lethbridge," I interrupted, " that's where I'm heading through today. It's only forty miles away!"

"We were closer than that! Halfway back, the hailstones were so bad that we had to turn round and head back to Lethbridge!"

"So you escaped?" I asked, stating the obvious.

"With the hailstorm hot on our heels! It's all about being in the wrong place at the wrong time!"

"But it's August!"

"Welcome to the Prairies!"

A couple of days later I met a twenty-three year old car mechanic called Mike. He was living out here in Alberta but missing his native British Columbia, where he used to race mountain bikes. He gave me his number and I rang him that evening, once I'd found a campsite in Medicine Hat. At half past six, Mike, his twenty-year old wife Tracie and their dog Taz turned up to camp for the weekend. When it became dark, Tracie put on a head-torch and made Taz run round in circles, chasing the beam.

"I don't know who's more crazy, the girl or the dog!" laughed Mike.

"Well, they're probably both missing the mountains!"

"No kidding. One thing we love to do is to go camping up the mountains in the winter. We often wake up to find the tent covered in fresh snow."

"Sounds like fun, but a bit cold!" I said, remembering my experience in New Zealand.

"It's okay when you've got the proper winter gear. Inside the tent, it's always toastie!"

"Once we woke up to some scary noises," shouted Tracie, in a dizzy spin. "We had a cougar prowling round the tent!"

"So how can you live in the Prairies after all that?"

"Man, we're dying out here!" Mike confessed.

"It's not too far to drive though, is it?"

"Well, as it happens, we were thinking about doing something fun this weekend," he announced. "How do you fancy going back to the Rockies?"

"Yes!"

"Cool! What do you think, Tracie, we'll set off in the morning!"

"Sounds good to me!"

That night, I woke up to another frightening thunderstorm, with the tent being blasted by a strong wind and ferocious rain. Mike called out to me to say we had to get out of there fast, as their tent was becoming flooded. I opened my tent and looked out, saying "Ooh 'eck!" What I saw was a veritable river, running right underneath, where an hour before the ground had been hard and dry. At least mine wasn't leaking this time. It's amazing what a full set of poles and a decent pitch can do!

We chucked everything into the back of their ancient Toyota Tercel and Mike (already soaked) waded in, almost knee-deep, to the tree where my bike was locked up. We threw the bike into the car and drove back to their place, aqua-planing on the way.

Their apartment was a typical adventure-cookie flat, with bikes and gear everywhere, and maps and expedition photos all over the walls. This was too good an opportunity to miss, and the next two days were to be my only non-cycling days in Canada. I crashed out on the sofa for what was left of the night.

Tracie made some awesome pancakes for breakfast, before we loaded the car again, for the drive north to Banff. After three hours we skirted Calgary and headed for the mountains. I was in the back with all the gear, on top of which, in various poses, was Taz, mostly watching the traffic over Mike's left shoulder! Within an hour of reaching the National Park, we saw three elk, and also a young bear, moseying about amongst the trees.

We hit a family restaurant, explored the Banff Springs Hotel, then got onto a campsite in the forest. In the morning we went for a walk up a canyon. The path was crowded at first, but the further we got, the more natural it became. The number of walkers dwindled, till we were on our own on a little muddy pathway.

A clear, fast flowing river dropped down the rocky waterfalls and through the canyon. The smell of the mountain air and the pines was invigorating; Mike and Tracie both said they felt alive again. Climbing out of the gorge, we came upon a high valley with soaring mountains all around. There we found the inkpots, a group of surreal blue and orange cold springs. Blue was the colour of the rocks and sand, curiously moving as if there was a serpent beneath the orange algae.

Sadly, we had to head back to the car for the drive home, leaving the Rockies behind again. At eight o'clock we drove into Calgary for a meal stop, passing the Olympic ski jump on our way in. We found a restaurant specialising in cheesecakes, very sneaky because you almost can't go there without having both main course and dessert. We carried on our mad conversations the whole time, like trying to work out how long a plate you'd need to serve a cow's tongue!

Only twenty miles from home, we came across some deer, and one of them ran across the road in front of us. Poor Tracie tried to screech to a halt but cried, "Oh no, we hit 'im!" as the deer toppled over and bits of fur went flying all over the place. Luckily he got up and jumped over the fence, so we reckoned he'd be ok. Just five minutes further on, we pulled up again because Mike had spotted the Aurora Borealis, streaking vertically upwards from the clouds on the horizon. We got out of the car to watch this magical spectacle, subtle colours stroking the northern sky.

"Wow!" I said. "Only a few miles from home and we're still having adventures!"

Mike, Tracie and Taz took me back to Medicine Hat in the

morning, to the same campsite that we'd left on the Friday night in the rain. Mike had taken the morning off work, but I don't think he'd told his boss. We did the decent thing and got a drive-thru McDonald's breakfast, then ate it in the car by the campsite. It was a sad goodbye as I got on the bike to pedal east again, and they drove back home.

The next day, as I later found out, they drove one hundred and eighty miles to try and find me again, only I was camping eight miles further on! I'd had a howling tailwind for those two days, so they didn't find me. I rang them every few days while I was still in Canada, and they charted my progress across the country.

The very night after the McDonald's breakfast, I pitched the tent by the road and became caught up in yet another storm. The wind started whipping the tent around as I was putting the last peg into the dusty ground. The sky blackened and the freezing cold rain came pelting down. The lightning flared up again and I jumped over a gate and ran into a steel tunnel under the road. As the lightning came closer, I was thinking, "What if all the cattle decide to run through this tunnel?"

With the lightning only a mile away, I decided to run for it, back over the gate and across the road. I was wearing sandals, shorts and a T-shirt, legging it in the freezing rain and howling wind, through the enormous puddles and onto private property. This was actually the campsite I'd been heading for all day, only to find that it had been closed down. The old toilet block had no roof, and I was scared to death by the lightning. I found an old static caravan at the end of the field and ran in. A bird was caught inside, flying backwards and forwards in a panic, banging and fluttering against the walls as the storm raged. A few cold minutes passed as the rain battered the caravan, then the storm rolled off as quickly as it had appeared, and the bird flew free, into a calm sky.

The idea of riding across the Prairies was something I'd always thought of as being really boring, but what with storms like these every other day, the killer mosquitoes at Reed Lake and the monster trucks, there was no time to be bored. I was now in Saskatchewan and the Trans-Canadian Highway rolled on and on, through Moose

Jaw and Regina, every town being hailed by the sight of another grain elevator on the horizon of cornfields, cornfields and more cornfields.

I had a strong wind every day, but it kept on switching direction right the way across Saskatchewan and Manitoba. One old guy told me, "There's always a breeze on the Prairies, it just depends on where it's coming from!" The awesome thing was that I was crossing time zones as I headed east, and every single day brought me closer to home.

In Winnipeg I went to a bike shop, the last one for another four hundred miles. I bought a rear view mirror and a new tyre, then asked if they knew of a campsite. One of the customers told me that there wasn't one within the city, but that I could stay at his house! He was called Stephen, and he said he was a medical student. He'd just had his bike fixed, so we were able to ride back to his house where he told me to make myself at home! His girlfriend Laurie came home and we had a curry.

Laurie said that she's in the Royal Canadian Air-force, and my room was full of books on how to become a flying instructor. They told me that the winters in Winnipeg are severe. Temperatures as low as minus forty are not that uncommon, and once there were one hundred and eight consecutive days below freezing point! Winnipeg is close to the American border, yet up in the north of Manitoba it gets truly Arctic. There are virtually no roads, and hardly any people. Manitoba is bigger than Britain, with only one and a half per cent of Britain's population!

We stayed up talking and drinking until the early hours, then in the morning we rode into town so I could get back onto the road to the east. Stephen showed me a couple of old buildings, one of which was a French chateau, the other a French church. We took a cheesy photo of the two of us next to a statue. The figure on top was Louis Riel, a local folk hero of the Metis people. These were half-caste French / Red Indian fur traders who tried, unsuccessfully, to resist being dragged into the new nation of Canada.

I said goodbye to Stephen and headed off. After thirty miles I realised that I'd finally succeeded in crossing the Prairies. The change was sudden and dramatic, from cornfields to trees, rocks, hills and thousands of lakes. This was the beginning of Ontario and the

Canadian Shield, beautiful but never-ending! Here, I left behind the frequent storms, but I was once again entering bear country, so I would have to be careful when free-camping, i.e. practically every night.

The heat was driving me doo-lally most of the time, and I kept getting de-hydrated, my water running low before I was anywhere near the next roadhouse or town. I'd go for a swim in a lake sometimes, or if I was really over-heating, I'd dump the bike and walk straight into the water and slump down, complete with watch, cap, shorts, T-shirt and sandals.

One month and two thousand miles since leaving Vancouver, I entered my fourth time zone so far in Canada, crossing the Eastern Standard time zone, at 90 degrees longitude west. I was still only half way across the country!

Dear Verena
Happy Birthday! Tim just phoned and told me that you're 26 today! I hope you celebrated in style.
Everyone's very well here – I'm playing lots of tennis - 4 games this week – and now my right arm is so sore I can hardly lift it!
Sally and Nick are on holiday in Italy, Janna and Richard are camping in Wales – still lovely days but it's getting dark early, and autumn is coming.
Looking forward to seeing you when Tim gets home – not long now!
Hope your Mum and Dad are well and – as usual – don't work too hard!
Lots of love – Berlie xxx

I rolled down into Thunder Bay, with a magnificent view of Lake Superior. Stopping at a video shop and asking about a campsite, I was again given a bed for the night. This time, it was a girl called Shelly, who rang her boyfriend to see if he had a spare room. It was a shared house and somebody had just moved out. The lad's mum turned up and it transpired that she was a keen traveller, having been to numerous far-flung places, including teaching English in Istanbul. She invited me to her friend's house for breakfast, just down the

road. When I got there in the morning, the friend, Linda, turned out to be a traveller as well, and we talked about Nepal over pancakes and maple syrup in her old wooden house. They took some photos of me outside, saying to each other;
"I'll take the picture; you can be in it!"
"No, you've got to be in the picture; you made the pancakes!"
"But you found him!"
"I didn't find him – Shelly found him!"
After the pancakes, I visited a bike shop and fitted new cones and bearings to the bike hubs before hitting the road again. I also bought new inner tubes, cycling shorts and a puncture kit. Just outside the town was a memorial to Terry Fox, the guy who set off from Newfoundland to run across Canada, doing a marathon every day. This would be no mean feat, but when you consider that he was dying of cancer and had already lost a leg to his illness, he became a national hero, raising twenty-four million Dollars for cancer research. He ran 3,339 miles but never completed the full route because the cancer defeated him, and he died aged twenty-three, on June 28th 1981.
The road continued along Lake Superior with staggering views, but never any hint of the far side; I saw a sign saying, "USA 7 days by canoe!" The forests crept up to the water's edge, dark green pines and deciduous trees turning red and gold at the end of August.

A waitress in a restaurant told me about what life is like here in the winter. She once got snowed in after a three-day blizzard. A snowplough cleared her driveway but there was still a fifteen-foot drift between the drive and her front door. It took her two days to dig a tunnel through it to escape from the house!
"Another time," she added, "one of the highway cuttings got jam-packed with snow."
"That must have stopped the traffic!"
"There was snow piled up to twenty feet deep and a mile long!"
"But surely they couldn't leave it! There's no other road!"
"Exactly. The guy with the snowplough thought he'd drive at it full-pelt to make a start!"
"That's a bit mad!"
"What did he do?" she invited me to guess.

"Err, he came to a standstill."

"He buried himself!" she laughed. "The only way they could shift the snow was to use dynamite!"

"Well, at least the roads are clear in the summer, except for the road works."

"There you go. We've got two seasons in Ontario. Winter and Construction!"

One time I approached a junction in the middle of the night. It was miles from anywhere, and yet there was a single streetlight, with two people standing under it, dressed in dark clothes. I stopped to ask them where the next restaurant was, and ended up spending an hour with them. They were a couple of young, excited hitchhikers called Ian and Laura.

They eventually got another lift, but in the meantime we had a laugh, joking around and telling stories. They were heading out west for the same reason as a guy I'd met the night before.

"I've been kicked out of home," said Laura. "But anyway, I don't get on with the people in Southern Ontario. All they ever do is watch TV, so they've all got messed up values."

The two of them were off to find jobs in British Columbia, but for the moment they were just trying to hitch a ride to Thunder Bay, where Ian's uncle lives. Every time a car or truck came, Laura was there, hitching up her baggy trousers, to which the driver would respond with a honk of the horn! I thought that, just on personality alone, they should have been picked up much quicker than they actually were. Their "Thunder Bay" sign was funky, and had taken them all afternoon to make.

When a car finally stopped for them, we shook hands and Ian said, "Thanks for the company." He told me that if they hadn't got a lift, they'd have ended up sleeping in the forest with no tent, as he'd managed to set fire to his tent once while making a campfire!

These two were typical of the people I met, drifting along the Trans Canadian Highway. One morning I crawled out of my tent by the side of the road, and a hobo walked by with nothing more than an old shoulder bag. He called out, "Did you sleep well? Too many bugs!" He was walking in the direction of White River, sixty miles back down the road, with nothing else in between!

I met other people who'd cycled across the country in previous

years. One van slowed down as it overtook me, the driver saying;
"I know what you're goin' through, man!"
"Cheers!"
"I once rode from Edmonton to Nova Scotia."
"That's cool!"
"Man – those trucks," he said with venom. "I cursed every single one of 'em!"
"Yeah – they're nutters, aren't they!"
"They don't want you on the road, that's why!"

For a week I followed the shores of Lake Superior, through red, gold and green forests, pitting my wits against the constant hills and headwinds. The Lake, a never-ending expanse of blue, would suddenly appear from around a corner. The road would sweep down to beaches of sand, pebbles and driftwood. There was even a tide, and it was hard to appreciate that this wasn't the sea. With water so clear you could drink it, the invitation was too great, and whenever I had the chance I'd go for a swim to cool off.

After almost twenty thousand miles, the bike was beginning to show its age, and there was a peculiar problem, which I just couldn't solve. For weeks, it felt that the brakes were on when I was on long hill-climbs in the heat. I would get off the bike and check, but the brakes definitely weren't rubbing! Then I decided that it must be the hubs, so I'd strip them down to clean, check and re-grease them, but to no avail. I even took the bike to a bike shop to have someone look at it, but he couldn't find anything either. If it wasn't the brakes or the hubs then it must have been the sealed bottom bracket, or a ghost, or else my imagination. I didn't want to get any new wheels at this late stage, even though the braking surface on the rims was practically worn through. The wheels had done a sterling job, and hadn't even broken a single spoke, the whole way round the world!

The further east I got, the worse the truck drivers seemed to be. I was constantly looking in my rear view mirror, ready to dive off the road, and the special wide-load trucks were no better than the rest; I could always tell that they weren't going to give me enough room, so I'd have to dive onto the gravel. Ontario was by the far the worst for this; I had to ride over thirteen hundred miles with no hard shoulder, following a six-inch band between the gravel and the wheels of the trucks.

Doing this for ten hours a day gets very tiring. I nearly copped it at one point, when I steered onto the gravel by mistake, then tried to correct it but caught the front tyre on the edge of the tarmac, sending me veering back into the road. The car behind me had to slam his brakes on and swerve hard to avoid me. This reminded me of one of the many scary moments I'd had in Turkey, when I lost concentration on a treacherous road and almost fell over into the carriageway. I'd just managed to unclick my shoe from the pedal to halt my fall, when a coach thundered past my left ear at full pelt, with inches to spare.

Dear Berlie!

Thanks for your birthday fax and sorry for being so terrible in writing back.

Tim rang me this afternoon – he's convinced there is a ghost in his bike, which is fed up of cycling. Something makes the pedalling really hard, but as soon as he turns the bike over to check it the wheels go round really smoothly!

Autumn has definitely made its way to Kirchschlag – it's cold, wet and horrid.
Bye,
Verena

Ontario was beginning to drag after over two weeks of lakes, pines and hills. I found myself doing mad things like singing Sheryl Crow songs in a comedy old-man accent, then repeating things to myself over and over again, little phrases that I'd made up in moments of insanity. Then I'd look down, and my feet would still be going round and round. I went through a low point when I'd crossed three thousand miles of Canada but still had another thousand miles to go. I decided that I needed to pep things up again, like I had in the Australian Outback. Over the period of three days I'd done three hundred miles, so I thought it would be cool to carry on and try to make it a thousand miles in ten days.

Suddenly, I was out of the never-ending province of Ontario and into Quebec, where I followed the vast St Lawrence River towards the Atlantic, passing through Montreal, Trois Rivieres, Quebec City, Rivieres du Loup, onto New Brunswick in yet another time zone, and finally Nova Scotia. I failed to do the thousand miles in ten days, as on the tenth day, with forty miles to go, I was offered a camping spot in a park belonging to the Lion's Club. Hurricane Floyd had been pummelling me for a couple of days, so I thought, "Sod it!"

What these ten days did, though, was to bring me out of the doldrums and into a different state of mind. I was gunning for it again, powering towards the end of the whole trip, like a sprint at the end of a marathon.

I loved Quebec, with its crazy, twisted French-ness. I'd entered a bright world, full of sunshine and character. Beautiful wooden houses, strung out along the road, were painted in colours of red, blue or green. All were perfectly kept, with their balconies, pillars, rocking chairs and odd metal roofs. I passed fields of corn, cattle and old barns with painted red doors.

The American feel of Southern Ontario was gone, and the cafes and restaurants were much more traditional and interesting. The mixture of my rusty French and the locals' rustic French and faulty

English lead to some funny conversations at meal stops. In one café I asked what the "Crème de Chou" was. The lady said, "It's Garbage…. No; Cabbage!" Also, The way they say things like "Sucre" sounds totally different from French-French, sounding more like "Su," with the end of the word missed off.

Hurricane Floyd had first hit me when I was free-camping in New Brunswick. After battering the American and Canadian coast for a while, it had now decided to move inland, though luckily it was losing some of its power. I'd pitched the tent in a ditch and woken up to find that it was a bit windy. It had been raining for hours and it was freezing cold. I packed up and dragged the bike out of the ditch and up to the road. Then the full force of the wind hit me. I managed to do eighty miles on this day, but God knows how!

I had breakfast in a restaurant and the man said ironically, "Nice day to ride a bike!" I rang Verena in Austria, and she said she'd already got her ticket to fly to England for my home coming, two and a half weeks hence.

"I just can't wait to see you, my Timmy!" she cried excitedly.

"I know lady, that's if I get there!"

"You will, I know it!"

"It's stupidly windy today," I grumbled. "The bike was getting thrown about so much that I had to put all of the heaviest stuff in the handlebar bag, just to keep the front wheel on the ground!"

"That sounds a bit scary. You will be careful, my honey!"

"Of course, lady! Only a few days left, then I fly to Ireland!"

"And how long will it take you to ride across Ireland? A week or so?"

"Oh, I don't know! I haven't got a map yet! But it'll be a tiny country after Canada…"

Whenever a truck went past, I would suddenly be shielded from the wind and would wobble violently the other way. After a few hours, the rain stopped but the wind continued, and I was actually enjoying it, in a mad kind of way! During the afternoon, the eye of the storm passed over, and I was able to make some headway.

In the evening I met some people in a café, and they told me about a picnic spot down the road. I almost missed it in the freezing cold rain. It was already dark, and the eye of the storm had passed. The wind was picking up again so I pitched the tent right up against a little woodshed. I was about to climb into the tent when a car pulled up, its headlights half blinding me. It turned out to be the people from the café, offering me a room in their bible school. I couldn't be bothered to take the tent down again, so I thanked them for their kindness, saying that I'd be fine.

This turned out to be a bad move, despite the shelter from the woodshed, as I suffered a very frightening night with the wind howling through the trees. I spent most of the night peeking out of the door of the tent, watching the huge trees being bent halfway towards the ground by the hurricane.

By eight a.m., the rain had stopped and I looked out to see a clear blue sky. The wind was no longer gale force, and best of all, it was now a tailwind, helping me to clock up another hundred miles. I saw the headlines in the day's papers and counted my lucky stars; "Floyd fades – Region relatively unscathed."

On reaching Nova Scotia, I headed north east, in the direction of Cape Breton Island. I stayed on a campsite in Pictou, where the lady told me that she loves her new found, laid-back lifestyle.

"I come from Southern Ontario," she explained. "They're all mad... everything's timed!"

"Well, I wasn't there for long and I didn't like it much!"

"They all rush around all the time, but they're going nowhere!"

"I know what you mean."

"I never wear a watch!" she boasted. "If I'm late, I'm late. If I'm early, good for me!"

"So you won't be returning."

"Down there, nobody's got any time for anyone... I'd never go back!"

My coast to coast ride was nearly over. I'd been able to smell the sea for a couple of days, when the wind blew the right way. At times I hadn't thought I'd make it, and as usual, the main danger was from the traffic.

My closest call here in Canada was one night at nine o'clock, when I left a restaurant in a town in Ontario. It was dark and I had my reflective gear and flashing lights on. A truck came bearing down on me from behind and my sixth sense told me that he hadn't seen me. I swerved off the road and the truck thundered right past the spot where I'd just been, before swerving way too late and nearly losing control. I later met a truck driver who said he'd seen me one evening. He apologised, or rather boasted, that he'd frightened me, saying that they all do it for fun. He was high on drugs and had just driven two and a half thousand miles without any sleep. It scared the life out of me, to think that my fate could have been held in the hand of a fool like that.

I'd spent most of my nights sleeping on any old bit of ground by the Trans Canadian Highway. Flattening the shrubs and dead branches to pitch the tent, I wouldn't care about whether or not the ground was smooth or flat. Often, I'd clamber on to the top of a cutting in the rock to sleep above the road, however uncomfortable the rocks were. It had been an epic journey, coloured by staggering scenery and some truly amazing characters.

As I approached Cape Breton Island, the mist shrouded the last few miles of the Canadian mainland. I reached the causeway and crossed the Strait of Canso. To the right was the Atlantic! I couldn't stop laughing out loud, in an almost evil way! The wind was so strong, and the rain so hard, that it hurt, but I didn't care.

I fought the wind for twenty miles from Port Hastings to Louisdale, before turning onto a small road to find a way down to the ocean at Petit de Grat. Wooden houses were scattered about on the wild, wet hillsides of this far-flung island. I crossed a little bridge and struggled in the wind to Samson's Cove, a tiny pebbled beach at the end of a track. There were a few old houses, some abandoned cars and some crazy dogs on long chains, running around barking at me as I rode down the track and onto the pebbles.

I'd dipped my toe in the Pacific nearly two months before, off Vancouver. This time, I had a much better idea. I clambered over the rocks as the cold waves crashed over them, the sea and the wind blasting me with an invigorating spray. Laughing my head off, I made sure that no one was around, then I crouched down behind a rock at the water's edge...

Dear Verena,

"Hear ye! Hear ye!
    Englishman
        Dips his bum
            In the Atlantic
                off Cape Breton Island,
                    Nova Scotia, Canada.
                        Hear ye! Hear ye!"

answerphone message just received from Tim!

lots of love – Berlie xxx

Dunmore Head, Ireland to Sheffield, England

I'd always wanted to come here, to County Kerry, and it was just as beautiful as I'd hoped it would be. I had to get cracking though; I'd left the tent on a campsite in Tralee, forty miles away, and it was already late...

It was three days since I'd reached the East coast of Canada. Curiously enough, the only other person here on this West coast beach in Ireland was a Canadian. He took a photo of me, as I dipped my nose in this, the other side of the Atlantic.
 "I can't believe it!" he said. "This place is awesome! I've never seen anything like it in my life."

I went back past Slea Head and along the dramatic cliff-top, past the pretty cottages and a handful of four thousand-year old "bee-

262

hive" houses. Damp, moss-covered walls lined the narrow lane, and the sunlight broke through the clouds, onto the steely ocean. I pedalled hard through Dingle, with its colourful pubs and houses, then over the mountains with a sublime evening light, and pink clouds fading into darkness.

"Lady! I'm in Tralee!" I yelled into the payphone.
"Is that in Ireland?" she guessed.
"Yeah! I got here yesterday, but I didn't have time to ring up!"
"Have you been to the sea yet?"
"Yeah, I've done that! It was my nose this time!"
"Cool! So you're heading for Sheffield now?"
"Yeah, well, not now, tomorrow!"
"I'm dead excited," she was jumping around on the other end of the phone. "I've already packed my bags for England!"
"But I'm not due for another week!" I explained, putting more coins in the slot.
"I know. October the fifth!"
"Exactly! Sally's twenty-eighth birthday. What a present from her big brother!" I laughed.
"You're not gonna run off again are you? I'm not going through all this again?"
"Well, I've still never been to Africa…"
"Timmy!" she interrupted.
"I was just gonna say, we could go together! No bikes allowed!"
"It's a deal!"
"We could do it in a year or so, just for a month. Tanzania would be cool. There's Zanzibar, the Ngorongoro crater and Kilimanjaro!"

The next morning, I left beautiful Tralee and headed up through Listowel and Tarbert to Limerick. Just as on my previous trips to Ireland, I was charmed by the old men in the pubs, and amused by the fact that road signs in kilometres and miles appear side by side. I stayed in a bed and breakfast, run by a Mrs Gladys Doherty. I told her that we'd got the same surname. I said I'd been intending to ride up to Ballaghadereen where my great grandfather, James Doherty, came from, but decided that I'd do it next time I was over.

Hellllllloooo!

Thanks for that last fax, Berlie!
Tim rang me last night:
As a result and continuation of his "dipping his bum in the Atlantic" –
He dipped his <u>nose</u> in the Atlantic from the most Westerly point of Ireland!!
Yippee – just a few days left now.
V.

I had breakfast at Mrs Doherty's with a shop-fitter from Cork, a lovely character who covered his eyes when the catwalk models appeared on the television. I followed the back-roads to the River Shannon, over-growing with trees and rushes, and in County Clare I went through the joint towns of Killaloe and Ballina with their picturesque churches and stone buildings, an old stone bridge linking the two across the Shannon.

I found a campsite near RosCrea, County Tipperary, and spent the whole evening in the kitchen, talking to the only other guests; a couple of Dutch hikers who'd spent the last three weeks tramping and trekking all over north eastern Ireland. By the next night I'd ridden across parts of County Laois and County Offaly, and into County Kildare, with its rolling hills, wheat fields and cattle. I tried to find Rathangan campsite, only to find that it had closed a year before. I knocked on a farmer's door to ask if he knew of another campsite.

"So you're lookin' for somewhere to camp?" he asked.

"I am!"

"Well, I tell you what you'll be doing!" he announced. "You'll be camping in one of my fields!"

"That's very kind of you!"

"There'll be no electricity or anything, mind! But I won't be letting the cows in till 9:30 in the morning!"

He said his name was William Champ, and he seemed very pleased to be able to help me in such a way. I woke up at nine o'clock in the morning to the sound of cattle. I took the tent down as quickly as I could, just as William Champ walked up the road with the cows.

"I overslept a bit!" I called over the hedge.

"I can see that!" he replied. "T'was a rough night!"

Later on, a road-worker called out, "T'is a dirty ol' marnin'!" The weather was wet, windy and horrible, but I didn't mind. It was October the first and, regrettably, my last full day in Ireland. I put the rest of my clothes on and continued to amble to Dublin. I followed the road to Dun Laoghaire harbour, where I symbolically dipped my finger in the Irish Sea, before finding a campsite. It really was bitterly cold and wet, and I decided that this would be my last night's camping for a very, very long time! I spent the whole evening in the pub, drinking Guinness, before running back to the tent, too drunk to care about the weather.

The last ferry crossing of the whole trip was a rough ride, but I was ecstatic when Wales came into view. I had a long-awaited portion of chips in Holyhead, then half-way across Anglesey I could see Snowdonia and the Llanberis Pass, a dramatic play of light and shade washing over the mountains. I crossed the Menai Straits and slept at the Bangor Youth Hostel. The next day was a fantastic ride, scenery-wise, though I hadn't done any big distances for days; I didn't want to get home before Sally's birthday!

Best of all, on this day, I crossed the border into England! I took some silly pictures of myself, hanging off the sign, but felt embarrassed because of the cars driving past. Then again, I didn't care if the drivers thought I'd lost it!

ENGLAND AT LAST! OCT 3RD '99

The Youth Hostel at Chester was a charming town house, where I met some independent Japanese back-packers, and spent the next morning furnishing them all with information on where they should go next in Britain! This felt wacky because, normally, I was the one asking other people where I should go.

"I don't want to go to London," said one of the Japanese lads. "It will be too quiet because everyone will be in the church, praying."

I had a look round Chester, with its Roman and Elizabethan architecture, thinking, "Blimey, there's nothing like this in Canada!" On the way to Congleton I met an old guy and got chatting to him. He asked where I'd been, so I told him.

"Well, I think that's damn marvellous!" he exclaimed. "Imagine that, cycling round the World! I think you deserve to put your feet up! That's damn marvellous, that is!"

I climbed up Wildboarclough, in a very low gear, as I wanted to savour every moment of it. This was the Peak District, at long last! The weather did it justice, with a clear blue sky and a faint breeze. Nestled away in a quiet little valley, along the back lanes, is Gradbach Mill Youth Hostel. Hindmoor and I used to ride out to stay there when we were school kids, so it was the perfect place to spend my last night on the road, only thirty-three miles from Sheffield.

The Youth Hostel man was a superstar, the same guy that was there fifteen years before. I told him about my trip and he didn't charge me! I spent the evening thinking about how lucky I'd been to cycle around the world.

For someone with eczema so bad that I used to be carried around school by the teachers, unable to walk because of the horrific wounds on my knees, this was a real achievement. In Physical Education lessons I'd be the only one allowed to keep my socks on, as they were stuck to my ankles with dried blood. Italy had stopped me in my tracks, but I'd been unable to leave it at that. Then there was the asthma, which would have me coughing my lungs up, short of breath for days at a time, and had been getting worse in the years leading up to my trip. This was why I'd raised the sponsorship money for Intermediate Technology. Maybe it was the reason why I did the trip in the first place.

But this sense of pride wasn't the most important thing I'd got from all of this. It was the experience, the learning, the wonderful places, and, most of all, the people. Whether I was in Greece, Pakistan, Canada, Indonesia or Myanmar, I would always be welcomed and treated well. I was met by kindness and hospitality in every single country.

Before I'd set off, excited but worried by the prospect, people had given me all sorts of advice. Somebody told me to "stick to Christian countries." But others had more positive advice. My friend Karen had told me;

"It's not until you jump off the cliff that you discover your wings."

Tuesday, October the fifth 1999 was a stunning day. The morning was frosty, with a clear blue sky. The only sounds were the river and the birds. There was no hurry whatsoever, as Verena would only arrive in Sheffield at three in the afternoon, and my dad would collect her. I'd told everyone about two weeks before that I'd arrive on Sally's birthday at four o'clock.

Dear Verena,
I don't know about you but I keep bursting into tears!
I can't believe he's so near home now!
Gerry will pick you up from the airport on his way home from school – he may be a little late but don't despair – he'll be there!
Lots of love –
Berlie x

I crossed Axe Edge, with a bird's eye view over the sun-drenched crags and green valleys of the Peak District. On the horizon, amidst the yellows and browns of wild moorland, I could just make out Stanage Pole, only five miles from home.

I dropped down into Buxton and almost couldn't remember the way! Through Dove Holes I ambled, then I turned off at Sparrowpit and up towards Mam Tor. I decided not to go down the one-in-five descent of Winnats Pass, as I was convinced that I'd be killed on this, the last day. The fact that my brakes didn't work wasn't much help. Instead, I took it steady down the old broken Mam Tor road, traffic-free, with a clear view of Hope Valley. It seemed unreal to be back here after all this time, especially on such a day.

I sailed through Castleton and Hope, basking in the autumn sunshine, then turned off the main road in Hathersage and up the steep climb past the Scotsman's Pack. At the top was Stanage Edge, crowning the moorland of golden grass and reddening bracken. Dry-stone walls, barns and cottages blended in as if they'd been there for all eternity.

I could hear the sheep munching on the grass as I rode up to Stanage Edge. On reaching the top of the climb I sat down on my favourite spot, to look back at Mam Tor, the Hope valley and Kinder Scout. What a way to get back home. No airport, no motorways, no bus journeys, just a relaxing ride across the Peak District.

I only had five miles left to go, but I reckoned that Verena would be there by now, so I got up and carried on, past Burbage Edge and across the moors. The road fell away and the view opened up on Sheffield! I could hardly contain my excitement;

"WOW! We've come round the whole world, Jimmy!"

I saw a man sitting in his car, on a lay-by. I knocked on his window and asked,
"Could you take my photo? I'm cycling round the World! I left home over two years ago and I've only got four miles left!"
"Well, tha's well on't way, then, in't tha!" he said.
He took my picture and I dropped down to Ringinglow. I went into a payphone and rang home to make sure that everyone was there. I could hear them all jumping around with anticipation, and I said I'd be there in ten minutes. I continued down the hill into the leafy suburbs, practically shaking, and still convinced that I'd be knocked off at the last minute.

I rode into Ecclesall and onto the last of 21,688 miles of cycling, to complete the circle. Turning the corner at the bottom of Banner Cross

Road, I pedalled slowly uphill, hardly able to believe my eyes! It seemed that half the street was out, including most of the neighbours I'd known since I was four. Outside our house was the whole family, including the birthday girl. There were big signs in the windows, banners and a "Finish!" line across the drive. There were shouts and cheers, party poppers and camera clicks. And there, standing quietly behind the finish-line looking very relieved, was Verena…

'WITH VERENA AT THE END'

About the Author

Tim Doherty was born in 1969 in Sheffield, England. On the edge of the city is the stunning Peak District National Park, and it was there that he developed his passions for cycling, photography and drawing. Tim comes from a very creative and literary family. His mother Berlie Doherty is one of the UK's favourite children's authors. So when Tim came up with the idea of cycling around the world, it was clear that he would write a book about it.
Now living in Austria, Tim is furthering his professional career as a car designer. He is married and has two children.